Liverpool

Forgotten Landscapes,

Forgotten Lives

by

John Hussey

Other books by John Hussey:

Cruisers, Cotton and Confederates
John Gibson
Finding Margaret
Liverpool, the Confederate Years
The Light of Other Days
Survivors

First Published 2016 by Creative Dreams Publishing (UK)
an imprint of World of Creative Dreams

54 St James Street
Liverpool
L1 0AB

worldofcreativedreams.co.uk

British Library Cataloguing in Publication Data.
A catalogue record for this book is available from the British Library.

ISBN 978 0 9935524 0 3

*If you only read the books that everyone else is reading
you can only think what everyone else is thinking.*

– Haruki Murakami

*A people without the knowledge of their past history,
origin and culture is like a tree without roots.*

– Marcus Garvey

Contents

Acknowledgments 7

The Kaleidoscopic City 9

Lighting Up The Town – The Illuminations of 1813 19

The Surgeon Henry Park (1745 - 1831) 35

The Duellists 51

The School For Sculptors 61

The Franceys' Sculptors 69

On Borrowed Time 79

A Family of Sculptors: The Father 87

A Family of Sculptors: Benjamin Evans Spence (1822 – 1866) 101

Slaves and Sculptures: The Forgotten Statues of Leighton Hall 117

The Brownlow Hill Bohemians 139

The Man Who Loved Animals: William Huggins (1819 – 1884) 163

The Man Who Bought the Tinted Venus 175

Room to Breathe 185

Wealth and Poverty – The Great Chasm 195

And The Rains Came Down 207

The Orphan's Tale 215

The End of an Era 231

Bibliography 240

Index 242

Dedication

This book is dedicated with love to my wife Doreen,
Andrew and Carmel,
Gas and Dawn
and
Leila and Gabe

Acknowledgements

What would we do without the magicians at Liverpool Record Office who regularly produce photos and files from their inexhaustible archives like rabbits from a hat – many thanks to them all, not least for their patience and courtesy.

It's almost impossible to think of Victorian writers scribbling away with pens they dipped into inkpots, no different to the ones we had in primary school, without marvelling at the great works they turned out. There was no cut and paste then which is why I give thanks for my computer and to Sein Khan who is in league with the necromancers of the new technology and has no fear of either hard copies or hard drives – thanks Sein.

I would like to thank the many people in museums, art galleries and churches here and abroad who have taken the trouble to answer my emails and replied, often with pictures which they have taken for me.

I would like to also thank Jean Emmerson who ran Countyvise publishing company with her husband John for so many years and continued to do so after his sad demise. Countyvise was quite unique and it's only now that it is gone that I realise just how valuable it was to the authors of Merseyside.

Last but not least, I must thank Suzanne Lau for continuing where she left off at Countyvise and bravely striking out on her own. Suzanne's book designs are second to none and without her expertise this book would not exist, but the best part is being able to work together in an atmosphere of trust.

John Hussey,
2016.

The Kaleidoscopic City

"Progress is impossible without change, and those who cannot change their minds cannot change anything."

– George Bernard Shaw

What It May Grow to in Time I Know Not

Liverpool has always had something of a kaleidoscopic nature and even in this writer's lifetime the city has changed beyond all recognition – not always for the best. Although the original framework of streets has never altered, the number of buildings which have been demolished is quite staggering, made worse in the knowledge that many of them were irreplaceable architectural gems. The post-war predilection for concrete and steel buildings, so beloved of Communist states and of no aesthetic merit whatsoever, has brought about the demolition of many Victorian buildings in the city and their replacements have subsequently been recognized as so ugly that those which remain have been draped in advertising hoardings to hide their shame. The worst example of post-war architecture was the universally despised Concourse which was not only depressingly functional but performed the dual role of hiding the classically Victorian splendour of Lime Street Railway Station – the unloved and unlovely concrete accretion rose and fell in mere decades costing more to erect and dismantle than a building of substance and style which should have been erected in the first place. Lamentations upon Liverpool's lost architecture are a diversion which can be expanded upon *ad infinitum* but if there is any advantage to be gained by such reflections then it may simply be to illustrate that if the city can become so difficult to recognize in a single lifetime then how much more difficult is it to picture in one's mind the Liverpool of two centuries ago.

The further back in time we go the more amorphous the city becomes and those who have taken the trouble to chronicle the layout of the city as they perceived it become rarer and rarer. The seasoned traveller, Celia Fiennes (1662 – 1741) was an unusual sight in Georgian England travelling around the countryside and writing down her observations as she went; in 1698, she visited Liverpool and wrote: *"Liverpool is built on the river Mersey. It is mostly newly built, of brick and stone after the London fashion. The original (town) was a few fishermen's houses. It has now grown into a large, fine town. It is but one parish with one church though there be 24 streets in it, there is indeed a little chapel and there are a great many dissenters in the town (Protestants who did not belong to the Church of England). It's a very rich trading town, the houses are of brick and stone, built high and even, so that a street looks very handsome. The streets are well paved. There is an abundance of persons who are well dressed and fashionable. The streets are fair and long. It's London in miniature as much as I ever saw anything. There is a very pretty exchange. It stands on 8 pillars, over which is a very handsome Town Hall."* John Wesley (1703 – 1791) said much the same thing when he met John Newton (1725 – 1807) in Liverpool, but it was left to the accomplished writer Daniel Defoe (1660 – 1731) to describe

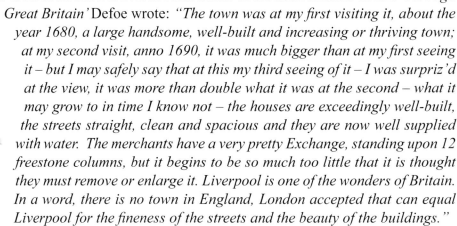

the town as he knew it over several visits. In his book entitled *'A Tour Through Great Britain'* Defoe wrote: *"The town was at my first visiting it, about the year 1680, a large handsome, well-built and increasing or thriving town; at my second visit, anno 1690, it was much bigger than at my first seeing it – but I may safely say that at this my third seeing of it – I was surpriz'd at the view, it was more than double what it was at the second – what it may grow to in time I know not – the houses are exceedingly well-built, the streets straight, clean and spacious and they are now well supplied with water. The merchants have a very pretty Exchange, standing upon 12 freestone columns, but it begins to be so much too little that it is thought they must remove or enlarge it. Liverpool is one of the wonders of Britain. In a word, there is no town in England, London accepted that can equal Liverpool for the fineness of the streets and the beauty of the buildings."*

Daniel Defoe

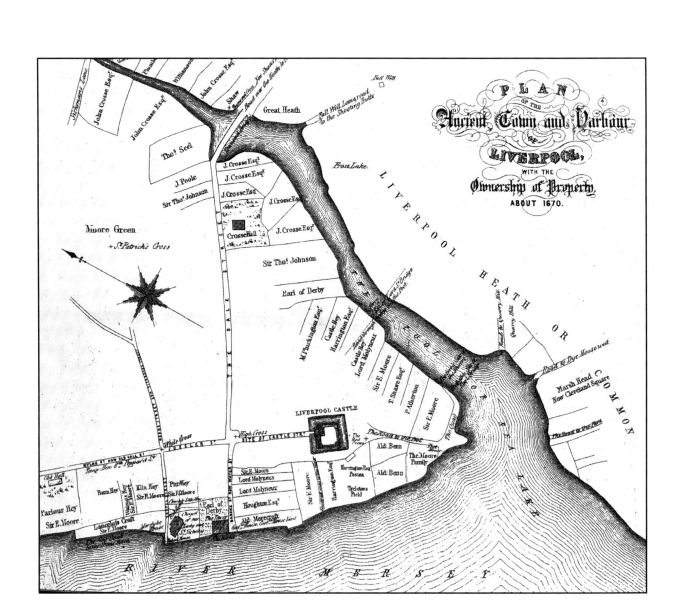

Liverpool 1670. Liverpool Record Office

The first of Liverpool's Town Halls could hardly be described as such in today's terms but it was a beginning and the thatched building that Reverend John Crosse presented to the town in 1515 stood for an astonishing 150 years. In 1673, Liverpool's second Town Hall or Exchange was built on the same site on the instructions of Mayor James Jerome and reflected the growing wealth of the merchants of the city not least due to the colonnades beneath the building where they conducted business. It was this second Town Hall or Exchange that Defoe admired so much.

*2nd Town Hall,
by G.W. Herdman,
Liverpool Record Office*

Although it seems churlish to dispute anything said by such luminaries as Fiennes, Wesley and Defoe, who had nothing to gain by their remarks, contemporary maps appear to display something more of an emergent fishing village than Defoe's *"wonder of Britain."* The Pool of Liverpool still bisected the township from Cleveland Square, meandering along what is now Paradise Street and Whitechapel and headed outwards from Byrom Street along Scotland Road. A bridge transversed the creek at the bottom of Dale Street in order for coaches from the inns along Dale Street to cross onto Shaw's Brow and out into the countryside for London and the provinces. Whitechapel was the home of thousands of frogs and was then called Frog-Lane. The original framework of seven streets which form the template for the city today had recently been laid out with Dale Street, the longest, running from the Exchange (Town Hall) to the bridge at the bottom of Shaw's Brow (now William Brown Street). Although it was falling into dereliction the Castle was still standing and Castle Street ran to the Town Hall as it does today, continuing onto Juggler Street and Old Hall Street. Moore Street and Water Street ran down to the river where the Church of Our Lady and St Nicholas stood as it always had near to the Tower where French prisoners languished in dreadful squalor. As for the remainder of what is now the city centre, the land was divided into rural plots owned by wealthy and influential families and beyond that there was a vast tract of countryside with the occasional mansion dotted here and there. On the southern side of the *"Sea Lake"* was Liverpool Common which led onto the old Deer Park – and apart from dwelling houses clustered near to the river, there was not much more to Liverpool than that. When Defoe wrote his complimentary tracts the town was just emerging from its fishing village origins and given that what he saw was only an embryo of what Liverpool would become, Defoe's vision of a future Liverpool displayed a rare prescience. However, the era of Georgian architecture which would define the wealth of the city throughout the 1700s was in a future which Defoe would never see but there was no doubt that even he would have been astonished at the speed in which Liverpool grew from the promise of its early days to the architectural splendour of the Georgian era, soon to be rivalled by the glories of the Victorian era.

A Century of Expansion in the Georgian Era

In the following years the town expanded rapidly and the increase in the numbers of ships in the river brought about the building of Liverpool's first dock; the Old Dock as it was called was built under the direction of Thomas Steers in 1715 and it not only provided a safe harbour but a fast unloading of cargo straight onto the quayside. In previous years ships' cargoes had previously been laboriously loaded onto Lighters and rowed to shore, often taking weeks to unload a single ship – the Old Dock was a pivotal part of the maritime trade in Liverpool and the beginning of the dock system which would in time stretch for miles along the waterfront; it could even be said that the Old Dock was the foundation upon which modern Liverpool was built. The Old Dock was also revolutionary for another reason which has been largely ignored; the Dock was built at the mouth of the tidal Pool and taking up a large portion of the waterway, it was the catalyst for filling in the creek which had run through the town for centuries.

Beginning with St Peter's Church consecrated in 1704 and the first building on Church Street, the 18th century was an unprecedented era of building which spread inexorably outward from the river, absorbing the farmland as it went and leaving in its wake a network of churches, warehouses, shops and streets, to be filled with an ever-growing population which grew from a mere 1200 in 1670 to 35,000 in 1770, 100,000 by 1815 and 375,000 in 1850. The Bluecoat Hospital was built in 1717 and near to where St George's Hall now stands there was a Seaman's Hospital, an Infirmary and a Lunatic Asylum. By 1726 the Castle had been dismantled and replaced by the Church of St George, consecrated in 1734, where John Newton once preached and the Mayor and Town Hall Councillors claimed most of the pews. St George's Church was just one of an astonishing proliferation of Churches built across the city during the 1700s – St Thomas's Church in Park Lane was consecrated in 1750 (in 1757 the spire blew down in a storm and at a later date the Church was struck by lightning causing the structure to become so unstable it was dismantled in 1822), St Paul's Church in St Paul's Square was consecrated in 1769, St Ann's Church, Great Richmond Street, built in 1772, was regarded as being out in the countryside, while St James's Church, built in 1775 at the bottom of Parliament Street, is still standing. St John's Church was built in 1784 at the top of what is now St John's Gardens but was demolished only 50 years later to make way for St George's Hall – the Church was universally condemned for its mediocre architecture and there were few complaints at its passing. It was an indictment of the widespread sectarianism that was still in existence that not one of the Churches built in the 18th century was Catholic. The house where William Roscoe (1753 – 1831) was born was on what were then the outer limits of the town at the top of Mount Pleasant; the building of The House of Correction next door to the Workhouse at the top of what is now Brownlow Hill intruded greatly on the rural nature of the area and was an indication of how land was becoming scarcer as the city expanded.

Bluecoat 1863

The increasing numbers of ships on the Mersey made the waterfront a hive of activity with shipbuilders, rope-walks, chandlers and seamen jostling for work and in 1753 the Salthouse Dock became the second dock in the city. Salthouse Dock was followed by George's Dock, King's Dock and Queen's Dock and by 1800 they formed the nucleus of a dock system which would expand beyond all expectations in the Victorian era under the direction of Jesse Hartley. As the city expanded outwards and the population grew accordingly, overcrowded houses, slum conditions and rowdy behaviour followed and the addition of thousands of seamen roaming around the many public houses made the waterfront less than habitable for respectable families. The wealthy moved outwards and the Georgian Houses of Gambier Terrace, Canning Street, Rodney Street, Parliament Street and many more, became the homes of shipowners, sea captains, merchants and shipbuilders who could bring up their families in luxury and safety while maintaining their businesses which were just a short walk down to the river.

Aim At the Goose!

Surprisingly, the second Town Hall lasted 50 years less than the original wood and thatch building and less than a century later the third Town Hall was erected in 1754, decorated with ornate carvings representing merchant endeavour, mostly of the maritime kind. Designed by John Wood of Bath, the 3rd Town Hall was funded by the merchants of the town, many of them engaged in the slave-trade, and the building was in effect little more than a gentlemen's club for the wealthy merchants and traders of the town.

John Wood was a member of a club of quite a different kind which held its first meeting in the Exchange Coffee House on January 15th, 1743. Given that membership was voluntary and the name of the club was The Most Honourable and Facetious Society of Ugly Faces with the motto *"Tetrum Ante Omnia Vultum"* or *"Before All Things an Ugly Face"* it was remarkable that the club garnered any membership at all. The rules for joining were also quite stringent.

1) That no person whatsoever shall be admitted of this society that is not a bachelor, a man of honour and a facetious disposition.

2) That a large mouth, thin jaws, blubber lips, little goggling or squinting eyes shall be esteemed considerable qualifications in a candidate.

3) That when a member marries he shall forfeit ten shillings and sixpence for the use of the society.

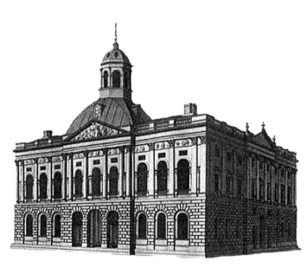

3rd Town Hall

Unsurprisingly, the Ugly Club lasted only a decade and folded up in 1754, the same year that Wood's new Town Hall came into existence.

In 1775, slave ships and merchantmen lay idle in the docks and Liverpool was filled with 3,000 disgruntled merchant seamen milling around the town, out of work because of The American War of Independence. In a masterpiece of indiscretion the shipowners reduced the wages of those that could work by a third and the already volatile situation escalated into a bitter strike. Peaceful meetings and delegations to the Town Hall by the seamen were met with hostility from the merchants who hired strike-breakers with the result that the incensed seamen dragged a number of cannon from the ships at anchor and began a bombardment on the Town Hall. The Town Hall had no defence against ship's cannon and may well have been badly disfigured but for a strange incident in which the Liver Bird may well have saved the day; the Town Hall frontage was decorated with carvings dedicated to the commerce of the town and one of these was a large Liver Bird high up on the façade of the building – an unknown member of the mob called out to the gunner *"Aim at the Goose!"* and the cannon did less damage by firing high. Four people were killed and several injured and there's no doubt that matters would have been made worse before a cavalry detachment of 100 men and officers of the 1st Royal Regiment of Dragoons arrived from Manchester and quickly subdued the rioters and arrested the leaders.

The Town Hall had had a narrow escape but there was worse to come in 1795 when the building was consumed by fire, the dome destroyed and the interior gutted. Although the shell of the building remained, the Town Hall was virtually rebuilt under the direction of the architect James Wyatt, opened again in 1797, and remains the building in use today.

3rd Town Hall in flames, by Herdman. Liverpool Record Office

The Vision Made Real

Within a century, Liverpool had grown out of all recognition to the township that Daniel Defoe praised so lavishly but it would be a mistake to believe that in 1800 the city's unprecedented growth had created some idyllic metropolis – in fact the gleaming sandstone buildings hid an unpalatable legacy of poverty. Most of the wealth derived from the maritime and commercial energy which consumed the city throughout the 1700s fell into the coffers of a wealthy élite of Merchant Princes, many of them slave shipowners, and the little that was left was grudgingly doled out in wages which were pittances to a starving workforce. The city had undoubtedly grown larger but the streets were narrow and unpaved and the smoke from thousands of chimneys was beginning to mix into a toxic smog which would suffocate its citizens for the following 150 years. Written in 1780, precisely one hundred years after Defoe's contemplations upon *"what it may grow into in time"* an American visitor to Liverpool, Samuel Curwen, Judge of Admiralty, partly answered the question with the following remarks:

"Entered into the city of Liverpool, so celebrated for its commercial character; houses by a great majority, in middling and lower style, few rising above that mark: streets, long, narrow, crooked and dirty in an eminent degree. During our short abode here, we scarcely saw a well-dressed person, nor half-a-dozen gentlemen's carriages; few of the shops appear so well as in great other towns; dress and looks more like the inhabitants of Wapping, Shadwell and Rotherhithe than in the neighbourhood of the Exchange, or any part of London above the Tower. The whole complexion nautical, and so infinitely below our expectations, that nought but the thoughts of the few hours we had to pass here rendered it tolerable. The docks however, are stupendously grand, the inner one, called Town Dock (the Old Dock) *lying in the centre of it, and filled with vessels, exhibiting a forest of masts; besides this are three very large ones* (George's Dock,

Canning Dock and Salthouse Dock) *lying in front of the city, communicating with each other by flood gates, intermixed with dry ones for repairing; the lower or new one* (George's Dock) *has a fine wide quay on its outer side; an agreeable walk, being lined with trees on either hand; below this on the river, is now building nearly finished, a circular battery with embrasures for thirty cannon* (The Old Fort)".

Defoe's optimistic view of Liverpool's future had come true to some degree as far as its architectural fabric was concerned but what he had never envisaged was that its commercial success would bring about unprecedented degrees of poverty and in his terse essay, Samuel Curwen, a complete stranger, had gone to the very heart of what Liverpool was all about and would remain so for years to come – maritime commerce at the expense of all else. The three docks that impressed Curwen so much were only the beginning of the future vast empire of the docks. The *"forest of masts"* was only a fraction of the ships that would eventually come down the river and the *"streets, crooked and dirty in an eminent degree"* were only a foretaste of the courts and slums which would overwhelm the city and its environs throughout the Victorian era and well into the 20th century.

Early Victorian Seamen

For every Georgian Town House there were a hundred slum dwellings and the charitable provision of a few alms houses to house seamen's widows or disabled seamen did little to alleviate a slum-dwelling majority whose numbers would swell to bursting point throughout the Victorian era. James Allanson Picton (1832-1910) who bequeathed Picton Library to the city has also left a vivid picture of life in the early years of the 1800s. In his own words: *"Imagine a town of 100,000 inhabitants without gas, without railways, without steam boats, without police – The streets were all paved with rough boulder stones – The miserable oil-lamps at long distances apart served only to make darkness visible – There were scavengers to sweep the streets. Their method was to sweep the mud into long parallelograms here and there about a foot deep which were then left for days – These heaps were called Corporation Beds – I have known as many as ten stand-up fights after dark outside our house."*

Even within this short account, Picton makes it clear that life as he knew it in Georgian era was uncompromisingly difficult and unpleasant and there's little doubt that he was relieved to have made the transition into the Victoria era. Picton's reference to rail travel indicates the tremendous changes that occurred in his lifetime in methods of travel and that he was well acquainted with the days when there were only coaches available for the very few who could afford them and just how uncomfortable a coach trip could be.

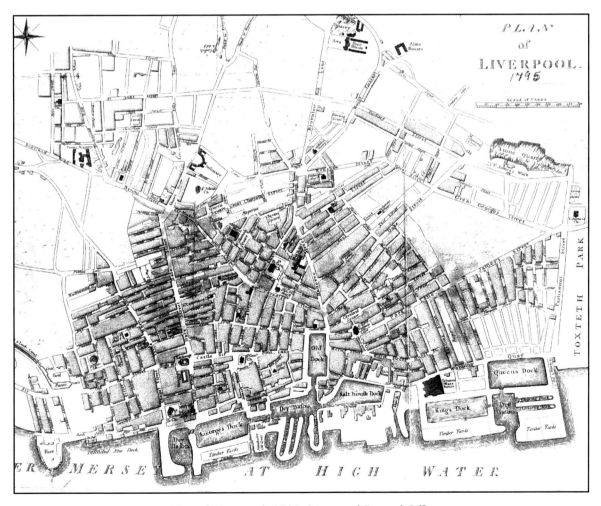

Map of Liverpool, 1795. Liverpool Record Office

In 1849, Herman Melville (1819 – 1891) wrote of a few weeks spent in the city as a lad of 16, in the pages of *"Redburn - His First Voyage."* Melville had taken along his father's journal which described the city in 1807 when he had previously visited, and attempting to follow in his father's footsteps using the journal as a guide, Melville was astonished to find that in a mere 30 years many of the sights his father had described were no longer in existence and others had altered beyond recognition. However, what is most noticeable is that Melville joins with other latter-day writers in contradicting Celia Fiennes' and Daniel Defoe's fulsome accounts of the town made just 150 years previously and writes of the poverty and drunkenness in great detail. Although it can be perplexing to find such different views of the town, the only logical conclusion to be reached is that while the city expanded architecturally and its maritime trade grew exponentially, working conditions and pay lagged far behind, leaving a legacy of grinding poverty which would linger well into the future – it seems that the tidal wave of progress is always fated to leave in its wake a backwash of poverty.

It was to this background of extreme wealth and even more extreme poverty that in 1813 the City Councillors came together – not to discuss the dynamics of the town or how they could improve its infrastructure or how they could help the needy, but to decide how they could best celebrate the downfall of Napoleon Bonaparte – even after so many years in existence the Town Hall remained the Gentlemen's Club that it had always been and it would be a long, tortuous process before the City Councillors thought less in terms of their own interests and assumed the civic responsibilities that came with the title.

Anyone who enters St George's Hall from the William Brown Street entrance will be confronted with a large staircase with a marble statue of a Victorian gentleman in a frock coat standing at the top. The sculpture is by William Theed and is a fine representation of Henry Booth (1788 - 1869). A closer inspection gives some clues as to why Booth merited a statue within the hallowed halls of Liverpool's finest building – at the rear of the statue can be seen a train coupling and there is a small sculpture of *The Rocket.* Booth was in fact just as instrumental in the formation of the railways as George Stephenson (1781 - 1848) but has somehow been forgotten with the passage of time. Two years before he died Booth wrote a short account of Liverpool as his father knew it from 1750 onwards – the following extracts add to our understanding of what the town looked like at that time. *"My father's master was a man named Dobson and he lived in Clayton Square which at that time was on the outskirts of town. The top of Church Street was the limit of the town in that direction: Bold Street with its splendid shops and the Lyceum library was not in existence; fields and waste ground extended in a south-easterly direction through the site of Great George's Square as far as Park Lane. The population at that date was under 30,000 souls but the commerce of the port was thriving. The African Trade including the slave-trade in regard to which Liverpool held a bad eminence had been established some thirty and the records state that 74 vessels sailed for Africa in the year 1764. In 1785, the 1st mail coach* was established between Liverpool and London, at that date Castle Street was so narrow that only two coaches could pass one another but the following year was widened and shortly became the most spacious and important street in the town. So Liverpool continued to enjoy a prosperous commerce and in natural sequence to increase rapidly in bricks and mortar."*

* The first mail coach started from Liverpool to London on July, 25th, 1785. It was to arrive in 30 hours at a cost of £3, 13shillings and sixpence. J.A. Picton

Lighting Up The Town

The Illuminations of 1813

"Look back over the past, with its changing empires that rose and fell, and you can foresee the future, too."

– Marcus Aurelius

The Glorious 1st of June, by Henry J. Morgan

The Devil Incarnate

Although the English had regarded the French as traditional enemies for centuries and had fought battles at sea and on land in many theatres of war, the storming of the Bastille in 1789 which heralded the French Revolution took the struggle to a whole new level and raised the stakes higher than they had ever been. The shock waves reverberated across the world, and in 1793 when the unthinkable became reality and Louis XVI went to the guillotine, every monarchy in Europe recoiled in horror. As reports of the excesses of the Revolutionary mob became increasingly disturbing the crowned heads of Europe's revulsion turned to trepidation and then to a real fear for their own crowns as the Revolutionary armies began to mobilise. Throughout the 1700s English and French merchant ships had fought running battles at sea in the guise of privateers and both sides justified their actions with Letters of Marque from their respective governments. Letters of Marque were issued so that merchant ships could legally engage an enemy at sea in times of war but both sides often ignored such niceties and fought whether war had been formally declared or not. The number of merchant ships leaving Liverpool as privateers throughout the Georgian era was extremely high – many of them never even bothering to carry cargo and engaged solely in capturing French prizes. In their turn, French ships attacked English ships whenever they were able and there are dozens of sea battles documented in which French ships have targeted English slave ships and their black cargoes; in fact the details of conflicts at sea between French and English ships are so numerous, not to mention exhilarating, that it seems to have been a customary rite of passage of every voyage. The highest prize ever taken by any English ship was that of the French ship *Carnatic* by Captain Peter Baker of *The Mentor* in 1788. The cargo was worth £400,000 with a cache of diamonds alone worth £135,000 and Captain Baker bought Mossley Hall, subsequently christened Carnatic Hall, on his share of the proceeds. While Liverpool ships, in every sense of the word, fought their way across the Atlantic, Liverpool shipowners lived in constant dread of losing their ships to disease, storms, shipwreck or mutiny and had even become inured to the fear of privateers, but the Revolution made life at sea even harder for merchant ships.

The Revolutionary Wars signalled the beginning of an epic struggle at sea between the French and the English in which the Royal Navy excelled in battle after battle; Admiral Howe destroyed 7 French ships of the line in 1794 at The Glorious First of June, Admiral Sir John Jervis made his reputation at Cape St Vincent in 1797, and Camperdown in 1797 reinforced English dominance of the seas. While the British fought the Revolutionary Navy at sea, a young Napoleon Bonaparte was fighting for the Revolutionary Army on land, making his name and reputation at Toulon in 1793, Lodi and Arcole in 1796 and Rivoli in 1797. However, his record of continuous successes came to a shuddering halt in 1798 when Napoleon discovered for the first time the power of the Royal Navy and his fleet of ships was annihilated at Battle of the Nile. English sea supremacy was something which frustrated Napoleon throughout his career, from his inability to invade England to defeat at Trafalgar in 1805, and in 1806 he attempted to strangle British trade with the Continental Blockade which was enforced by his order that every merchant ship must first stop at a French port in order for the cargo to be checked. It was a major setback for British merchant ships although many of them ignored the decree and with typical Napoleonic hubris one nurseryman in Hammersmith was granted permanent free passage to supply Fuchsias to Josephine's gardens at Malmaison. Nevertheless, the Napoleonic Wars had a catastrophic effect upon British merchant shipping and Liverpool shipowners were affected more than most – it should also be remembered that the Abolition of the slave-trade in 1807 also impacted greatly on Liverpool's mercantile trade, making the Napoleonic era a time of depression for shipowners and seamen alike and to Liverpool merchants Napoleon was nothing less than the devil incarnate

The Battle of The Nations – Leipzig 1813

Although Napoleon's defeat at Leipzig was celebrated across England at the time, the battle as such, has never entered into the annals of British military history in the way that Blenheim,

Napoleon defeated

Waterloo or even Dunkirk have done and it has faded from national consciousness. The reason lies in the fact that although England was a part of the Coalition, consisting of Russia, Prussia, Austria, Spain, Portugal and Sweden and 18 other countries, at the time of the campaign Wellington and his Spanish and Portuguese allies were still marching into western France fresh from victory over the French at Vittoria, and took little part in the key battles – in fact the only British contingent at Leipzig was a battery of Congreve rockets which acquitted themselves well. There's no doubt that the Peninsular Campaign was a major force in keeping Napoleon's forces stretched to the limit and played a great part in allowing the Leipzig Campaign to take place but the true origins of the battle lay in Napoleon's disastrous débacle the previous winter in the snows of Russia, when for the first time the nations of Europe realized that his armies were far from invincible. Following the retreat from Russia, the sight of Napoleon's bedraggled army staggering back across Europe was the inspiration for the conquered nations and they rose up as one against their oppressor. Nevertheless, the battles of the Leipzig Campaign were always hard fought and were not always victories but little by little the French troops were pushed back to the borders of France. The defining battle took place at Leipzig in Germany on the 16th to the 19th October, followed by running battles across virtually every country in Europe until in 1814 the Coalition entered Paris as victors.

With over 100,000 casualties the Battle of the Nations was the bloodiest in Napoleonic history, surpassing Waterloo by far. The battles of Dolitz, Markkleeberg, Wachau, Liebertwolkwitz and Leipzig have entered into the folklore of the nations that took part in those conflicts but all of them today are virtually unknown in England. They were however, writ large in England at that time, and even as late as 1898, Thomas Hardy (1840 – 1928) was moved to write the recollections of the battle in an epic poem called *Leipzig*. It begins with an old man recalling his Leipzig mother telling him as a boy the emotional impact of the battle, compounded by the fact that her husband was a German Hussar in the fighting:

> *And as I grew up, again and again*
> *She'd tell, after trilling that air*
> *Of her youth, and the battles on the Leipzig plain*
> *And all that was suffered there.*

But like many before and after, Hardy was not immune to the mystique of the Bonaparte legend and the remainder of the poem is a paean to Marshals Ney, Marmont, Poniatowski, Murat, Augureau, and the Emperor himself.

> *Against the first band did the Emperor stand;*
> *Against the second stood Ney;*
> *Marmont against the third gave the order-word;*
> *Thus raged it throughout the day.*

These are just two stanzas of a poem which deserves to be far better known and would undoubtedly be so if the subject was British but like the Battle of Leipzig Hardy's poem has faded into obscurity.

Liverpool Mercury Newsman 1818. Binns Collection, Liverpool Record Office

A Commercial Break

The *Liverpool Mercury* of Friday, December 13th 1813, was replete with surprisingly detailed reports of the fighting across the Channel, most especially in Holland where 250 Russian Cossacks were reported to have entered Amsterdam. The Cossacks were the spearhead of much larger Russian forces but were unable to attack the occupying French army until reinforcements arrived; they evidently had little faith in the peasant army 20,000 strong armed with farm implements, and a force of 3,000 students led by a renowned professor. Nevertheless, it was expected that the French would soon be expelled from Holland with the news that the French fleet had surrendered at the Texel. There was also the startling news that no less than 750 ships were in the Channel awaiting a fair wind to blow so that they could sail into English ports – there was no reason given as to why there were so many ships or who owned them. One enterprising journalist had filed a report of Napoleon reviewing what was left of his troops in the Tuileries gardens and had spotted the Emperor's son in dress uniform among the Old Guard. The King of Rome was the two year old son of Napoleon and Marie Louise and otherwise known as the Duke of Reichstadt or L'Aiglon (the Eaglet).

The advertisements in *The Mercury* told a tale of their own with patented flue-covers for sale which came highly recommended for high buildings but were *"professed not to work in every instance, such as high winds"* and there were new pocket-lights without phosphorus *"cheaper than the common tinder-box."* There was manganese *"for potter's use"* and a host of intricate maritime paraphernalia for sale by Smith and Co. of Pool Lane, all *"manufactured by themselves."* But the most intriguing advertisement by far had the startling heading *"Prime Bang-Up"* which turned out to be the name of one of the numerous coaches working out of the city. It has been said that prior to the Industrial Revolution London was a *"city of horses"* and it is largely forgotten that across the country in general horses were commonplace both for commercial and private ownership; in a Liverpool which increasingly employed horses for all manner of transport, and most especially the docks, horses must have been as numerous as people. The following reproduction of *The Mercury* advertisement for coach travel is a fascinating glimpse into Liverpool's past.

PRIME BANG-UP

Cheapest travelling from the Saracen's Head Inn, Dale Street, Liverpool, by the following Post Coaches at reduced rates:

Manchester Volunteer Post Coach. Every Morning at six o'clock to the Star Inn, Deansgate, Manchester – Fares inside five shillings, outside three shillings.

Manchester Post Coach every afternoon at 2 o'clock.

Chester & Holyhead Royal Mail every afternoon at three o'clock: sets out from Mrs Cookson's Woodside Ferry Boathouse. Nova Scotia.

CHESTER & SHREWSBURY BANG–UP Post Coach (carries only four inside) every morning at eight o'clock, by way of Rock Ferry, Chester, Wrexham, Ellesmere, to the Talbot Inn, Shrewsbury – goes a nearer road by 5 miles than any other Coach between Liverpool and Shrewsbury.

London Light Post Coach, every Sunday, Wednesday and Friday Mornings at six o'clock which carries only four insides to the Golden Cross, Charing Cross, in 34 hours, being only one night out, well-lighted and guarded – at reduced fares.

London Royal Liverpool Coach, every Tuesday, Thursday and Saturday Mornings at six o'clock to the Golden Cross, Charing Cross, in 34 hours, being only one night out, well-lighted and guarded – at reduced fares.

London Expedition Coach, every Evening at six o'clock to the White Horse Cellar, Piccadilly and the Saracen's Head Inn, Snow Hill, lighted and guarded – at reduced fares.

Birmingham Light Post Coach, called the Bang-Up, every Morning at six o'clock, (Sundays excepted) to the Saracen's Head Inn in 14 hours, only four insides.

Bristol and **Bath, Lord Wellington Post Coach,** every morning at six o'clock by way of Birmingham, Bromsgrove, Worcester, Gloucester, to the Bush Inn, Bristol.

Despite the enticing wording of the advertisements coach travel was never anything but uncomfortable and expensive and went completely unmourned and unmissed when train travel began from the 1830s onward. A certain romanticism around galloping horses, creaking leathers and colourful postillions persists to this day but the facts were very different and by 1850 most of the coaching inns in Dale Street had vanished into the mists of time.

Pickpockets and Paupers

Marshall Ney and the Old Guard by Adolphe Yvon

However, the advertisements which were so mundane then and are so fascinating now were only a small section of the *Liverpool Mercury* and the headlines that day were dominated by a meeting at the Exchange in order to organise the celebrations of Napoleon's downfall, despite the fact that he was still in the Tuileries and would remain so until March 1814, when the Allies entered Paris. But to all intents and purposes, throughout the country the Napoleonic era was deemed to be over and a triumphant Liverpool City Council was buzzing at the news. Sir John Gladstone (1764 – 1851), the father of William Gladstone, opened the proceedings with a Churchillian speech *"celebrating a series of events great and unexampled in the history of the world."* For those who may have been ignorant of current events, Gladstone gave a brief but accurate summary of the events leading up to Napoleon's downfall, beginning with the Emperor's entry into Moscow and the disastrous retreat of 1812. Gladstone made sure that his audience knew of Napoleon's flight back to Paris in disguise leaving his tattered army to straggle on through the snows of Russia and detailed how the Allies had come together *"to seize the propitious moment and throw off the yoke of the tyrant."* The battles in the Peninsular were given a special mention and with Wellington's armies advancing into Bordeaux, Sir John praised his advance into France as *"a march which has astonished the world."* Although Sir John commended the Russians, the Allies and Wellington to an enthusiastic audience which often greeted his remarks with loud cheers, he was far less complimentary towards the Dutch and in a scathing condemnation stated: *"Though the Dutch, however, feel that love of liberty common to all mankind and which so much distinguished their ancestors, yet I am sorry to find that they have parted with the French functionaries rather with the civility of persons who are taking a polite leave of a departing guest than with the indignation of men who are shaking off their old oppressors."*

Orange woman

It was a sign of the times that not one of the City Councillors noticed the inherent hypocrisy in Gladstone's lofty reference to *"the love of liberty common to all mankind"* when many of them were active in the slave-trade and Sir John himself owned plantations in Jamaica and Demarara, worked by his own slaves. Nevertheless, Sir John's noble words and stirring speech contained in places startling similarities to those made after Dunkirk and The Battle of Britain, 130 years in the future, and evocative phrases that he used such as *"England – a beacon of liberty"* have a familiar ring to them. But no matter how much his audience enjoyed the jingoism, Gladstone eventually came to the kernel of his speech which was how greatly Liverpool had benefited from the defeat of Napoleon and how commerce in all its forms was already booming in the city and in what manner they could celebrate their return to prosperity. It seems that the decision had already been made to illuminate the town and all that remained was to decide where the funding was to come from. After celebrating the good fortune of men who were already far wealthier than any average citizen of the town, it seemed grossly inappropriate to ask for money from the man in the street, but in a startling example of bigotry, esteemed members of the medical profession had been asked to make an inventory of the financial health of the people of Liverpool and reported that *"the major part of the inhabitants are in a state of pauperism."* Even the City Councillors were appalled when Gladstone joked that *"under these circumstances it would be highly inappropriate under the pretext of illuminations to pick their pockets still further"* and when they made their feelings known with *"clamours of disapproval"* Gladstone hastily returned to his patriotic theme. Apart from the poverty in the town there was no mention whatsoever of soldiers returning from the Napoleonic Wars, disabled and forced to beg on the streets.

It took several more meetings to decide that the illuminations in the Town Hall would be paid from the Councillors' pockets with the remainder of the town each funding their own individual buildings and the event was to be divided into three sections over three days; The first day would see the town illuminated, the second would be devoted to a *"splendid charity ball for the ladies"* and the third day there would be a number of public dinners for tradesmen who were encouraged to treat their workforce to a day's holiday and a *"repast."* One of the *"repasts"* has been noted as being in the potters' dwellings in Grafton Street and Wellington Road in Toxteth where the workers were sat down to a meal of bread, cheese and a barrel of ale. The houses had been built for the workers at the Herculaneum Potteries and were still standing in 1965 until the wholesale demolition of the houses and long-standing communities in the area.

One man who had more reason than many to rejoice at Napoleon's downfall was John Caspar Lavater of the firm of Dixon, Werther and Lavater and a son of the great Swiss poet, theologian and physiognomist Johann Kaspar Lavater (1741 - 1801) – the herbaceous plant Lavatera is named in his honour. Lavater père had been shot in 1799 by a French grenadier on the streets of Zurich when he had attempted to remonstrate against the French occupation of the city – he had lived on for over a year but eventually succumbed to the bullet he had received. John Caspar Lavater, his son, lived at the top of Mount Pleasant, in a house which is still standing today, opposite the Wellington Rooms. One of Lavater's neighbours was John Mather who somewhat ironically was a collector of Napoleonic memorabilia which he bequeathed to the Free Public Museum.

Even a Cockney Would Have Stared

Illuminations were nothing new to the town and several precedents had been set when successive mayors threw illuminated banquets in the Town Hall, followed by two grand affairs in 1789 to celebrate and give thanks for George III's recovery from another bout of his long-standing illness. The first was an illumination of the Town Hall and the town on the 26th March, 1789, which began with a twenty-one gun salute from the cannon at the Fort and ended at midnight with a repeat performance from the guns. The second was a far more elaborate ball and supper arranged for the following month. The ball and supper was a glittering affair which began at 7 o'clock in the evening of the 16th April, 1789, signalling the lighting of the Town Hall and several other key buildings in the town. The invited guests consisted exclusively of the great and the good of Liverpool with the gentlemen wearing patriotic crowns and mottos on their jackets and collars, and the ladies outdoing the men as always by sporting bandeaus and colourful favours pinned to their elegant gowns. But the real star of the show was the Town Hall itself, with every room gaily decorated in every imaginable way – coloured lamps were festooned from the ceilings, pilasters were wound around with more lamps in the shape of crowns, royal cyphers and ornamental flowers, and from the chandeliers polished metal stars glittered and sparkled as they slowly circled around in the heat given off from the room. In the upper rooms painted glass transparencies with lanterns placed discreetly at the rear gave a luminous and three dimensional effect with one of the most outstanding being a representation of the Town Hall as it was illuminated in March. There was a full-size transparency of the King, another of Brittania, two transparent urns engraved with appropriate mottoes, triumphal arches surrounded by lamps, vases, ornaments and a table arrangement of Mercury bringing the news of the King's recovery to Neptune.

Town Hall illuminations, 1813.
Liverpool Mercury

The guests had each been welcomed at the door by the Committee and country dancing begun at 7 pm proceeded until 9 pm, when the guests were ushered into the ballroom which was by mutual assent the pièce de résistance of the whole sparkling ensemble. The tables had been ingeniously arranged so that the whole company of 800 guests could sit down together beneath and surrounded by a breathtaking display of illuminations which covered every inch of the room. No less than 10,000 lamps and 1,200 wax candles in different shapes and colours adorned the chandeliers, hung in festoons from the ceilings, covered the walls, pilasters and cornices and decorated the tables. Toasts were given to the King and the Royal Family, followed by more to the prosperity of Liverpool and its commerce and all agreed that the whole evening had been *"the greatest spectacle of the kind ever seen in the country."* The tables had groaned with the profusion of food on offer and filled to the brim with the fine wines the company finally made their way home at 4 am of the following day, with a suggestion that they should do it all again for the King's Birthday on the 4th June, ringing in their ears. The newspapers all reported on the banquet in detail with Gore's General Advertiser summarising the whole thing as follows: *"Eight hundred well-dressed persons of both sexes, commodiously sat down to an elegant supper, all at one time, in one superb room, splendidly illuminated with ten thousand lights was a sight at which even a Cockney would have stared, and his more exalted and refined neighbours at St James's would have admired and been surprised at."*

The celebrations of 1813 had a lot to live up to, but on this joyous occasion it was planned for the whole town to participate. Whether or not Napoleon's downfall took precedence over George III's health is a moot point but there's no doubt that the commercial aspects of all the celebrations were never far from the surface and the merchants and shipowners of Liverpool were enthusiastic participants in anything which furthered their business concerns.

Liverpool En Fête

On Friday, 17th December, with a headline entitled **The Illumination** the *Liverpool Mercury's* pages were filled with detailed descriptions of the decorations on the main buildings in the town. In a lengthy and verbose introduction replete with celebratory phrases, the words *patriotism, exaltation, splendid, glorious, joyful, rejoicing* and so on were sprinkled liberally throughout every sentence. The only jarring note was an allusion to a journalist writing for a rival newspaper (probably *The Courier*) who had climbed to the heights of Everton, looked down on the lights of the town and declared the scene to be reminiscent of the burning of Moscow. *The Mercury* took the opportunity to condemn the offending *"afflictive recollection,"* consoling its readers with the forecast that London and Liverpool would never meet with such a fate. Evidently, *The Mercury* journalists had also viewed the illuminations from a distance and offered the fanciful idea that *"the prospect of the town from Edge Hill, Low Hill and Everton gave to the spectators the idea of a city fabricated by the hands of fairies from the very substance of light itself."* Warming to his theme of magic in the air, the columnist then compared the scene to something from the Arabian Nights before describing each of the principal displays in detail.

Although by today's standards it's easy to dismiss the illuminations as primitive, in an age when the darkness was only ever dispelled on moonlit nights, the coloured lamps of the town must have been a stirring sight, and it says a great deal that despite their minor internecine squabbles every newspaper and journal in the town reported on the illuminations and they were all as one in declaring them a breathtaking success. Given that the lamps which formed the basis of the displays were simply thousands of oil-lamps supplemented with vast amounts of candles, the ingenuity and energy that had gone into the illuminations was staggering. The beautifully painted transparencies on glass were works of art in their own right and the finest artists in the city had given their services to create the translucent dioramas which were so much a feature of the celebrations. Joseph Wright of Derby (1734 – 1797) who pioneered paintings of scientific subjects and chiaroscuro scenes sometimes used back-lighting which gave the appearance that the flames were actually flickering in a foundry for example; strangely it's an art which has gone out of style. Sadly, there are very few contemporary drawings of the illuminations and we must take it on trust that the Liverpool celebrations of 1813 were a wonder of the Georgian era which will forever remain a tantalisingly ephemeral and elusive event. However, what we do have are our own imaginations and a remarkably detailed account of each display by the *Liverpool Mercury*.

The Town Hall – The Exchange was the focal point for the illuminations and the whole of the front of the building was decorated with coloured lamps. The triangular pediment at the top of the façade contained the words *'Europe Liberated'* in variegated coloured lamps with a laurel wreath in the centre overlooked by a large Crown. In the windows behind the balcony were three complex transparencies – one represented Britannia leaning on her shield, holding her trident entwined with the symbols of commerce, indicating England's sovereignty of the seas and extended trade with the world; the second had an allegorical Victory dispensing her Crowns to the nations allied against the tyranny of France with the fallen Eagles and Colours of the enemy lying at their feet; and the third had an allegorical Independence leaning on a cornucopia roused by a herald proclaiming *'Commerce is Free'*. Altogether, the trio formed a triptych which could be viewed as one single picture. The right and left wings of the building were emblazoned with the initials *G.R.* (George Rex) and *P.R.* (Prince Regent) and above the main door were the words *Orange Boven* (Orange is on top) flanked by the words *Leipzig and Vittoria* on each side.

The original Athenaeum, Church Street

Athenaeum – The Athenaeum was built in 1798 and originally in Church Street around the corner from School Lane. The small frontage allowed only the letters *G.R.* with different coloured lamps spelling out the motto *'Europe Free'* in large letters.

The Union News Room – Situated at 105 Duke Street, the building was named for the fact that it came into being on the 1st January, 1801, on the same day as the Union of England and Ireland was ratified. Designed by John Foster, the austere and magisterial building was England's first public library and now listed, still stands on the corner of Duke Street and Slater Street. The sheer size of the façade and the inordinate number of windows allowed a more lavish display than any other building in the town and the proprietors took full advantage of the space at their disposal. In the upper brickwork were emblazoned in large, colourful lettering the words *'By Union A Good Cause Triumphs'* and in the three windows which divided the words were transparencies of *England, Scotland* and *Ireland.* The lower windows were painted in imitation of ground glass with coloured lanterns at the arches spelling out *God Save Our Good King* in ultramarine blue, and in each window were the words *Wellington, Graham, Vittoria, Salamanca, Alexander, Blucher, Moscow, Leipzig* in alternate colours of gold and carmine with coloured stars in each corner. The whole display was overlooked by a huge *Prince's Plume* resting on the *King's Arms* in coloured lanterns, at the highest point of the building. Mr Leigh of Duke Street was congratulated for painting the transparencies without payment.

The Lyceum – Situated at the bottom of Bold Street, the Lyceum newsroom had every window illuminated and a transparency of *The Prince Regent.*

The Lyceum 1828. Liverpool Record Office

The Post Office – The original Post Office was in 1775 a simple dwelling-house located in North John Street with apertures on the outside for receiving and delivering letters. The Post Office later moved to Lord Street until 1800 when it moved again to Post Office Place where it was situated during the illuminations. Apart from the ubiquitous coloured lamps the centrepiece of the Post Office display was a large transparency representing *Britannia receiving a Victory Wreath from a Cherub – at Britannia's feet the British Lion trampled a French Eagle with a broken staff.* In the distance a messenger is approaching Britannia with an olive branch and the whole scene is overlooked by the *Eye of Providence.*

The School for the Blind – Originally built in Commutation Row, the school was situated in London Road in 1800. For the illuminations the school exhibited a transparency with the moving words – *'We can participate in the general joy, though we cannot see the general blaze'.*

The Music Hall – The original Music Hall was opened in 1786 on the corner of Bold Street and the aptly named Concert Street to the strains of Handel's Messiah. The building which housed 1300 spectators was demolished circa 1850 and replaced with the present building which was also a music hall and in latter years home to a large Waterstones bookshop. The celebratory display in 1813 was a modest Crown in variegated lamps and coloured lamps on the cornices.

Freemasons Hall – Situated in Bold Street, the window display was a transparency of the Duke of Kent, suitably attired in his Freemason's Robes as Grand Master.

The Theatre – There were several theatres in the town and *The Mercury* is not specific as to which one is referred to here but it is probably the Theatre Royal in Williamson Square. Given the skill of the props-men working in the theatre, the decorations would have been carried out with little difficulty and they took the opportunity to festoon the frontage with coloured lamps with a large transparency in the centre proclaiming *"Hail to the heroes, to Wellington, to our brave allies, for the independence of nations, for victory, for the prospect of peace and prosperity. All Hail!"*

The Excise Office – Situated at the bottom of Hanover Street, the Excise Office chose a Crown with a star each side, a Plume of Feathers and an Anchor in coloured lamps and a transparency proclaiming with a subtle humour *May the Proof Spirit of the British Nation ne'er be lowered by French Adulteration.*

Messrs Roscoe, Clarke and Roscoe's Bank – In Castle Street was elegantly decorated with coloured lamps.

Castle Street, 1786.
Liverpool Record Office

Messrs Heywood's Bank – Brunswick Street was decorated with *Anchors* and a *Crown* in crystal lamps and the words *'Peace and Plenty'* in coloured lamps.

Messrs Moss, Dale and Co's Bank – In Dale Street was decorated with coloured lamps festooned across the whole frontage.

Mrs Billinge – Presumably a shop in Castle Street had a transparency of *Lord Wellington* with the words *'Peninsula, Our Brave Allies'* and *'Leipzig'* painted on three windows and illuminated with lamps.

The Dispensary – The original Dispensary was in Princes Street/North John Street but was relocated to Church Street, next to the Athenaeum in 1782. The display was that of *Britannia seated on a Cannon with Trident in hand and a Majestic Lion at her feet.* Painted on the windows was an ambitious attempt at a poem which one suspects could have quite easily become an epic if not for lack of space.

Europe Rejoice! The Tyrants' Gilded Fame
Is now the empty shadow of a name
Russia, Prussia, Sweden, rose with might!
And turn'd Napoleon's day to darkest night!
Briton's Rejoice! Your loudest voices raise
In strains harmonious of exalted praise.

Concentric Society – The *Mercury* gives no indication where the Concentric Society was situated but they had spared no effort in their display with no less than four transparencies of allegorical paintings representing the *Liberation of Europe,* the *Restoration of Commerce,* and the *Trade of Liverpool.* Between the painted allegories were the mottoes *'In Haec Signo Vinces, Europe Be Free, The People, The King May he Reign for his People'* and keeping to the Latin theme *'Vis Populi, Vis Regum.'*

Mrs Bartington's Backbone Club House – In Liver Street, seemed to have missed the point of the celebrations and chose to advertise her own club with the words *'Backbone Club'* picked out in coloured lamps.

The Mystic Society – at Mrs Forshaw's in Hale Street, settled for a simple *A, B,* and *C* picked out in lamps, and true to her profession, left passers-by mystified as to what it represented.

Mr J. Gore – Castle Street – the offices of the famous *Gore's General Advertiser* and prized reference book today is a wonderfully detailed window on the past. Gore's chose a transparency of the *Duke of Wellington* with the words *'Britons Rejoice'* across the frontage.

The Courier Office – In Castle Street, was emblazoned with patriotic motifs in every window with a regal *Crown* and *Plume of Feathers* at the top of the building. The left window had a complex transparency of fortitude resting on a pillar with a background of a turbulent sea, a deserted city, Moscow in flames with lightning flashes above the words *'England Has Saved Herself by Her Firmness and Other Nations by her Example.'* The right hand window contained a no less complex transparency of the Genius of Britain holding up a Star of Independence to the Oppressed Nations of Europe with Wisdom and Valour at her Feet and the wording *'That Ray Which has Shone with such a steady lustre from our own happy shores is now rapidly diffusing throughout the whole Continent.'* The four windows above exhibited the words *Vittoria, Leipzig, Moscow,* and *Dennevitz* – and at this point even *The Mercury* which had reported the event in the minutest detail became tired of recording the remainder of the *Courier's* emblems and ended with etc, etc, etc.

Offices of the Liverpool Mercury are still standing.

The *Liverpool Mercury* – Was no less extravagant in its choice of decoration with a complicated transparency in which Liberty dressed in pink with an orange coloured cap on her spear and attended by the British Lion is in the act of presenting a ribbon to a Dutchman inscribed with the words *'Orange Booven'* and *'Get Up! Stand Up Like a Man!'* In the same transparency a Mynheer, dressed in traditional costume is arising from a prostrate position, with one hand on the British Lion and another on his hip, crying out *"Oh My Poor Backbone!"* The Mercury appeared to have adopted the same attitude to the Dutch as Sir John Gladstone and continued with another picture of John Bull standing on a rock inscribed *'The People Have Triumphed'* exhorting the Hollander to get up by shouting *"Up With the Rumps!"* Another transparency which presumed that Liverpudlians could read French, has Napoleon as an imp, running away while exclaiming *"La Liberté Morbleu! Il faut que je m'en aille"* while a Russian Eagle hovers over the fleeing Emperor. The side windows were painted with the mottoes *'Peace and Plenty and Free Press.'*

The Past is Another Country

The *Liverpool Mercury* list of illuminated buildings was by no means a comprehensive list of all those that took part in the illuminations and many were omitted. However, the most prestigious buildings were highlighted and it is quite telling that not one of them existed in Defoe's day apart from the Town Hall and even that was a very different building to the one that Defoe knew – in fact, even the streets were unknown in his time. If the shade of Daniel Defoe could have in some way reappeared to find the answer to his rhetorical question *"What it may grow to in time I know not"* then he would have seen the skeletal beginnings of the town that he was familiar with, fleshed out and spreading in every direction. And if he had been astonished at the many changes that had taken place then he would have been in a state of wonderment at the explosive growth of the Victorian era which would bring about an architectural and industrial revolution which would change the face of Liverpool forever.

The extent of the celebrations marking the downfall of Napoleon, in Liverpool and the country in general, were indicative of just how much he was feared and in Liverpool particularly, how trade and commerce had been affected. Over and over again, the words, *"commerce"* and *"trade"* appear in the illuminated wordings and in the press, and for a city of merchants whose wealth was dependent on maritime matters their joy was boundless. It was quite ironic that at the time the celebrations were taking place that Napoleon was still in the Tuileries and would remain so until the Allies entered Paris in March, 1814, when the Ogre would be condemned to exile on Elba. But it was even more of an irony when One Hundred Days later, Napoleon escaped from Elba and the whole game would be played out on a different battlefield and on a different day – and the lamps and illuminations done all over again.

Plus ça change

The people of the town did in fact contribute to the celebrations but it was an entirely voluntary contribution; following salutes from the cannon of the men-of-war anchored in the Mersey and the pealing of church bells, on Tuesday, 14th December, the good people who lived on Everton Brow, who it has to be said were wealthier than most, decorated the windows of their houses with transparencies. Each house vied with the other for the best transparency and it was said that the glow could be seen as far away as Chester. In the evening there was a grand firework display. On the following Saturday, similar celebrations took place on the slopes of Edge Hill. It was quite astonishing how the downfall of Napoleon had electrified the town and in the general euphoria ships returned to sea with no fear of privateers, a grand plan for re-paving the whole town was begun and Richard Westmacott's sculpture of Lord Nelson was unveiled on October 21st, on Exchange Flags. There was even a discussion on the building of a tunnel beneath the Mersey which was soon forgotten when the government gave the town a magnificent grant of £60,000 for *"its loyalty and faithfulness"* in order to improve the dock system. Even the East India Company was infected with the general optimism and when the company threw open their commerce to private enterprise it was not difficult to guess who would be the first to take advantage. Sir John Gladstone was the owner of a large ship called the *Kingsmill* and on May 27th 1814, the ship sailed for Bengal with a full cargo, returning 15 months later with a valuable cargo of sugar, cotton, ebony, indigo and spices and *'a few shawls and muslins for the ladies.'* It was the beginning of a trade which would grow to *'colossal proportions'* and further enrich the man who had proposed to pay for his own good fortune by donations from the public.

The Surgeon

Henry Park (1745 - 1831)

*"It is the surgeon's duty to tranquillize the temper, to beget cheerfulness,
and to impart confidence of recovery."*

– Sir Astley Paston Cooper

St Nicholas Church and the Tower, 1760 by W.G.Herdman – Liverpool Record Office

Daunting Prospects

Born in Water Street nearly 300 years ago, although the topography is unchanged and the hill remains as steep as ever, Henry Park would find very little that he would recognize of the area today. He would no doubt be overwhelmed by the grandiose buildings and wonder why he could no longer see the river, but he would at least recognize the name Tower Buildings which was the site of the castellated Tower which he knew so well. He would also recognize the tiny lane which leads to the Church of St Nicholas called Tower Weint and could not fail to notice that the Mersey no longer laps at its walls. The Water Street that Henry Park was born into was little more than a medieval street which was unpaved and ran down to a small, sandy shore which was covered by the Mersey at high tide, and Liverpool itself was still recognisable as the fishing village it had been for centuries.

*The Tower 1804 by Herdman after a
drawing by James Boardman.
Liverpool Record Office*

It was a sad fact that the era Park was born into was less than conducive for his future profession of surgeon and given the constraints that they worked under, the working lives of surgeon Park and his colleagues were nothing less than heroic. It was a strange coincidence that the year that Park was born, 1745, was the same year that the ancient profession of Barber-Surgeons became defunct and the law was passed making surgery a profession in its own right; the Guild of Barber-Surgeons had been in existence since the 15th century practising their strange mixture of skills which included amputation, leeching, dentistry, bloodletting and of course hair-cutting – the distinctive barber's pole dates from the time of the Barber-Surgeons with the bright coloured, red wrapping on a white background advertising that bloodletting was practised here. Henry Park's surgical skills would be far removed from the dubious practices of the Barber-Surgeons but they would still be a world away from the surgery of even Victorian times which was greatly advanced but still left a lot to be desired. Park and his colleagues were in fact trapped in a curious interval in time where surgery was moving away from the medieval quackery of the past but would never attain the most basic knowledge of the Victorian era. One of the greatest problems that surgeons wrestled with at that time was the lack of knowledge of anaesthetics followed closely by a lack of even the most basic practices in hygiene and Henry Park would be shackled by both these difficulties throughout his lifetime; the first operation using a general anaesthetic of ether did not take place until 1846 and chloroform came into use the following year – prior to that the only things available were the administration of opium, large amounts of alcohol, various herbal remedies or *in extremis* a blow on the head with a wooden mallet (by all accounts ether had been used at a much earlier date than the mid-Victorian era and it appears that the doctors in the Liverpool Infirmary allowed a great opportunity to slip from their grasp when they turned down the use of ether as early as 1776 – a Dr Matthew Turner who worked at the hospital was advocating the use of *aether* but unfortunately he sold the drug at the exorbitant rate of 2 shillings per ounce. Because of the high price, Turner's colleagues became sceptical of the drug's alleged properties and refused to pay, denying patients an anaesthetic for years to come and throwing the chance of fame and fortune to the winds).

As far as hygiene was concerned, it was virtually non-existent until Florence Nightingale preached it as a religion during the Crimean War.

Liverpool was still little more than a cluster of streets, alleys and courts when Henry Park was born, with a population of around 20,000 inhabitants. Church Street had a large orchard on the south side, a legacy left by the castle which had been demolished in 1715 – St George's Church was on the site in Park's day – Clayton Square had not yet been laid out, Bold Street did not exist and it was just a short walk into a pleasant countryside of fields surrounding the town. The main throughfares of Dale Street, Castle Street and Tithebarn Street were still only 18 feet wide until they were widened in 1786 and when Henry Park was aged 20 the streets were still the unsanitary pathways they had always been, while in 1768 the *Liverpool Chronicle* reported that it was still common practice *'to empty privies into the streets.'* Contaminated water supplies were commonplace, which was not unexpected when the main water supply was the Fall Well – situated on the corner of Lime Street and Roe Street. The Fall Well was subject to a number of contaminants with the brickwork often crumbling and falling in the water below and people washing their clothes and sometimes themselves, thereby introducing dirt and soap into the drinking water. Sewerage was non-existent, malnourishment was commonplace and many of the inhabitants lived in overcrowded court dwellings – all elements which contributed to the many diseases which were prevalent such as tuberculosis, typhus, smallpox and cholera, not to mention the high child mortality rate.

It's difficult to escape the belief that Liverpool in the 18th century must have resembled one of today's third-world countries and remarkably it would be a long time before anyone would make any connection between the relative robustness of the farming community just a short distance outside the town and the sickly pallor of the closely-packed inhabitants close to the river. It must have been a daunting prospect to take up surgery and doctoring when faced with such a battery of diseases with so few tools to combat them.

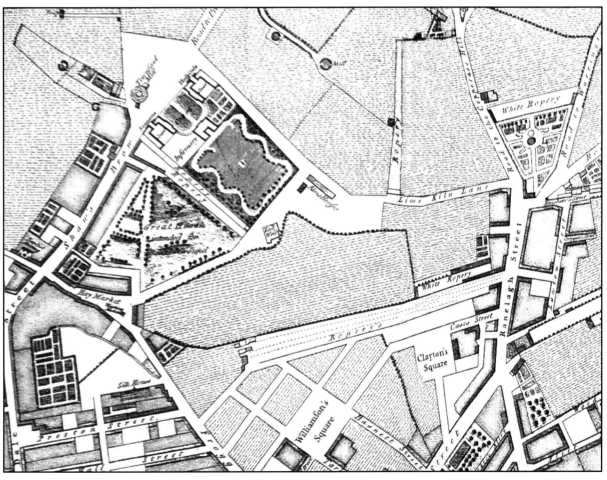

Eyes' map of 1765 showing location of Infirmary. Liverpool Record Office

The Poor Law Acts beginning in 1601 had made each parish responsible for its own poor with a system of outdoor relief and the provision of money to needy people but the system became too complex, expensive and inefficient and in 1723 led to the building of the first workhouse in Liverpool which was situated on the corner of College Lane and Hanover Street. There had also been some effort at relieving poverty in Liverpool and elsewhere with the provision of Almshouses – there were Almshouses where the Queensway Tunnel now stands and others at the top of Shaw's Brow, Hanover Street and Dale Street, with many of the inhabitants the widows and children of seamen lost at sea. However, the fact remained that the best efforts of the authorities, charitable organisations and philanthropists could not keep up with the ever-growing population, and poverty and the diseases which accompanied it were endemic throughout the lifetime of Henry Park and beyond.

There was however, light in the darkness, and it was yet another strange coincidence that one year prior to Henry Park's birth, in 1744 a subscription was begun in order to raise funds for a much needed hospital – an institution which would play a great part in Park's life. The building of the hospital which would be called the Liverpool Infirmary was not something unique to Liverpool but was part of a national initiative in which hospitals sprang up in major towns and cities across the country.

There was no shortage of donations to the hospital fund and the first list of subscribers and philanthropists enrolled into the scheme numbered 121 names; in any undertaking of that period in time, it was always a curious phenomenon that among the list of lawyers, doctors, merchants and clerics there was inevitably a sprinkling of names of men engaged in the slave-trade who were always generous to a fault, and foremost among the subscribers were the names of Thomas Seel whose gift of £86 was the highest of all the donations, Richard Gildart, Samuel Ogden, John Hardman, Foster Cunliffe and John Atherton, all men who had earned their fortunes from the slave-trade – in the list of subscribers they were diplomatically marked down as merchants.

Building of the Infirmary began in July, 1745, on a site named Oyl Mill Field which was roughly where St George's Hall stands today. Briefly interrupted by the Jacobite Rebellion the Infirmary was completed on the 25th March, 1749, and officially declared open by the Earl of Derby. The first Senior Surgeon elected was James Bromfield. The hospital was a handsome building with wings on each side devoted to the care of seamen and gardens to the rear – it would remain on that site until 1826 when it was relocated to Brownlow Street.

Infirmary and Seaman's Hospital with Folly Fair in foreground by Herdman.
Liverpool Record Office

Le Jeune Médicin

The Tower in 1816 by Herdman. Liverpool Record Office

Henry Park was born on March 2nd, 1745, in Water Street, one of two boys and three girls, and he was baptised in the nearby St Nicholas Church. Henry's father was an apothecary but his sudden death while away from home had a devastating effect on the family which was greatly exacerbated by the fact that he left no will; in the days when women were disenfranchised in every conceivable way, her husband's estate which lay more in land than in money, devolved to his eldest son, Edward, who was no more than three years old, leaving Mrs Park (née Lyon) with a vastly reduced income and five children to care for – Mary aged 12 was the eldest and Henry who was the youngest had not yet reached his first birthday. Despite her financial woes, Henry's mother ensured that both of her sons received a good education, beginning school at a very early age in the school run by the Reverend Henry Wolstenholme. Henry was barely three years of age when he started school and at the same time began a friendship with another boy who would become the Reverend H. Roughsedge. The two boys were in the habit of calling each other Harry and Bob and were still doing so many years later in a friendship which would last an astonishing 80 years – Henry was always known thereafter as Harry to his associates and friends. The standard of education at Wolstenholme School was extremely high, and after mastering the basic subjects Harry Park went on to study Greek, Latin and mathematics at which he excelled. Harry remained in the school until the age of 14 when he was placed in the care of Mr Bromfield at the Liverpool Infirmary. Dr James Bromfield was an uncle by marriage but in later years when Park was vastly more experienced he looked back on his early days in the Infirmary and was less than complimentary about Bromfield's skills as a doctor. Park was probably correct about his mentor's lack of expertise but may not have realised that Bromfield's true role lay in politics, and it was his political acumen which first gained the Oyl Mill Field as a site for the proposed Infirmary. Bromfield had been Mayor in 1746 and as a Town Councillor knew only too well the necessity for a hospital in the town and he had contributed generously

The Prison Weint 1810 by Herdman.
Liverpool Record Office

both to the building fund and the maintenance fund. Despite Park's misgivings, Bromfield remained in his post as Senior Surgeon from the opening of the Infirmary in 1749 until 1763 when he retired – he died the following year. Although Park may have been a little harsh on Bromfield, he was undoubtedly correct when he surmised that the level of care by the medical officers was sadly lacking; Park was always known for his sunny disposition and his criticisms came in the form of comic tales of his early years working in the Infirmary which, in his own unique way, were more revealing and scathing than any formal critique. The deficiencies of the medical officers left Park very much to his own devices at the Infirmary but he turned the situation to his own advantage by devoting himself to practical and theoretical studies of medicine revealing an unusual aptitude for the profession. Park was barely 17 years of age when, as part of his apprenticeship, he was given the responsibility of caring for the prisoners-of-war incarcerated in the Liverpool Tower, the greater number of them French prisoners from the wars of 1746 in North America, sometimes called King George's War. It was indicative of how little the prisoners were cared for when Park found himself the only doctor in a prison housing 600 inmates, all of them suffering from malnutrition and living in appalling conditions. It was an onerous burden to shoulder without help or supervision but far from crumbling beneath the strain the young Park thrived among the prisoners whose cheerful and positive attitude mirrored his own and as he worked among them the young man came to admire the fortitude and spirit of the French prisoners who called him affectionately *le jeune Médicin*. Park took the opportunity to learn the French language while he worked in the Tower while the prisoners made their own diversions carving cocoa-nuts and beef-bones with their pen-knives into works of art which were highly-prized outside the prison. The prisoners were later allowed to sell their carvings outside the prison walls but at that time selling was forbidden and they showered their carvings on Park as a means of thanking him for his efforts on their behalf. In the belief that the presents would be never-ending Park was in the habit of giving them away to friends, but the supply dried up when the prisoners were one day removed to another prison and the young doctor regretted all his days that he had never kept some mementoes for himself – he realised too late that they were remarkable works of art which are still prized today by collectors.

A Second Apprenticeship

Park's main successes at the Tower were not strictly speaking of a medical nature but the improvements he made to the cleanliness and ventilation of their surroundings and the quality and quantity of their meagre provisions went some way to alleviating the prisoners' sufferings. Park compensated for the lack of practical training on offer and his solitary existence by reading each evening, and many hours were spent poring over books on anatomy, surgery and chemistry. Park described the first three years of his working life in the Infirmary as his *"first apprenticeship"* and an example of *bad* practice, in other words *"how not to do it"* but things were about to change dramatically when he embarked upon what he called his *"second apprenticeship"* when still only 17 he went to live in the London house of the eminent surgeon, Sir Percivall Pott (1714 - 1788). Sir Percivall Pott was one of the leading surgeons of his day and had introduced many improvements into surgical practice, not least his reluctance to follow the customary practice to amputate limbs when there were distinct possibilities of alternative treatment. There are still several diseases which carry the name *"Pott's"* before them including Pott's Fracture and as a specialist in diseases of the joints he introduced many principles which are still in use in modern medicine. Pott was an innovator in many ways and was one of the first surgeons to recognize and identify the correlation between diseases and occupation. As a mainstay of Bart's Hospital for many years it says a great deal about his influence on the hospital that nearly 250 years after his death there is still a ward named the Sir Percivall Pott ward.

Henry Park's training mentored by Sir Percivall Pott was a world away from the lackadaisical days of his *"first apprenticeship"* and laid the foundations for his future success. Gaining invaluable practical experience at St Bartholemew's hospital, Park thrived under the tutelage of Pott who he idolised, and from the age of 17 to 20 his practical and theoretical learning was first class. Besides following Pott's medical teachings, Park revered the eminent doctor to the point where he paid him the great compliment of adopting many of his mannerisms. It was something which Park did unconsciously but it became so ingrained that many years later many of Pott's traits and peculiarities lived on through Park and were noticeable to their mutual friends who pointed them out as quite strange. In the final year of his apprenticeship and after three years spent with Pott, Park travelled to Rouen where he was again impressed by the quality of his tutors, in particular Claude-Nicolas Le Cat (1700 - 1768), Chief Surgeon of the ancient and prestigious Hôtel Dieu. Park attended all of Le Cat's lectures and wrote every word down in a book he called *Chirurgical Observations and Remedies*. From Rouen, Park spent the final months of his learning in Paris, after which time he was ready to embark in practice on his own account and put his accumulated knowledge into practical use. On his return to London, Pott tried to persuade the young doctor to set up practice in the capital where he would have undoubtedly earned fame and fortune, but Park's devotion to his mother and attachment to the town of his birth made his mind up for him and he returned to Liverpool clutching the London Diploma in Surgery, the only surgeon in Liverpool to have attained one.

Sir Percivall Pott

Births and Deaths

Park returned to Liverpool at the end of 1766, aged 22, when he immediately returned the expenses of his education back to his mother. In his turn Edward relinquished his claims to his inheritance and divided the property equally before his untimely death soon afterwards when he was around the age of twenty-five. Part of the inheritance was a portion of land called Jericho Strawberry Gardens and this was allotted as Mary's share; Mary who had *"passed the best years of her life as her mother's right-hand help, the judicious counsellor, as well as partner in cares and anxieties under adverse circumstances"* was especially fond of this place *"lying close to the water side where the Mersey expands so as to have the appearance of a lake, and being enriched by much fine timber which has since been felled, possessed uncommon beauty."* As the eldest child, Mary remembered more than her siblings the summers spent there enjoying the company of her father and the evenings of music and dancing in the company of the Woodward family.

Henry Park

In 1767, a place became available at the Infirmary and Park took up the post of surgeon in the hospital where he had begun his apprenticeship. With a sound background of practical and theoretical surgery Park was eminently suited to the post which was principally involved in caring for the labouring classes of the town. Aged just 22 and full of energy and exuberance, he became a favourite among his patients, and known for having an iron constitution, he worked unsociable hours whenever he was needed. Park's powers of endurance were remarkable and he often worked excessive hours and studied whenever he found time but his energy was not confined to work and on social occasions he would dance until the early hours and then rise early to follow the hounds. However, in 1776, at the age of 31, Park sold his hunter and vowed never to mount a horse again except for carrying out his duties; it seemed a strange decision to relinquish the sport he loved but it was just one of many things which changed when his marriage came about. Henry married Elizabeth Ranicar, the eldest daughter of John Ranicar and Ellen Ranicar (née Ellen Green) of Westleigh Hall, Leigh, in a ceremony which took place at the Church of St Mary the Virgin, Leigh, on the 1st May, 1776, with Park's great friend Joseph Brandreth as one of the witnesses. The couple set up home in Basnett Street which was at that time perceived to be out in the country and one year later in 1777 Park went into partnership with another surgeon at the infirmary, Edward Alanson, working from a room in Park's home in Basnett Street and still employed at the Infirmary. As difficult as it is to comprehend now, Park's private patients grumbled at the distance they had to travel as Basnett Street was so far out of town.

Henry and Elizabeth's first child was born in 1777 and named after Elizabeth's mother's maiden name, she was christened in St Thomas' Church as Ellen Green Park. Every year thereafter another child was born in Basnett Street until by 1786 Elizabeth had brought into the world seven girls and two boys.

Henry Park seemed to have a particular talent for the care of infants and midwifery and in 1769 he had begun to detail the names and dates of the children he had helped into the world – it was in effect a Register of Births and neatly handwritten in columns were the Names and Addresses of each patient, Date of Birth, Class of Labour, and Notes. So that a typical Class of Labour would say *"natural birth"* or *"abortion"* which was rare, or *"breech"* which was also uncommon, while the notes would include such comments as *"twins"* or *"jaundice"* and all too often would state baldly *"consumption"* or *"cholera."* One of the better known names in the book is William Ewart Gladstone who was born in Rodney Street on the 29th December, 1809, but the remainder of the book is a fascinating document of the people and places in Liverpool in the Georgian era. The book begins in Haymarket in January 1769 and ends in June, 1830, at an address in Colquitt Street, but in-between the 123 pages are a host of names and addresses ranging from every street in the town centre, homes on the Wirral and as far away as rural Woolton, totalling nearly 1400 births; in an era when it was not considered quite decent to allow men to carry out midwifery the statistics reveal the trust that Park had engendered in his patients over the years. Revealing a wry sense of humour, Park called his remarkable Register his *Book of Genesis*.

Henry and Elizabeth Park's children were as follows:

Ellen Green Park born 5th March	1777 -	died 3rd April, 1854	-- aged 78
Mary Lyon Park born 7th June	1778 -	died 4th June, 1795	-- aged 16
John Ranicar Park born 11th May	1779 -	died 14th Dec, 1847	-- aged 68
Elizabeth Park born 25th August	1780 -	died 1781	-- aged 1
Ann Park born 2nd August	1781 -	died 1781	-- aged 3 months
Elizabeth Park born 18th Dec	1782 -	died 6 June, 1855	-- aged 72
Ann Green Park born 5 April	1784 -	died 4th July,1862	-- aged 78
Henry Park born 13th April	1785 -	died 1790	-- aged 5
Charlotte Catherine Park 19 July	1786 -	died 14th Jan, 1872	-- aged 86

It's quite clear from the above that although Henry Park was an eminent surgeon his family were not immune from the ills that made life such a lottery in those days and while the first Elizabeth lived for just one year the second Elizabeth lived to 72; Mary Lyon Park died young aged 16 but Henry only lived until the age of 5 and while the first Ann died at a pitiful 3 months, the second Ann made it to the ripe old age of 78. While it was always excruciating for any parents to watch their children wither on the vine, the high mortality rate of yesteryear was accepted as a way of life and Henry and Elizabeth could weather the storms while they could take comfort in each other. Henry was devoted to Elizabeth and their marriage brought them both happiness so that when she died on the 21st November,1786, just 4 months after the birth of Charlotte Catherine, it was a disaster which none of his medical skills could avert and still brought tears to Henry Park's eyes over 40 years later.

Carrying On

Soon after Elizabeth's death, Henry invited his mother and his sister Mary to live with him and at the same time employed a Governess to look after his five daughters. He worked on as he had always done and it was around this time that he published a small book entitled *The Excision of Carious Joints*. It was almost certain that Park had emulated Sir Percivall Pott's reluctance to amputate limbs and appalled by the numbers of soldiers returning from the American War of Independence and the interminable wars with the French with limbs missing that he resolved to try other methods rather than amputate which often meant certain death. Park's alternative was to remove damaged bone and tissue and allow the limb to heal itself and he first performed the *excision of a joint* on a man chosen for being *"a strong, robust, Scotch Sailor, age 33."* Although the operation left the sailor with one leg ¾ of an inch shorter than the other the operation was an unqualified success and allowed the man to continue his life at sea – sadly, fate was never kind to the *"Scotch Sailor"* who went on to be shipwrecked twice, suffering many hardships, and finally drowning in the River Mersey. Several further operations met with the same success as Park's first subject and when Park's colleagues began to copy his technique it was the beginning of the end for needless amputations.

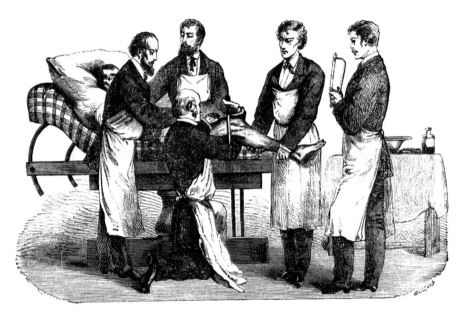

Surgery in Park's era

In 1788, as a means of taking his mind off his loss, Henry's sister Mary persuaded him to build a house in Bold Street which was then sparsely populated. Park enjoyed designing and he built his house to his own specifications on the corner of Newington Street near to the house of Ann Renshaw which stood on the opposite corner and he would soon have Joseph Brandreth as his next door neighbour. Joseph Brandreth (1746 - 1815) established the Dispensary in Church Street in 1778 and was a colleague and friend of Park at the Infirmary. Today, the bottom floor of Park's house which he occupied for 32 years has been converted into shops, but the original brickwork can be seen at the top floor and to the rear. Park threw himself into his work but Elizabeth would have been dismayed at how little he looked after himself; his meals were snatched and eaten at irregular times, he slept fitfully and endangering his life travelling across the river in stormy weather, he endangered it further by allowing his clothes to dry on his body on his return. Park's reckless behaviour extended to the Infirmary on an occasion when he volunteered for an experiment to test the effect of heat on the human body. One man had already died during this experiment but Park entered the 9 foot square chamber undeterred, enduring a temperature of 202° Fahrenheit and frying three eggs in the same room. After blistering his fingers when he touched the thermometer, Park then ate the eggs before emerging from the chamber and the left then Infirmary to walk over Everton Hill in a severe frost.

Park owned a piece of land which had been in his family for centuries situated on Smithdown Lane when it was a rustic landscape of trees and gardens. Divided from the city by two miles of farmland, Park found pleasure in cultivating his garden and would spend the evenings there with his children whenever he could get away from work. He often mused over the idea of building a retreat here for his retirement years but his plans never came to anything more than dreams. The landscape has changed so dramatically that it's difficult to imagine the area around Tunnel Road, Smithdown Road and Earle Road as woodland, farmland and gardens but circa 1800 it was a bucolic place of beauty. It was so beautiful in fact that Thomas Earle (1754 -1822) had already bought up most of the land and when Henry Park decided to sell his portion in 1797 Earle purchased that also, building his mansion called Spekelands at what is now the top of Earle Road, where he overlooked a demesne as grand as that of any feudal lord.

In 1779, Park joined the committee for the addition of a Lunatic Asylum to the Infirmary. The very name Lunatic, which is offensive today, was then in common use for anyone with mental disorders and with psychiatry not even in an embryonic stage treatment of mental patents was virtually non-existent. However, the fact remained that in the wards of the Infirmary the patients with mental illnesses disturbed the other patients and at that time the only known remedy was exclusion from society. The Lunatic Asylum wing of the Infirmary opened in 1792 with its entrance on St John's Lane. Park was also responsible for the exclusion of other patients from the hospital wards but few could argue with the logic that it was lunacy of another sort to allow Typhus and Cholera sufferers among the other patients and Fever Wards were constructed which kept those with contagious diseases apart from the rest of the hospital.

The Dispensary, Church Street, 1798, by Herdman. Liverpool Record Office

For many years Park had been a passionate advocate of a medical library for the use of students and doctors within the Infirmary and he worked many years to achieve his aim. Strangely, Park's medical library had its origins in the unlikely setting of the Dispensary in Church Street where books were often donated which would later form the nucleus of Park's collection. But first he needed to find a suitable place to house his collection and also gather the money together to fund the project. Over several years Park was constantly inventing new ways of funding his pet project, and although he always denied it, on many occasions he used his position as a member of the board which issued licences to doctors sailing aboard slave ships, by collecting a *"donation"* along with every licence fee. The medical library finally came into being in a room above a gateway into the Infirmary where it remained until 1824 when it was in danger of being lost amid the chaos of the planned demolition works for the proposed St George's Hall. Park was long retired by that time but he ensured the collection would not be lost by finding a new home for the books in a building across the road on a site which he would never have dreamt would soon be built on as Lime Street Station. However, there were others who valued the collection and when the time came for the building of the station and Park was no longer around, the books were moved to the Medical Institution opened in 1837, where they can be found today, including Park's *Book of Genesis.*

Early Retirement

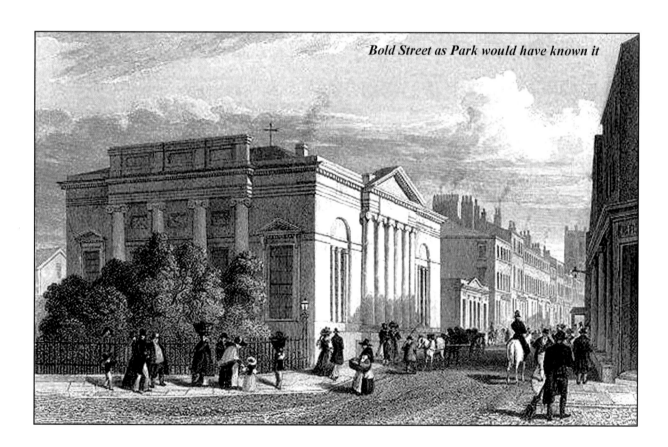

Bold Street as Park would have known it

Park held the post of surgeon at the Infirmary for 31 years, in which time the hospital had attracted competent medical officers far removed from the bumbling doctors that Park encountered when he first entered the hospital as an apprentice. But in the year 1789, aged just 53, Park resigned his post, leaving behind him a great number of respected colleagues, and close friends such Joseph Brandreth. There's no reason given as to why Park resigned at such an early age but it is quite within the bounds of possibility that he felt worn out – Park had always been conscientious to a fault and worked exceptionally long hours. Alternatively, he often yearned for a rural retreat and may have thought of pursuing this aim, and given that life expectancy in the 1700s was a lot shorter than it is now Park may have thought that time was running short. But if his reason for leaving the Infirmary was to cut down on is workload then he was in for a rude awakening as his workload actually increased, and the same year that he resigned, Park took on the role of Surgeon to the Liverpool Corps of Artillery Volunteers; despite his respect and liking for the French during his time among the prisoners-of-war he was at one with the Englishman's aversion to Napoleon and donated £100 to the war effort against the tyrant. There was also Park's private practice which kept him busier than he expected in which he was as conscientious as he had always been often to his own detriment. There was one occasion when Park went out to a patient on a winter's night and fell in the snow, *badly spraining his ancle* (sic) but crawling the rest of the way, he attended his patient before limping home to attend to himself.

Park had always had an alarming tendency to suffer accidents and his *ancle sprain* (sic) was a minor mishap compared to some of his other injuries. He had, for instance, early in his career at the Infirmary fallen down some stone steps, severely fracturing his right elbow and dislocating the joint. Park immediately pulled the joint back into place before it could swell and the fracture healed in time but he could never bend his elbow afterwards beyond a right angle. Park said himself that he had broken every bone in his body *"except one arm and one head."* Park was nearing 60 when he suffered one of his worst accidents attending a patient on the Wirral. He had taken the ferry across the river and hired a horse on the other side, but some way into his journey he was thrown by the horse causing him to break every rib on one side of his rib-cage, some of them in two places. It was in this condition that Park then abandoned his horse and walked a mile to his patient's house, attended to his patient, and then walked two miles to the ferry, crossed the river and then walked to his house in Bold Street where he at last put himself to bed. His recovery took a long time but Park's injuries eventually healed successfully and he returned to work with little changed apart from his avowal to give up riding and some capitulation to comfort with the purchase of a carriage. Park's reputation went before him and from the age of 60 to 65 he found his practice growing and he was working harder than ever, not only in his private practice but in offering a free vaccination service two days per week to the *"wives of the labouring classes."* Twice a week 50 or 60 mothers congregated at his house with their children for the treatment which was almost certainly a smallpox vaccination following the discoveries by Edward Jenner in 1796.

The obvious solution to this heavy workload was a younger partner and many came forward offering large sums of money to go into partnership with such a highly esteemed surgeon. But Park refused them all on the vague principle that *"he entertained too high a sense of the responsibilities of his profession to risk a disappointment in abilities which, however promising, he had not seen sufficiently tried."* It was not until he reached the age of 70 that Park surrendered the high moral ground and took as a partner James Dawson, a surgeon that he knew and respected.

The North front of the Infirmary, 1770, by Burdett. Liverpool Record Office

Retirement at Last

As Park grew older the siren-sound of his fabled retreat in the country became louder and more persistent until he could resist it no longer and finally fulfilled his dream of a life in the country in 1820 in the bucolic outskirts of Wavertree when he finally retired aged 75. Park called his house Wavertree Lodge or Belle Vue (also Olivebank Cottage at some stage) and Charlotte and Elizabeth, his daughters, both in their 40s, also lived there, cultivating a friendship with Felicia Hemans, the poetess who lived on Wavertree High Street and exchanging gossipy letters with John Gibson, the sculptor, from his studio in Rome. It's not clear if Park ever bought any Gibson sculptures but he had certainly contributed towards his life in Rome when he left Liverpool in 1817, donating to a fund to give the sculptor his start. Henry Park enjoyed eleven years retirement and could look back on a career which spanned nearly 60 years, having the satisfaction of knowing that he had alleviated the sufferings of unknowable numbers of people with his alternative to amputation alone; Park's willingness to embrace new techniques was the reason why many Liverpool children were saved from the ravages of smallpox; thousands more had been helped in his work in the Infirmary and his private practice and his midwifery skills had aided thousands of mothers when childbirth was a far more hazardous process than today; there were also the many committees Park served on and his work at the Liverpool Night Asylum For the Houseless Poor as told in a report giving thanks for *"the unwearied attention of Mr Park, surgeon, Edge Hill, and other friends of the institution, the former regularly in the afternoon and the others in the evenings of the Sabbath, to give religious instruction to the homeless, is above all praise."* The date of the letter is the 26th December, 1831, which tells us that even in the final days of his retirement Park was still working for the less fortunate in the community. He also had the honour of a medical term named after him called *"Park's Aneurism"* which is still in use today. Born during the reign of George II, during the era of the

Jacobite uprising and Culloden, Park lived through the tumultuous 60 year reign of George III when the American War of Independence had impacted upon Liverpool shipping, and was in retirement during the ten years of George IVs undistinguished reign. Park had seen Liverpool when it was only just emerging from its almost medieval shackles (the Castle had only been demolished 30 years before his birth while the Tower was demolished in 1819) and had moved into the Georgian era of architecture which can still be seen surviving today dotted around the city – and in the final years of his life Liverpool was at the heart of a railway system which would one day span the globe.

During his days in Wavertree Lodge, Park found time to read, enjoy visits from old colleagues and delight in his garden which he loved, but his real joy in life was to see his grandchildren and great-grandchildren around him. Of his children, Mary Lyon Park had died aged 16, John Ranicar Park had become a theologian and surgeon and married and moved to London, the first Elizabeth had died aged 1, Ann had died aged 3 months, the second Elizabeth appeared not to have married, Ann Green Park had married George Burgess Wildig in 1820 in Holy Trinity Church, Wavertree, and had one child born in 1822, Henry had died aged 5, and Charlotte Catherine appeared unmarried.

Of all his children it was his eldest daughter, Ellen Green Park, who came nearest to emulating her mother by having a large family. Ellen Green Park married Peter Berthon (1772 - ?) on the 9th November, 1797, at St George's Church, Derby Square, and from 1798 to 1814 they had 11 children together. Of all Ellen Green Park's children it was her third child, Ellen Sarah Berthon, born in 1801, who would follow her mother and grandmother by marrying aged 18 and having a large family of 10 children; the first of Ellen Sarah's children, Robert Berthon Preston, was born in 1820, the same year that his great-grandfather, Henry Park, purchased Wavertree Lodge. The lives of Robert Berthon Preston and his mother, Ellen Sarah Berthon, are outlined in a later chapter.

Late in 1830, Henry Park began to have disturbing symptoms which he diagnosed himself as Schirrous pylori, and he knew that it was the beginning of the end. With Christmas nearing, he never told his children of his condition but it wasn't long before he could no longer hide the fact that he was gravely ill and in his final weeks he fretted over making sure his affairs were in order before he passed away on February 2nd, 1831, at Wavertree Lodge. Henry Park was duly buried in St James Cemetery and Solomon Gibson, the brother of the renowned John Gibson, sculpted a memorial tablet which is still within the Oratory. Doctor John Rutter wrote a moving obituary of the friend and colleague that he had known many years with one sentence placing Park as *"one of the finest surgeons of his time."*

The house that Park moved into is still standing as the bowling club in the triangle between Mill Lane, Olive Lane and Long Lane, Wavertree.

Liverpool, 1820, by William Daniell

The Duellists

"It has a strange, quick jar upon the ear,
That cocking of a pistol, when you know
A moment more will bring the sight to bear
Upon your person, twelve yards off or so."

— Lord Byron,
from Don Juan (canto IV, st.41)

Duels at Dawn

As the preservation of a code of honour among gentlemen, duelling had been an element of the English aristocrat's world for centuries, with pistols or swords the usual choice of weapons. Although the practice was condemned by the Catholic Church and frowned upon by an intelligentsia opposed to violence, duelling had persisted from the 15th century and was still in place well into the 19th century. Over the years duelling had acquired a code of practice in which the accused party was allowed the choice of weapons, seconds would be present on behalf of each of the duellists and a surgeon would be on hand to tend to the wounded. While duelling was not illegal at this time, in an odd form of logic the legislation was such that if a protagonist killed his opponent then he could be charged for murder, and for this reason alone most duels took place at dawn in out of the way places; although it is true to say that the law was rarely applied, not least because there was a reluctance to prosecute members of the ruling classes.

English duelling pistol, circa 1830

It would have almost been inconceivable to prosecute either George Canning (1770 - 1827) or Robert Stewart, Viscount Castlereagh (1769 - 1822) when they met on Putney Heath at 6.00 a.m. on 21st September, 1809, to iron out their differences with pistols; both men were highly esteemed government ministers whose Parliamentary disputes led to a grand finale in which Castlereagh, who was acknowledged as one of the finest marksmen of his day, challenged Canning who had never fired a pistol in his life. The first round of shots ended with both shots going wide, and following a refusal by Canning to apologise to the aggrieved Castlereagh, a nerve-wracking few minutes were spent waiting for the pistols to be reloaded – Canning's second was reported to have been shaking so much that Castlereagh's second loaded the pistol on his behalf. The second round of shots was fortuitous for both men when Canning's shot was deflected by a button on his opponent's coat and Castlereagh's shot struck Canning, wounding him in the fleshy part of his thigh when it could so easily have severed an artery. There were no charges laid against either men but the affair damaged Canning's political career for many years afterwards, and when he put himself forward as Prime Minister to George III shortly after the duel, he was refused the post. Spencer Perceval (1762 - 1812) was the man chosen to be Prime Minister in October, 1809, earning the dubious distinction of being the only British Prime Minister to have been assassinated; in a strange twist of fate, but for his duel with Castlereagh, it could so easily have been Canning who stared down the barrel of John Bellingham's pistol on that fateful evening in the House of Commons on the 11th May, 1812. In 1822, following a scandal involving the then heinous crime of homosexuality, Castlereagh committed suicide by cutting his own throat, and in 1827 Canning finally achieved his ambition to become Prime Minister, unfortunately dying in the same year and earning the dubious claim to have been in office the shortest time of any Prime Minister, a mere 119 days.

If the Canning/Castlereagh duel had been a *cause célèbre* then a duel 20 years later involving the Duke of Wellington (1769 - 1852) was nothing less than a sensation, particularly in view of the fact that the Duke was a national hero and happened to be Prime Minister at the time. Wellington's greatest act while in office was to further the cause of Catholic Emancipation which would herald the end of Catholic repression and the beginning of civil rights to a people who had hitherto been treated as second-class citizens. There were of course many opponents to the Emancipation Act and none were more vituperative than George Finch-Hatton, the Earl of Winchilsea (1791 - 1858) who accused the Duke's reforms as being *"an insidious design for the infringement of our liberties and the introduction of Popery into every department of the State."* Wellington's response was a challenge to a duel which took place on 21st March, 1829, on Battersea Fields with pistols as the weapons of choice. Wellington was the first to fire his pistol and missed by a substantial distance, prompting the belief that he had done so on purpose, while Winchilsea never fired at all according to a prearranged plan with his second. Winchilsea subsequently wrote the Duke an apology but in the final

Contemporary sketch of
The Duke of Wellington's duel

analysis his decision not to fire his pistol was a wise one – nobody in their right mind would have wished to go down in history as the man who killed England's national treasure.

By the 1840s legislation was well in progress to make duelling illegal but that never bothered the notoriously belligerent and bad-tempered Earl of Cardigan (1797 - 1868) who challenged a former Captain in his regiment, Captain Tuckett, who had written some offensive letters to a newspaper highly insulting to Cardigan. The meeting took place on Wimbledon Common on the 12th September, 1840, in which Tuckett was wounded. By this time, the law was not prepared to make allowances even for an Earl and Cardigan was brought to trial in January, 1841. However, after convening a jury and a great deal of paperwork was amassed in preparation for the trial, Cardigan was acquitted on a legal technicality when the prosecution got Tuckett's name wrong.

Liverpool Duels

Duels had been a part of the lives of aristocrats for centuries in every country in Europe and travelled as part of the culture of imperialism wherever the French and British built their colonies. The list of celebrated politicians, authors and poets who have taken part in duels in England alone is quite astonishing and includes Ben Jonson, The Duke of Buckingham, Richard Brinsley Sheridan, Lord Byron, William Pitt the Younger, to name but a few, and Liverpool was not exempt from its own duels which were fought *"on the most frivolous occasions and for the slightest possible affronts, intentional or supposititious."* James Stonehouse summed it up succinctly saying that *"in those days duelling was very prevalent and small words brought out pistols and coffins for two."*

A Major Edward Brooks, who appeared to revel in the drama of life or death occasions, played a part in three of Liverpool's most notorious duels.

Everton Beacon stood on the site of St George's Church

Throughout the time of the Napoleonic Wars, it was always feared that Napoleon would invade England and the southern coastal towns were always on alert to repel the French; the danger was not without foundation as Napoleon had built a fleet of barges and prepared an invasion force as early as 1803. In Liverpool there was also the fear that French ships would one day sail down the Mersey and bombard the town, hence the numbers of warning beacons across the area on high points such as Everton, Woolton (Beaconsfield Road) and Bidston. When rumours of Napoleon's projected invasion travelled north, several Liverpool gentlemen, in an admirable display of patriotism, took it upon themselves to form their own regiments to defend Liverpool and repel any Napoleonic invaders. The shipowner Thomas Earle formed *"Colonel Earle's Regiment of Fusiliers"* and at the same time West Indies trader John Bolton formed his *"Regiment of Royal Liverpool Volunteers"* – it was a measure of the wealth of both men that the uniforms, food and pay of their respective regiments were all paid for out of their own pockets. It was also true that purchasing a regiment was not merely playing at toy soldiers and the regiments were drilled and prepared as any other regiment of the British Army with all the same problems and sometimes the same insubordination. There was an incident on 12th June, 1804, when the troops were drilling on Copperas Hill and preparing for firelock practice, and a Captain Carmichael spoke to Thomas Earle *"in an insulting and impertinent manner."* It was behaviour which could never be tolerated particularly in view of the fact that Carmichael had spoken loudly in front of the whole regiment and was ordered to keep quiet, but far from backing down Carmichael persisted in disobeying orders to a degree which forced Earle to act. Carmichael was ordered to a court martial which took place in the following month of July, lasting all of five days and ending in a remarkably light sentence which was *"to be reprimanded at the head of his regiment."* Carmichael had John Bolton to thank for the mercy shown by the court and it said a great deal about Bolton's humanitarian nature that he spoke well of the man, extolling his virtues and past record – Bolton's forbearance would be severely tested in the following months when he came within the malevolent sphere of Major Edward Brooks.

The Anonymous Letter

Major Brooks had already crossed Captain Carmichael some months earlier in a meeting which resulted in a duel on Bootle Sands. Evidently words had been exchanged over very little of consequence but Brooks' fiery temperament had brought about the duel which ended unusually with both men emerging unscathed. There is not a great deal known of the details but it is probable that Brooks had fired his pistol and missed and Carmichael had then fired into the air. However, it seems that Carmichael's merciful act met with little gratitude from Brooks who was heard to exclaim *"D--- it, why don't you fire at me—we did not come here for child's play!"* Some time later Brooks was involved in a duel of a very different nature and although he was not directly involved in the duel there is no doubt that it was his mischief-making which instigated the incident which may never have happened if he had kept his own counsel.

*William Sparling
by Frank Daniell,
Colchester Museum*

The beginning of the story began well enough, with the courtship of William Sparling and Ann Renshaw in the months of 1802, leading to a promise of marriage. William Sparling was the son of John Sparling (1731 - 1880) who made his fortune in the slave-trade, land speculation and building work in Liverpool. In common with many other slave-traders the name of John Sparling, who lived in Duke Street, two doors down from York Street, was added to the long list of Lord Mayors of Liverpool in 1790. As the only son, William Sparling who was a lieutenant in the 10th Regiment of Dragoons, inherited his father's estate part of which was the St Domingo estate, and he lived in St Domingo House which his father was so proud of that he made it a clause in his will that future heirs must live in the mansion. Ann Renshaw, the daughter of the Reverend

54

Samuel Renshaw, lived with her father on the corner of Bold Street and Newington Street – the house is now demolished and has been replaced by a building of glass and steel of nondescript design. With money no object and a mansion house for their future home, life was set fair for the engaged couple, until the day William Sparling found a letter in his post-box which would not only shatter their dreams but bring about a sequence of events which would end in tragedy – the contents of the letter which was unsigned, were later described by Henry Park as *"the purport of which was too horrible to mention."* From the time that William Sparling picked up the poison-pen letter both his and Ann Renshaw's happiness spiralled into a maelstrom of misery which would encompass the lives of many of their friends and relatives and eventually read like a plot from a Maupassant short story.

Sparling realised that much of the letter discrediting his fiancée consisted of lies and was inaccurate in parts but by his own account there were other parts which were unacceptable to him; after some deliberation and soul-searching, Sparling wrote to Reverend Renshaw informing him that he was breaking the engagement. Renshaw was naturally bitter about the situation and wrote to Sparling to tell him so.

Sticks and Stones...

The matter should have ended there but Mr Edward Grayson, an eminent shipbuilder of the town, was greatly offended by Ann Renshaw's treatment – she was after all his niece – and began to verbally abuse Sparling for deserting her. In December, 1802, Grayson was travelling to his home in Wavertree accompanied by Major Edward Brooks who he was about to entertain to dinner when he began to berate Sparling to Brooks and used a phrase which would come back to haunt him when he called Sparling *"an infernal villain."*

If Grayson had left it at that then a situation in which he was only a peripheral figure may well have blown over and life moved on, but apart from making an outburst in front of Brooks, Grayson compounded his mistake by denouncing Sparling on the steps of the Athenaeum which was then in Church Street, where passers-by could hear every word. As time went by, instead of leaving the situation to cool down, Grayson became further emboldened and obsessed about Sparling's alleged *"infamy"* he began to make veiled threats about *"chastising him."* In the early months of 1803, the affair became a source of local gossip and Sparling left Liverpool for 5 months, travelling to London and Paris, presumably to distance himself from the rumours. However, in April, 1803, Edward Brooks insinuated himself into the situation once again by meeting Sparling in London where he informed him of the situation in Liverpool. At the trial later on, under cross-examination from Henry Park, Brooks admitted to informing Sparling of the general situation but denied that he had exacerbated matters by detailing Grayson's outbursts.

Grayson's indiscretions eventually became too much for Sparling and on the 19th September, 1803, he wrote a long letter from London to Grayson which outlined every threat and insult that Grayson had made stating clearly *"my authority is Major Brooks"* and he finished by challenging Grayson with the time-honoured words *"you know where to find me."* The problem was that Grayson didn't know where to find him as Sparling was moving around so much, and over the next few months a flurry of letters travelled back and forth each more belligerent than the last. By the tone of his final letters Grayson wanted to get out of the situation, pointing out to Sparling that *"I am twice your age"* but extricating himself from the situation was hardly possible without losing face and duelling was after all a matter of honour. In the end Grayson threw caution to the wind and stated *"If I had a thousand lives I would forfeit them all sooner than retract in an ungentlemanly way the language you accuse me of."* And tellingly, he averred that *"I consider myself justified in the eyes of God and man for what I expressed to Major Brooks"* but there is more than a hint that Grayson regretted ever confiding in Brooks and there's no doubt that Brooks relayed every detail of Grayson's words to Sparling while they were in London.

Death in the Dingle

During the whole of the year 1803 the whole sorry saga seemed to have taken on a life of its own and as momentum gathered there was a certain inevitability that at some point the situation would escalate into more than a war of words and on Sunday the 26th February, 1804, the matter came to a head. The fateful day began before 7 a.m. when Henry Park was rudely awoken by a frantic ringing of his doorbell and an agitated Dr John McCartney urged Park to get dressed quickly and he would explain everything as they travelled in his carriage. As they travelled along, McCartney explained that the duel between Sparling and Grayson was finally about to take place and Captain Samuel Martin Colquitt R.N. whose frigate *Princess* was anchored in the Mersey, was acting for Sparling. McCartney explained that he would be present as a doctor and he wanted Park, as an eminent surgeon, to also be available if there should be anyone wounded. Henry Park informed McCartney that he would never have entered his carriage if he had known he was travelling to a duel and when they reached their destination Park refused to leave the carriage which McCartney had placed a few yards outside the Ancient Chapel of Toxteth. Sparling and Colquitt arrived soon afterwards in a carriage and when Grayson and his servant arrived on foot they all entered the gate into the field across the road and made their way to the beauty spot known as Knott's Hole (there is some confusion as to the site of Knott's Hole and the river frontage today is unrecognisable from days gone by. Most agree that the beauty spot was still there in the 1950s as the *"cast-iron shore,"* which attracted children from miles around – the site is now the river side of the Garden Festival).

*Sketch of Knott's Hole
by Robert Griffiths, 1907*

Soon afterwards Park heard two shots followed by an agitated Sparling and Colquitt who were running towards him shouting *"Make haste, for Grayson is badly wounded!"* and then they both fled the scene. Sparling and Colquitt made their way to Duke Street where they found Ralph Benson, the son of Moses Benson, and gave him the news before heading for the river where a boat was waiting to take them out of reach of the authorities. Park made his way to where Grayson was lying face down on the ground in great pain with blood pouring from a wound in his thigh. McCartney and Park managed to get Grayson to the carriage and drive him to his home. Park, McCartney and another doctor named Lyon did their best for the stricken Grayson but they all agreed that the ball had *"perforated the thigh bone"* and they were unable to extract it from the wound. There was little that could be done for poor Grayson and he expired at 3 a.m. in the morning.

Sparling and Colquitt were indicted for murder in a trial which took place at Lancaster Assizes on the 4th April, 1804, presided over by Sir Alan Chambre. The trial took more than a week in which anyone with any knowledge of the duel and the events leading up to it was cross-examined thoroughly so that the whole sorry picture revealed itself as the days went by. Henry Park cross-examined Major Brooks, deftly bringing out his whisperings to Sparling, and was himself asked for his own version of events before the trial ended with the jury taking just 20 minutes to pronounce both Sparling and Colquitt not guilty. Henry Park was a reluctant participant in the penultimate duel to take place in the city but he was soon to find himself embroiled in the final duel which would take place in Liverpool and once again Brooks would be involved.

The Liverpool Croesus

Colonel John Bolton (1756 - 1837) the son of an apothecary, was born in Ulverston. He was educated at the Town Bank Grammar school in Ulverston and on completing his education he was apprenticed to the firm of Rawlinson and Chorley, West India merchants and shipowners. Three years into his apprenticeship, at the age of 17, Bolton was sent to St Vincent by his employers, where in the early years an acquaintance described him as wearing a sailor suit and selling potatoes and cheese in order to survive. From these humble beginnings Bolton began to thrive, so much so that in 1786 he had amassed enough money to return to England and set up in business on his own account in Liverpool. Bolton became an extraordinarily successful shipping merchant, earning the astronomic sum of £38,000 in most years. Trading in slaves, rum, sugar and cotton, to St Vincent and Jamaica, Bolton eventually purchased three ships, the *John*, the *King George* and the *Gudgion,* all three of which in 1799 set out for Angola with the object of taking on board 402 slaves on the *John*, 550 on the *King George* and a mere 374 on the *Gudgion*; that single enterprise alone was worth a king's ransom. Bolton's career was very similar to that of Moses Benson, a successful slave-trader who lived just a few yards away in a mansion in Duke Street which was so large that its frontage was between Kent Street and Cornwallis Street – the Lake District seemed to be a breeding ground for maritime merchants as Benson's father was also from Ulverston.

Bolton's home was a double-fronted mansion at 116 Duke Street where he made his house the Tory Party Headquarters – his friends George Canning and William Huskisson (1770 - 1830) were frequent visitors with both of them often making political speeches from the balcony attracting crowds numbering into the thousands. It was ironic that Huskisson was once heard to say that *he could never countenance a web of railway lines criss-crossed across England* – Huskisson's bronze statue by John Gibson is tucked away across the road from Bolton's mansion in a square called Cooper's Court where it is rarely seen by the public. Extremely patriotic, Bolton also formed his own regiment, called *Bolton's Invincibles* which he often paraded on Mosslake Fields with bands playing and flags waving in a colourful display of hubris. It was a measure of Bolton's wealth that his Invincibles consisted of 10 complements of 60 men, all of them clothed, equipped and armed out of Bolton's own pocket. Disbanded in 1806, Bolton retained his rank of Colonel for the rest of his days.

Moses Benson's mansion on the corner of Kent Street and Duke Street

Married to Elizabeth Littledale (1741 - 1796), Bolton purchased a mansion aptly named Bolton Hall in Lancashire but soon lost interest when he purchased another Mansion named Storr's Hall on the banks of Lake Windermere in the Lake District. Bolton and his wife spent much of their time in the Lake District furnishing their house with the finest mahoganies from the West Indies and entertaining their friends – on one memorable occasion they hosted a regatta on Lake Windermere which included George Canning, Robert Southey, Sir Walter Scott and William Wordsworth who described his host as *"The Liverpool Croesus."*

Quite Enough Income

However, in 1804, Major Edward Brooks cast a shadow over the life of John Bolton, just as he had done in the Sparling/Grayson affair and once again it was his vindictive and devious nature which would bring about another tragedy. When Bryan Blundell died, the office of Customs Jerker became vacant and Colonel Bolton recommended Major Brooks, formerly of the Lancashire Militia, for the post; Brooks was also from Ulverston and Bolton may have felt some loyalty to him for that reason. Soon after taking up the post Brooks applied for an increase in salary and his application came before the West India Association, an organisation of which Colonel Bolton was President. Brooks' request was denied by the Association but in a display of monumental effrontery, Brookes blamed Bolton for the decision, when he heard that Bolton had commented that *"£700 a year was quite enough income for a comparatively young, unmarried man."* Considering that Bolton had been instrumental in him obtaining the post in the first place, Brooks' petulance was entirely misplaced, but matters sank to a new low when Brooks insulted Bolton each time they came into contact. Bolton was eventually forced to respond and a duel was arranged for the 20th December, 1804, at Miller's Dam, off Aigburth Road – not quite 12 months after the Sparling/Grayson duel. However, the meeting was interrupted when both participants were arrested before a shot could be fired, and brought before the courts and bound over to keep the peace for 12 months. The perennially volatile Brooks immediately turned on Bolton, blaming him for informing the authorities, but it was later discovered that it was one of Brooks' own friends who had done so, in a bid to avoid a fatality.

John Bolton 1835,
by Thomas Crane.
National Portrait Gallery

The cooling-off period handed down by the courts made no difference whatsoever to Brooks who continued to insult Bolton with increasing virulence on every occasion that their paths crossed. On a winter's day in 1805, when the 12 months court directive was nearing its expiry date, Colonel Bolton was walking down Castle Street accompanied by Thomas Earle when Brooks approached from the opposite direction and subjected Bolton to another tirade calling him *"a name which no gentleman could put up with."* Bolton was once again forced to challenge

Brooks and once again the authorities heard of the situation, holding both Brooks and Bolton in custody and enforcing their bail conditions. But Bolton was by this time beyond restraint and Brooks was as defiant as ever with the result that on the day they were both released Brooks sent a friend to Bolton to arrange a meeting to settle the matter that same afternoon. And on the 20th December, 1805, the two men finally came together on a field not 200 yards away from Brooks' home in Daulby Street – the whole area has changed out of all recognition in the 210 years that have elapsed since the duel and it is difficult to pinpoint the site with certainty but it was somewhere between Pembroke Place and Prescot Street, near to St Judes Church which was demolished in the 1960s to make way for the Royal Teaching Hospital. It was dark by the time seconds were arranged and Bolton took the precaution of picking surgeon Henry Park up in his carriage for another reluctant presence at a duel. The seconds had some difficulty in loading the pistols at 6 p.m. which only served to turn the tension up further but eventually Colonel Bolton's 18 months of humiliating vituperation from Brooks was about to come to an end, one way or another. Brooks fired his pistol first and missed altogether, but Colonel Bolton never offered the mercy that Carmichael had when he fired in the air, and Brooks died instantly as a ball struck him in the right eye. There was no trial on this occasion, Brooks' friends all stated that he was fully to blame for his own fate, and an enquiry stated that Colonel Bolton had acted with courage, gentlemanly behaviour and forbearance throughout. It was the last known duel in Liverpool.

Low Hill by Herdman as it was at the time of the duel

The School For Sculptors

"Trying to imagine the Liverpools of yesteryear in all their various guises, is like chasing butterflies without a net."

– John Hussey

London Road and Gallows Mills, 1803

The Changing Face of Liverpool

If ever any proof was required of Liverpool's shifting landscape then an impartial observer need look no further than Brownlow Hill, which is a perfect example of the kaleidoscopic nature of our city and a place where buildings have appeared and disappeared over many years for no apparent reason. Within my own lifetime most of the buildings on each side of the hill and within the side streets have been swept away only to be replaced by nondescript architectural oddities with no aesthetic value whose only redeeming feature is their lack of durability which will ensure their own destruction within a few years. But if we could see Brownlow Hill even further back in time over 200 years ago at the beginning of the 19th century, which in the great scheme of things is a relatively short period of time, then the only recognizable thing in sight would be the unchanging topography of the road up the hill.

Herman Melville's eponymous hero Redburn left us a graphic description of the area in 1840, when tiring of the poverty and squalor of the inner-city, he set out to find something of the English countryside which he had read was renowned for its beauty. In this instance Redburn was not disappointed, with his first foray into the rural hinterland of Liverpool beginning at the bottom of London Road which he described as *"a dusty road with white cottages dotted here and there."* As he walked further on with *"nothing in sight but meadows and fields"* Redburn was entranced by the countryside he had heard so much about in America, and somewhere in the region of what is now Edge Hill, near to a Church, he was welcomed into a cottage by an old man seated at his door – *"Come, come"* said he *"you look as if you had walked far; come take a bowl of milk. Matilda (his daughter) my dear, (how my heart jumped) go fetch some from the dairy." And the white-handed angel did meekly obey and handed me – me, the vagabond, a bowl of bubbling milk which I could hardly drink down for gazing at the dew on her lips."* Redburn stayed for a meal and discovered that the old man had another two daughters both of them as delightful as the first and he later claimed that *"to this day I live a bachelor on account of those ravishing charmers."*

Most of the area on the outskirts of the town fitted Redburn's description but a building erected here and a field sold there, were the beginnings of a slow erosion of the countryside surrounding Liverpool. The rustic landscape of Brownlow Hill had been disturbed as early as the first quarter of the 1700s when a brick building called the Liverpool Powder Magazine was erected on the area where Russell Street now stands (Russell Street was constructed circa 1815, Clarence Street was laid out between 1796 and 1803). It gradually became apparent that a building filled with 800 tons of black gunpowder could cause a great deal of damage if it was ever ignited not only within the building itself but on its way through unpaved roads down to the ships in the river, and circa 1750, the Powder Magazine was moved to Liscard, which was presumably more expendable than Liverpool. However, the citizens of Liscard understandably objected to the explosives in their midst and the powder was later placed aboard ships in the river which was hardly an ideal solution. The original Powder Magazine on Brownlow Hill was later put to use as a place to house French prisoners of war until it was demolished in the 1760s.

The Adelphi Midland Hotel

Further down the hill, on the site which is now occupied by the Adelphi Hotel, Ranelagh Gardens was built as a pleasure gardens in the last quarter of the 1700s following the pattern established by Vauxhall Gardens in London. Open to the public as a place where they could wander around wooded paths, listen to music and watch firework displays, the gardens soon attracted rowdies and prostitutes and by 1826 the pleasure gardens had been replaced by the hotelier James Radley's Adelphi Hotel which would remain a landmark until it was replaced in 1876 and called The Midland Adelphi. The present hotel was opened in 1914. The original Adelphi had originally been a line of mansion houses which James Radley had bought one by one and then brought them together to make the hotel but the road opposite was named after Ranelagh Gardens; although Ranelagh Street sounded quite grand, in 1825 it was still lined each side by houses which were little more than cottages until one by one they were replaced by shops. To the rear of the Adelphi, between Hawke Street and Blake Street stood the Church of St Nicholas (not to be confused with the Church of Our Lady and St Nicholas on Chapel Street) which was erected in 1815, acting as Liverpool's Co-Cathedral from 1850 to 1967, when it was demolished following the building of the Anglican and Metropolitan Cathedrals. Prior to the building of St Nicholas, St Nicholas Catholic School occupied part of the site and in the 1840s Father Nugent founded a Ragged School next to the Church. In the same year of 1826, on a part of what was Ranelagh Gardens, St David's Welsh Church was built within a maze of shops and houses between Hawke Street and Tobin Street although it attracted so few Welsh people that services were held in English. The building work which began at the bottom of the hill gradually moved up the slope between 1800 and 1825 forming a line of houses and shops each side of the road although the land to their rear remained unbuilt on as yet.

St David's Church, Hawke Street

Despite the building works at the bottom of the hill, further up the slope, many of the gardens still clung on to their rustic origins, and on the Mount Pleasant side of the slope the fields still extended to the very top of Mount Pleasant. The juxtaposition of large buildings adjacent to the cottages and their gardens was an odd mix but it would have been difficult to argue with the aesthetic value of Churches and the old Adelphi was undoubtedly a handsome building. However, the local inhabitants had no voice in Council matters and the rectangular lines of Brownlow Hill Workhouse, built in 1770, jarred with the pleasant buildings at the bottom of the hill; and if the very nature of the Workhouse made it a place to be avoided, its austere façade ensured that it was positively forbidding to any prospective visitors. But the sad fact was that there was never any shortage of inmates and although it was built to house 1,800 inmates, an average figure of 4,000 souls who inhabited the place spoke volumes about the level of poverty in Liverpool at that time. Nathaniel Hawthorne (1804 – 1864) had a morbid fascination for the squalid areas of Liverpool and he visited the Workhouse in 1856 only to be appalled at the plight of its destitute and downtrodden inhabitants; moved to pick up and comfort a small child begging him for attention, Hawthorne later wrote of *"a sickly, wretched, humor-eaten infant, the offspring of unspeakable sin and sorrow."* The Workhouse was demolished in 1931 to be replaced by the Metropolitan Cathedral and the only thing remaining is the bell which summoned its unfortunate inhabitants to dinner, now a part of the Cathedral carillion.

For many years the base of the triangle where Brownlow Hill meets Mount Pleasant had been a picturesque rural backwater which Redburn would have appreciated as a flavour of Olde England – it was at that time called Martindale's Hill. There were two rusticated taverns each with a bowling green and they were located at the very edge of the town where a large area of water meadow called the Mosslake was used for cutting peat – the Mosslake would later be drained circa 1840 to make way for Abercromby Square. William Roscoe (1753 – 1851) was born in one of the taverns and spent his early years helping his father at his nearby market garden. Roscoe loved working with his father and such was the effect of the place of his upbringing that he was moved to write a poem called *Mount Pleasant* when he was aged 16, just a few years before the shadow of the Workhouse intruded upon the idyllic scene. The Workhouse was not the only building which altered the rural aspect of Mount Pleasant's country inns and bowling greens which had been in place since circa 1650, and the Medical Institution now stands on roughly the same area of Roscoe's inn. Further down the slope, a sturdy row of mansions opposite the Wellington Rooms are now the property of Liverpool John Moore's University.

*Liverpool Victoria
redbrick university*

Little by little the gardens and fields were built over and a fever hospital and the Lunatic Asylum, which was originally part of the Infirmary, was built in 1831 across the road from the Workhouse, further eroding the countryside and extending the boundaries of the town. Backing onto the Lunatic Asylum, between Pembroke Place and Brownlow Street was the Infirmary also moved from its original site in Lime Street – built in 1824 the neo-classical building was replaced by the present Gothic building in 1887. The Lunatic Asylum and the fever hospital were replaced in 1892 by the Redbrick Victoria Building of Liverpool University; the hundreds of students that criss-cross the campus each day would no doubt be horrified at the term Lunatic Asylum and perhaps see the irony of a University taking its place.

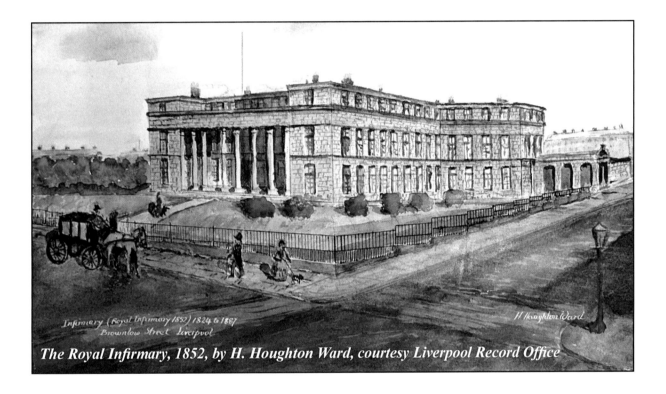

The Royal Infirmary, 1852, by H. Houghton Ward, courtesy Liverpool Record Office

By 1850, a glance at a map of the town reveals that the *"Roses and Honeysuckle and fields"* that Redburn had described had vanished and had been replaced by an urban sprawl which covered both sides of Brownlow Hill and all its side-streets. There was very little attention paid to the suitability of buildings and their juxtaposition to each other hence the erection of an Abattoir in the area of Bronte Street. The Abattoir had previously been meant for a site behind the Adelphi but James Radley had rallied his friends to object and the Abattoir remained on the site of the old rope works from 1834 until 1867 when it was removed to its present site on Prescot Road. Among the myriads of buildings, large and small, there were very few of note and today that situation has changed very little; the merits and demerits of the Metropolitan Cathedral have been debated *ad infinitum* but there's no denying the integrity of the Victoria Building which stands among many others in the city as a monument to the quality of Victorian building technique and architecture which has to this day never been surpassed. Apart from the Cathedral and the University buildings, today the remainder of Brownlow Hill's buildings are merely functional and the slope is drab in comparison to the rustic charm of a bygone age.

There is, however, one other building which has survived and is older than any in the area – Pleasant Street School, built in 1830, is tucked away as if in hiding from the wrecking–ball and recalls a time long before school attendance was compulsory.

The Sculpture Academy

When Samuel and Thomas Franceys decided to open their Marble Works in 1802, Brownlow Hill was on the fringes of the town and retained its rustic atmosphere of gardens and fields with the only real building of any size being the municipal workhouse which overlooked the flower-filled slopes like some medieval castle.

Strangely there is today very little known of the Franceys brothers or Mary Franceys who was employed as a sculptor at the Marble Works, although it is probable that they were related to Samuel Franceys who was employed on decorative plasterwork at Melbourne Hall, Derby, in 1760, and as for the Marble Works itself it has vanished from the face of the earth as if it had never existed – yet it was so well-known in its day that there was a nearby Franceys Street which is still in existence.

The Franceys' yard was situated between Pleasant Street and the newly built Clarence Street, directly opposite Ainsworth Street, upon the site of an old bowling green and they opened for business with an advertisement in *The Billings Liverpool Advertiser* of the 1st November, 1802, which read:

> *Statuary, Marble Veined and Dove, in blocks of large finall*
> *dimenfions and of good quality.*
> *Apply to S and T Franceys at Clarence Ftreet who have alfo on fale, a twelve-yard house*
> *and garden at the back of Clarence Ftreet, fuitable for a genteel family.*
> *Immediate poffession may be had.*

The quaint grammar and the ancient use of *"f"* in place of *"s"* places the Franceys firmly in the Georgian era and over 200 years ago when the brothers were first opening the Marble Works, Liverpool was still deeply mired in the slave-trade and would be so for the next five years until it was abolished in 1807. George III was King of England and Louis XVI had been executed a mere 9 years earlier, Napoleon Bonaparte had just been made First Consul and the Peace of Amiens was a short respite in the Napoleonic Wars which would culminate in the Battle of Waterloo, thirteen years hence. The Franceys brothers lived in interesting times but in 1802 they were more interested in making a living than following the fortunes of Kings and Queens and their Marble Works were at the very forefront of the building works which would transform Brownlow Hill's bucolic charms forever.

The birthdates of the Franceys family can only be guessed at with Gore's Advertiser of 1790 showing Samuel Franceys to be living at 4 Fontenoy Street, St James Street and 2 Webster Street in that same year and making his living as a *"stucco worker."* By 1796 Samuel had moved to Pleasant Street and in 1803 Thomas is also listed as living in 10 Pleasant Street as is Mary Franceys.

The Franceys brothers, originally specialised in the manufacture of decorative ceilings and chimney-pieces and soon expanded their range of items on sale in the yard into marble tables and various sculptures in marble, bronze or artificial stone – in fact they catered for any taste and manufactured whatever their customers required. The quality of their work and the growing reputation of the Marble Works attracted several apprentice craftsmen and carvers in stone who honed their skills under the direction of the brothers and went on to become celebrated sculptors in their own right. John Gibson stated that although the name *"Franceys"* was often carved on statues and memorials the brothers were businessmen and not sculptors and although apprentices were allowed to indulge in sculptures of their own devising or classical subjects ordered by various clients, the stock-in-trade of all such establishments was the creation of Marble Memorials. Most of the sculptors were required to work on Memorial Stones and many of them were allowed a free hand in the subject matter, resulting in many instances in elaborate and moving masterpieces of the genre. In some ways the Memorial stones, which were invariably large and heavy, were of more interest than conventional sculptures as most of them told a tale of some Victorian triumph or tragedy and in their own way are valuable insights into historical events.

Varying Fortunes

One of the Franceys' protegés was a young sculptor named Robert Ward, who entered into the Marble Works circa 1817, showing a great deal of promise. A bust of Huskisson had proven to be so popular that several casts were on sale in Franceys' shop but Ward was never destined to proceed much further in his career as he sickened and died at a very young age and his latent talent died with him. Too young to have made his mark on the world, James Allanson Picton lamented upon Ward's early death while holding a bas-relief of a *Sleeping Venus* he had bought from the young sculptor.

Dr Stevenson memorial, the Oratory

In complete contrast to the brevity of Robert Ward's life as a sculptor, the career of John Alexander Patterson McBride (1819 - 1890) was a long and fulfilling one – and for that reason alone it remains a mystery why so little is known of McBride and his work. McBride entered Franceys Marble Works at a stage when William Spence had taken over the running of the business and he trained under Spence until he left for London for some years, returning to Liverpool in 1846. McBride was a prolific sculptor and exhibited his work at the Great Exhibition of 1851, the Liverpool Exhibition and the Walker Art Gallery but never seemed to receive the acclaim that came the way of other sculptors – although he must have been highly regarded by his peers to have been elected Secretary of the Royal Academy in Liverpool when he voted for Holman Hunt for First Prize in 1851. McBride married Sarah Ryder and they had a daughter in 1857 they named Florence but apart from that there is little else known of his family life. In 1861, McBride had some initial success in competing for the commission to sculpt the statue of Wellington atop the Wellington Column in William Brown Street but he was eventually overlooked in favour of George Anderson Lawson, a decision which caused some controversy as Lawson was the brother of the designer of the Column, Andrew Lawson. Most of McBride's work has been *"lost"* with the passage of time but his best known works are *Lady Godiva* which the Liverpool Art Union awarded copies as prizes in 1850, A bust of *John Laird* for Birkenhead hospital in 1863 (Laird was an active patron of the hospital where many of his workers found themselves in the days before Health and Safety), a bust of *Dr Raffles* for Great George Street Chapel (Raffles lived in a house adjacent to the great tunnel-digger, Joseph Williamson, in Mason Street and had been active in the Church for over 50 years), and in 1854 a memorial tablet to Doctor Stevenson shown taking a pulse (after serving in the Peninsular War, Doctor Stevenson was the first medical officer in Birkenhead – the memorial was originally placed in St Mary's Church, Birkenhead but was removed to the Oratory, St James' Cemetery when it was demolished in 1977).

Fortunately, a great deal more is known about the remaining sculptors who served their apprenticeships at Franceys Marble Works and their stories are detailed in the following chapters.

Chapel Street in Victorian era, by Herdman

The Franceys' Sculptors

The gable end of the Lyceum with reliefs

Frederick A. Legé (1779 – 1837)

Frederick Legé was a German born sculptor who joined the Franceys brothers as early as 1803 when he sculpted the three medallions on the gable end of the recently built Lyceum (1800) at the bottom of Bold Street. The three sculptures representing *Navigation, The Arts* and *Commerce* can still be seen today in Waterloo Place. Although Legé who lived first at 51 Brownlow Hill and later at 5 Pembroke Gardens remained working for the Franceys for about 9 years, there is little to be seen of his work in Liverpool and he probably worked on memorials and headstones or in conjunction with other sculptors. He is credited with sculpting the ornate coat-of-arms which in 1805 was placed over the entrance to the Union Newsroom in Duke Street and in 1812 he sculpted *The Model of a Female Hand Holding a Pen* for Circus Street School, now in Salford Museum and purchased in 1865. The *Hand* sculpture was made for the school to be given as a prize for good handwriting and along with the three others made by Legé illustrates the range of work undertaken at the Marble Works.

The Union News Room, 1800.
The sculpture on top now removed

The Hand for Circus Street School now in Salford Museum.

Legé left the Franceys employment circa 1812, presumably to work for himself and a sculpture of *Satan* was exhibited at Edinburgh and the Royal Academy, London, in 1814. The statue of *Satan* (now lost) earned critical acclaim but it can only be assumed that Legé was unable to make a living on his own merits and in 1814 he found employment as one of several assistants to Francis Chantrey (1781 – 1841) who was at that time one of the foremost sculptors in the land. Chantrey was unusual in that he had never worked in Rome and for that reason alone was something of a hero to Regency and Victorian admirers in an age when Jingoism played a part in every aspect of the English way of life. On the other hand, John Gibson, who was the leading light among a colony of English sculptors in Rome, was critical of Chantrey for missing out on what Gibson regarded as an essential learning process. The press fanned the flames of the two men's rivalry and whenever Exhibitions were held or particular sculptures came up for discussion, they invariably extolled the virtues of any sculpture made by a sculptor of the *"English School"* as opposed to anyone based in Rome. Chantrey was such a prolific sculptor and had so many commissions that he employed several assistants who were skilled craftsmen in their own right, sculpting and polishing works to Chantrey's design and encouraged to use their own initiative. It is an indication of how highly Legé was regarded that Chantrey gave him full responsibility for a large memorial sculpture depicting the heartrending tragedy that befell the Robinson family.

Ellen-Jane Robinson's three year torment began when her husband, the Reverend William Robinson, died of tuberculosis in 1812 while still in his thirties, leaving his wife and their two daughters alone in the world. The following year, in 1813, Ellen-Jane and her eldest daughter

The Sleeping Children can be seen in Lichfield Cathedral

also named Ellen-Jane were on a trip to Bath. While preparing for bed, the daughter's nightdress took light from the flames from an open fire and she died of her extensive burns. The trilogy of tragedy was completed the following year in 1814 when Ellen-Jane's youngest daughter Marianne took ill and died in London – within a three year period, Ellen-Jane Robinson had lost her entire family.

In her distress the distraught mother turned to Chantrey to create a fitting memorial to her daughters and had a great deal of input into what would be the finished design – it was Ellen-Jane who informed the sculptor that the two children often fell asleep in each others arms and that was how she wanted them to be remembered. Following his preliminary clay model for the statue Chantrey handed over most of the work to Legé and it was at Legé's suggestion that a posy of marble snowdrops was placed in the hand of the youngest daughter. Quite apart from its obvious aesthetic merit the statue appealed greatly to a sentimental Victorian audience who were no strangers to tragedies of their own in a world where health was a lottery and diseases now eradicated struck without warning – so that the finished work was described as *"sensational"* when it was exhibited at the Royal Academy in 1816. The statue was then moved into its own final resting place, beneath the memorial to the Reverend William Robinson in Lichfield Cathedral where it can be seen to this day.

Frederick Legé was never a prolific sculptor and of his 23 known works only 7 survive. The memorial to Ellen-Jane Robinson's daughters, *The Sleeping Children* was undoubtedly his finest hour and he is often credited as the sole sculptor.

Patronised

Throughout history sculptors and artists, both in England and abroad, have benefited greatly from patrons who were invariably wealthy. Many of these rich patrons were true art enthusiasts while others merely followed the fashion for paintings and sculptures as decorative talking points for their often palatial homes. There was a third group whose motivation for commissioning sculpture was to create facsimiles in marble of their wives and children and themselves as three-dimensional studies in their favourite poses – naturally, the sculptor rarely enhanced any physical defects and enhanced the more favourable aspects of their subjects. A fashionable sculptor may well have found himself inundated with requests for *"family busts or statues"* which was undoubtedly lucrative but had the downside of taking him away from his real interests which may have been anything from neo-classical sculpture to municipal commissions for war memorials. Whether a sculptor had many patrons or just one, there were very few who survived without their financial input and the lack of patronage may well have been the reason why Legé worked for other, better-known sculptors. It was a problem which John Gibson never had and throughout his life he was supported in every way by a host of patrons and admirers.

John Gibson R.A. (1790 – 1866)

John Gibson was undoubtedly the finest sculptor to work for the Franceys brothers and although he went on to earn fame and fortune over a period spanning 60 years he never forgot his Welsh roots or his formative years in Liverpool. Gibson was born in Conway *"in the shadow of Conway Castle"* into a family which spoke mostly Welsh but in 1799 his parents decided to emigrate to America and the family made their way to Liverpool for the transatlantic crossing. However, the frenetic bustling of the Liverpool dockside was a far cry from the serenity of Conway and Gibson's mother Jane took fright at the prospect of boarding one of the flimsy looking sailing ships and refused to go any further. The family found a place to live in Green Lane off Clarence Street and inadvertently placed Gibson near to the place where the Franceys would begin their Marble Works which would soon become the nearest thing to an academy for aspiring sculptors – Gibson's father who was a Methodist Minister could well have said that it was pre-ordained.

John Gibson by Henry William Pickersgill, 1850.
National Library of Wales

The young Gibson had always sketched and drawn from his early years in Conway and he continued to do so during his schooling in Liverpool which finished when he was aged 14 and he was apprenticed for 7 years to a firm of cabinet-makers, William Southwell and Jonathan Wilson, based at No.1 Coventry Street. Initially, Gibson was quite happy with the novelty of woodcarving but he later became disenchanted with the work and a chance meeting with a sculptor friend who showed him his carvings of roses in marble made him greatly unsettled. The same friend introduced Gibson to the Franceys brothers and it was a visit to their yard that decided where his future lay. Gibson was desperate to work in marble and the Franceys allowed him to mould in clay a head of *Mercury* by Legé with the resulting work exhibiting to the Franceys the young man's latent talent. However, Southwell and Wilson also valued his talents and refused to release Gibson from his apprenticeship until following some unpleasant wrangling the Franceys purchased the apprenticeship for the then considerable sum of £70, indicating clearly their confidence in his future development. Gibson had joined Southwell and Wilson in 1804 and joined the Franceys in 1808 – ironically he would have never completed his apprenticeship anyway as Southwell and Wilson went into liquidation in 1810.

Among Gibson's many attributes was the ability to get along with most of the people he came into contact with which served him well when he required patronage which was never in short supply. Gibson corresponded with a great number of people, many of them remaining friends throughout his lifetime, and over the years he wrote an astonishing number of letters. This ability to make friends easily was no small thing and manifested itself from a very early age; when Gibson first arrived in Liverpool he continued to sketch just as he had always done and he bought his materials from John Turmeau (1777 – 1846) whose shop was then in Church Street. Born in 1777, Turmeau was descended from a Huguenot family of artists and jewellers which had settled in London. A painter of miniatures, Turmeau's name first appears when he exhibited at the Royal Academy, London, in 1794 and was living at Villiers Street, Strand. Turmeau settled in Liverpool circa 1800 and his name appeared on the first list of members of the Liverpool Academy in 1810 continuing until 1834, during which time he was President from 1812 to 1814 and treasurer from 1823 to 1834, exhibiting miniatures throughout that period. In the days preceding photography, miniatures were a popular way of keeping portraits of loved ones and skilled miniaturists such as Turmeau made a good living at their trade. Many of Turmeau's miniatures regularly come up at auction to this day, some of them named and others of unknown subjects.

A Turmeau miniature

Miniature of lady by Turmeau

From Church Street, Turmeau moved shop to Lord Street and then Castle Street where he ended his days – his best known portrait is one of Egerton Smith, the founder of *The Liverpool Mercury*. Turmeau was married and had 9 children, one of whom, John Caspar Turmeau born in 1809, followed in his father's footsteps as an artist in landscapes and architectural drawing, exhibiting one work in 1827 at the Liverpool Academy. Although John Gibson was only around 12 years of age when he had first known John Turmeau, the aspiring artist and mature shop owner remained friends and when Gibson was established in Rome, it was this enduring friendship that led to John Caspar Turmeau working under the now famous Gibson in his studio. Turmeau remained several years in Rome but later gave up art and returned to Liverpool where he set up in business as an architect and in that recurring theme of the age died in 1834, a full 12 years before his father.

From the moment that Gibson walked through the door of Franceys Marble Works he never looked back and his initial remarks that *"I began my delightful employment in high spirits, and I was truly happy, modelling, drawing and executing works in marble"* could quite truthfully have been written when he was in the twilight if his career. Gibson soon justified the Franceys' faith in his talent and he quickly became adept at carving ornate memorials and sculptures. William Roscoe was a frequent visitor to the Marble Works and in a scenario which would be repeated throughout Gibson's lifetime, the celebrated abolitionist and art historian admired the sculptor's work and requested a marble fireplace for his home at Allerton Hall. Roscoe was the first of many patrons that Gibson would attract but as time went by he became more of a mentor to the young man and as Gibson became a frequent visitor to the house in Allerton, Roscoe allowed him the freedom of his extensive library where Gibson spent hours copying rare prints of classical art.

In 1817, Gibson left Liverpool and set out for the Promised Land – Rome, which he regarded as the Mecca of sculpture. Letters of introduction from Gibson's many admirers in Liverpool and London paved the way for a place in the studio of the great Antonio Canova (1757 – 1822) where Gibson found to his dismay that while he may have been celebrated in Liverpool, in Rome he was just one of a multitude of aspiring sculptors and his true apprenticeship was only just beginning. Gibson was determined to succeed at his chosen profession and applied himself to everything that Canova taught him until the day finally came when he was encouraged to create a full-size statue of his own design. It was in effect, the culmination of everything he had been taught by Canova and the end of his apprenticeship when he produced *The Sleeping Shepherd Boy* which can be seen today in The Walker Art Gallery. By 1819, Gibson was working in his own studio and after sculpting the 7 foot tall statue of *Cupid Restraining Mars* he could hardly wait to begin on his next design – from that time onward, Gibson turned out an ever-increasing flow of statues, medallions and bas-reliefs, all of them based upon classical themes. In an age when men and women were punished with transportation to Australia for the most trivial of offences, on the other side of the yawning gulf between rich and poor was an upper-class aristocracy which thought nothing of spending on a sculpture a sum of money which would keep a family for a year. Marble sculptures were the height of fashion in the homes of the very wealthy and as they travelled extensively across Europe many of them visited the studios of popular sculptors and artists purchasing or commissioning works as they went. Gibson's studio was fast becoming well-known to collectors from England who preferred to buy from a fellow countryman but his standing rose enormously when the 6th Duke of Devonshire first entered his studio and immediately chose *Cupid Restraining Mars* for his newly built sculpture gallery at Chatsworth House, Derbyshire. The statue is in the same place in the sculpture gallery that the Duke placed it on delivery in 1820 and is a favourite of the cleaning ladies who will enthusiastically attest to the fine physique of Mars. The Duke bought several of Gibson's works which are also on display at Chatsworth.

Cupid Restraining Mars.
Chatsworth House

The Arch of Titus
by Fred Richards

Gibson never tired of neo–classical statuary and year after year he sculpted a pantheon of legendary Greek Gods which were immediately purchased by English collectors for their palatial homes. In 1838, Henry Robertson Sandbach (1807 – 1895) and his wife Margaret visited Gibson's studio seeking works of art for their mansion called Hafodunos, in North Wales. Gibson found an immediate rapport with Margaret Sandbach (1812 – 1852), not least because she was a lover of poetry and the arts and especially the sculpture of Gibson himself, but also because she was the grand-daughter of his first patron, William Roscoe. A statue called *A Hunter and His Dog* was the first of many that the Sandbach's would order for Hafodunos and in the years following, Margaret became Gibson's greatest devotee, exchanging letters which would lead to Gibson visiting the mansion in order to see his own works displayed. In the early years of the 1850s, Margaret's letters became less and less ardent which was a surprise to Gibson as she had always been as passionate as himself concerning classical sculpture, but it still came as a shock when he was informed that Margaret was suffering from a terminal illness. Gibson always used euphemisms for the more unpleasant aspects of life and when Margaret died in 1852, Gibson wrote that it was due to *"one of the most painful ills to which flesh is heir"* – she had in fact died of breast cancer and Gibson had lost his soulmate.

In 1831, the year after the death of William Huskisson (1770 – 1830) beneath the wheels of *"The Rocket"* Gibson was requested to sculpt a statue of the popular politician to be placed within a circular mausoleum based on a classical theme, in the centre of St. James's Cemetery, Liverpool. Eliza Emily Huskisson (1777 – 1856) was impatient to see the statue of her husband and travelled to Rome where she met Gibson for the first time and broke down in tears when he showed her the unfinished statue of which she approved greatly. Gibson and Eliza became great friends and she persuaded him to visit Liverpool to see the statue, eventually collaborating with him to produce three statues of William Huskisson in total. It was a feature of Gibson's persona that his patrons almost always became friends for life and the odd pairing of the eccentric sculptor and the upper-class matron were often seen together trundling around London where Eliza introduced Gibson to her high-born friends and acquaintances. It was Eliza Huskisson who calmed his nerves when Gibson was first summoned to meet the Queen with a view to sculpting a statue in her image.

Windsor Palace was the venue for Gibson's meeting with Queen Victoria and Prince Albert in 1844, and Eliza accompanied him in his carriage to make sure that he did not opt out at the last minute. To Gibson's great relief, the interview turned out to be a great success culminating in a commission for a full-size statue of the Queen. The statue was the first of several commissioned for the Royal family and most of them remain where the Queen first sited them at Buckingham Palace, Windsor Castle, The Palace of Westminster and Osborne House.

With commissions for his sculptures from the Royal Family, it seemed that Gibson's star had reached its zenith and his legacy would be the considerable numbers of neo-classical sculptures he would one day leave to the world. However, while this was all true, Gibson had yet another surprise to spring upon an unsuspecting world and he knew that there would never be a better time than at the height of his career. For many years Gibson had held the firm belief that the ancient Greek sculptors had painted their statues and those white eyes and that white marble were the base for colours which made the flesh glow, the eyes shine and the hair and clothing to whatever the artist desired. In addition, Gibson believed that in some cases coloured gems were used for the eyes and other materials for the nails, which in addition to the painting, made those who decorated the statues into artisans in their own right. As ridiculous as it may seem today Gibson knew that if he followed his long-held desire to follow in the footsteps of the ancient Greek sculptors it would cause a storm of protest and possible ridicule which is why he had held back for so many years. The unbending Victorian art critics who delivered their verdicts on works of art from Olympian heights were critical of any innovations and were capable of making or breaking reputations but when Gibson threw caution to the winds the result was *The Tinted Venus*, the statue he is best remembered for. It was quite a coincidence that the statue which would define Gibson's career was commissioned in 1850 by a Liverpool couple, Robert Berthon Preston and his wife Eleanor, and its first home would be 10 Abercromby Square, just a short distance way from its final home in the Walker Art Gallery over 160 years after its conception. Gibson was correct in his forecast that *The Tinted Venus* would cause controversy and the art critics fought skirmishes and running battles for years until commonsense finally dictated that Gibson had been right all along.

Although Gibson made several trips to London, usually as a guest of one of his many patrons and once for the opening of the 1862 London International Exhibition where *The Tinted Venus* was being exhibited, he remained in Rome for the rest of his life. It is a strange fact that despite working in Rome for over 50 years not one of his sculptures can be found in that city today – all of Gibson's sculptures were purchased by a legion of wealthy patrons in England where they were proudly exhibited in mansions and palaces across the country. It is another strange fact that, although they never set out to do so, the aristocrats who purchased Gibson's works effectively preserved them for future generations of art lovers. Mansions and palaces require a constant input of money and one by one many of them fell into disrepair until in the early years of the 20th century they fell like dominoes and were either demolished or given over to the state or into trusts. The result is that many of Gibson's works can be seen in galleries across the country – The Walker Art Gallery, The Victoria and Albert, Cardiff National Museum, The Lady Lever – while a very few can still be seen in their original settings in the great houses of England which still thrive. In the years that Gibson spent learning his art in the employment of the Franceys, Gibson complained on a visit to Liverpool that many of his sculptures had been signed at the base as done by the Franceys – one of these is high up above a door in Sefton Parish Church which was one of the subjects of Gibson's complaints. There are very few other works identifiable to Gibson prior to his leaving for Rome; the bas-reliefs outside the Wellington Rooms (built in 1815 as a homage to Wellington's victories) are one of his final works before he left for Rome in 1817 and are typical of his later bas-reliefs in marble. The commissioners of the building must not have consulted the sculptor as to the design as the sculpture appears to have nothing at all to do with Wellington but everything to do with Gibson's obsession with all things neo-classical.

The Tinted Venus.
Courtesy Walker Art Gallery

On Borrowed Time

"The answer to old age is to keep one's mind busy and to go on with one's life as if it were interminable. I always admired Chekhov for building a new house when he was dying of tuberculosis."

– Leon Edel

The Franceys' policy of taking on promising young sculptors to cut their teeth on the bread and butter design and sculpture of memorials and minor works benefited the firm as they would almost certainly have paid lower wages than an experienced sculptor, and it also benefited the journeymen sculptors who learnt their trade from the bottom upwards. Several of Franceys' sculptors, namely John Gibson and Benjamin Spence, would go on to achieve fame and fortune on the international stage but most of the apprentice sculptors would fall by the wayside for one reason or another and remain as competent sculptors capable of earning a living within their own sphere. It was an indication of the Franceys' reputation that young sculptors travelled from far and wide to work alongside established sculptors in the Marble Works.

Thomas Duckett of Preston (1804 - 1878)

Thomas Duckett, Senior Holy Trinity sculpture

Thomas Duckett was born in Preston to a family whose forebears were of farming stock. Originally apprenticed to a local plasterer, Duckett cancelled his indentures and went to work as a wood-carver for the cabinet-makers Gillow and Company, based in Lancaster. Details are sketchy regarding Duckett's arrival in Liverpool to work for what was then the firm of Franceys and Spence, but his first work, a bust of the Reverend J. Dunn (now lost) was exhibited at the Liverpool Academy in 1828 when Duckett was aged 24. John Gibson had left for Rome long before Duckett arrived in Liverpool but he certainly knew William Spence as his employee. There are probably memorial stones scattered around Liverpool carved by Thomas Duckett but there is little evidence of any of his work carried out for Franceys and Spence before he departed to work for Francis Webster and Sons of Kendal where he managed the sculpture department. At some point, Duckett returned to Preston, setting up home in Cannon Street and a studio in Avenham Road. Duckett specialised in funerary monuments and portrait sculpture – several of his busts of local dignitaries can be seen in the Harris Museum in Preston and local churches have monuments carved by Duckett on the walls. Thomas Duckett was far from being prolific and it is difficult to see how he made a living from such a low output. His portrait busts and funerary monuments show a level of proficiency which would have pleased his patrons but Duckett never progressed much further than that and although he does have one major work on display, as a work of art it leaves a lot to be desired; his commission for a statue of *Sir Robert Peel* was a popular choice at the time as Peel's abolition of the Corn Laws in 1846 made him a champion of the poor and combined with Peel's death in 1850 there was an unusual enthusiasm for the public subscription required. The statue carved in limestone was unveiled in 1852 at Winckley Square in Preston where it can still be seen today atop a large plinth. Duckett's statue of Peel, however, does not stand close scrutiny, and the sculptor appears to have vacillated between carving his subject in modern dress and neo-classical robes – the resulting work falls between two stools and was obviously too ambitious a project for Duckett.

Nevertheless, the unveiling was a proud event for the town and a huge crowd turned out for the event which was also attended by Duckett's second son from his five children – the twelve year old Thomas Duckett junior.

Wasting Away – The Romance of Tuberculosis

It is of course common knowledge that cholera, typhus, smallpox, scarlet fever and many other diseases were rampant in Victorian times, so much so that they have become woven into the fabric of the age, and universally feared, there was little about them which could be construed as romantic. Now and again, smallpox scars (if they were not too disfiguring) were worn as a badge of honour for having survived the disease, but tuberculosis was unique in being romanticized as a motif of heroic suffering and many of its icons have been immortalized in Victorian literature, theatre and art. Most of the diseases prevalent in the Victorian era we now know were caused by contaminated water, contaminated foodstuffs, malnourishment and not least, polluted air – all of which Liverpool possessed in abundance – but at the time, physicians had only a vague idea that some mysterious *"miasma"* was the cause and the only advice they could offer was to escape to some milder climate.

The nature of tuberculosis as a lingering disease invested the sufferer with a heroic fortitude and those unfortunates who had succumbed followed the great British tradition of carrying on in the face of adversity. The glittering eyes, pallid cheeks and hacking cough became symbolic of courage and endurance and were seized upon by artists as motifs for invoking poignancy – although the early death of Dante Gabriel Rossetti's wife and muse, the ill-fated Elizabeth Siddall was a little too close to reality. The world of literature and in particular Victorian novels was littered with heroes and heroines wringing the last ounce of compassion from contemporary readers who identified quite readily with subject matter culled from their own experience – Charles Dickens, Elizabeth Gaskell and the Brontës all used tuberculosis as a device for illustrating the ravages of poverty. But romanticising tuberculosis was not confined to the British Isles and the tragic Mimi from Puccini's *La Boheme* left audiences in tears as she died in the final scene, while Fantine, the wretched mother of Cosette in Victor Hugo's *Les Misérables* was the epitome of misery as a single mother abandoned by society and left to fall lower and lower into the depths of poverty until she too died, one of literatures most enduring icons of pathos. Across the Atlantic, cities such as New York, Boston and Chicago all contained poverty-stricken rookeries no less disease-ridden than their European counterparts and novelists such as Upton Sinclair used tuberculosis in novels such as *The Jungle* in which the plight of the Chicago meat-packers was little different to the workers in Lancashire cotton mills. Even Doc Holliday, immortalised by his exploits at the O.K. Corral, became a symbol of fortitude transferred to the American West, although it is true to say that in general Americans regarded the disease with a mixture of revulsion and fear rather than compassion.

On that day in May 1853, the future looked bright for the small boy watching his father's triumph as his statue of *Robert Peel* was unveiled to applause from the onlooking crowd. Nobody could have envisaged that the boy whose environment and upbringing was far from poverty-stricken would one day soon be facing his own demons but tuberculosis was a respecter of nobody and in the random lottery of Victorian life the young boy's life story would be as poignant as any of those fictional characters.

The dying Fantine by Margaret Bernadine Hall. Courtesy of Walker Art Gallery

Thomas Duckett Junior (1839 - 1868)

Thornycroft's Boadicea on the Embankment, London

Golden Opportunities

Thomas Duckett senior married twice, and his son, also Thomas, was the 2nd of his five children with his second wife Margaret (Ellwood). The young Thomas first worked at his father's studio in Preston showing a rare talent for sculpture, sketching and painting. He soon graduated to work under the acclaimed sculptor Thomas Thornycroft in London which was a great honour and wonderful opportunity for an apprentice sculptor and in 1860 Duckett enrolled in the Royal Academy Schools where he would exhibit works from 1861 to 1867. At the invitation of Queen Victoria, Thomas Thornycroft (1815 - 1885) accepted an honour which John Gibson had turned down, which was to sculpt one of the corner groups for the Albert Memorial and in 1867 he completed the group of *Commerce* as his part in the massive memorial. In 1869, Thornycroft once again sculpted a memorial to *Albert* with his equestrian statue standing in the front of St George's Hall, Liverpool, and followed it with the perfect counterpoint of an equestrian statue of *Victoria* on the same plateau. Thornycroft's best known sculpture is the famous statue of *Boadicea and her Daughters* standing as an eternal symbol of British defiance atop a huge plinth on the Victoria embankment. Another friend and mentor of the young Duckett was the Irish sculptor John Henry Foley (1818 - 1874) who was invited to carve the centrepiece of the Albert memorial which depicted a gilded Albert overlooking the symbols of the Empire. Duckett was extremely fortunate to have been tutored by Thornycroft and Foley who were two of the finest sculptors in England and their influence was beginning to bear fruit when their protegé won a prize of £30 and 3 shillings for a work entitled *Alfred in the Camp of the Danes* and carved an ambitious group called *Night and Twilight* which was shown at the 1861 Preston Arts Exhibition. Still in his early twenties, the future looked golden for the aspiring sculptor and it seemed that life could not get better when he married Elizabeth (Lizzie) in September 1863. Shortly after their marriage, Thomas and Lizzie travelled to Rome where Thomas entertained hopes of working under the guidance of the now famous John Gibson at his studio. In some ways Duckett's Rome interlude was a strange thing to do – certainly Gibson was always receptive to young sculptors especially those who had some association with the Franceys and Liverpool – but for some reason things never worked out and sometime in 1864 Duckett returned to Thomas Thornycroft's studio where he executed a sculpture called *Sister's Pride* which was exhibited at the Royal Academy Exhibition in 1865.

Desperate Remedies

It can only be speculation as to why Duckett returned to England – possibly the imminent birth of his daughter Lucia in 1864 was a factor or perhaps the onset of the tuberculosis which was to be his nemesis for the rest of his days. Certainly the incipient tuberculosis became more a factor in Duckett's life throughout 1864 and it could only have been an act of desperation which decided the young man to leave his daughter and pregnant wife Lizzie behind and set out to Australia. On the 13th February, 1865, the 26 year old consumptive boarded the *Winifred* in Deal and set sail for Melbourne in a quest to regain that most precious of all things, his health, and it was a measure of Duckett's despair when he was prepared to travel 10,000 miles on a voyage which could take 3 to 4 months to achieve his aim. As things worked out, the sea breezes blew away Duckett's symptoms, so much so that he spent his spare time sketching ship-board scenes and was commissioned by the Captain to paint four watercolours and carve two wooden medallions.

Twilight and Night (1861).
Thomas Duckett Junior

On arrival in Melbourne, Duckett befriended Eugène von Guérard who was the foremost painter of landscapes in Australia and counted him as his *"best friend here"*. By August, 1865, Duckett had modelled his friend's portrait medallion which was later exhibited at the 1866 Melbourne Intercolonial Exhibition along with three photographs of sculptures he had done in England but his initial expectations were doomed to disappointment when he was commissioned to design a seal for the Melbourne Public Library which the trustees refused to sanction as an engraving, If Duckett had entertained hopes that sculptural commissions would come easily in such an outpost as Australia he was to be sadly disillusioned and turned to finding work wherever he could which included a drawing of *Volunteer Manoeuvres by Moonlight* for the illustrated press

– it was work which he found boring. The drawing was required to be transferred to a woodcut which Duckett knew little about and was overjoyed when von Guérard once again came to the rescue and *"worked on the trees for me, putting in magical, fairily delicate touches until they had a freedom and style quite exquisite."* Unfortunately, the work which he had begun to take such a pride in was ruined by the engraver and both Duckett and von Guérard were duly disgusted at the published sketch. It seemed that Duckett had little choice but to continue sketching for the same employer and completed drawings of Chinese woodcarvers, sometimes including himself in the drawings, in August, 1866. But overall, Duckett was disappointed in Melbourne and wrote to Thomas Thornycroft's daughter, Helen, that an ape in a local circus was *"the nearest approach to a human being ever seen in these colonies."* But Duckett's aversion to Melbourne society and his difficulties in finding work paled into insignificance by an unusually severe winter and the enervating effects of the ocean voyage were dispelled by an onset of his original symptoms. On medical advice, early in 1867, Duckett set up camp at Emu Creek, Mandurang, and wrote in February to a friend in England, Mrs Pearson, that he had done no carving or sketching for two months *"certainly the longest abstinence of my life."*

The End of the Line

By May, 1867, Duckett had recovered enough to take up his sketch-pad and travel to Launceston where he remained *"modelling medallions, making drawings and nursing myself"* until in June he made his way to Sydney, seeking work once again. There was always a living to be made making portrait busts and Duckett's fortunes changed for the better when he received commissions for busts of Sir John Young, John Fairfax, David Jones and finally a bust of the Governor with the expectation that a full-size statue would follow. Duckett was beginning to forge a career in Sydney and in the summer of 1867 he received his largest commission to date which was to provide sculptures for the Haslem Creek Receiving Station in the centre of Rookwood Cemetery. The officials of Sydney had found an ingenious way to solve their problems of the increased number of burials required in the city with the Mortuary Train which ran from central Sydney outwards to Rookwood Cemetery picking up mourners and coffins at several stations along the way – eleven miles outside the city centre, the Receiving Station terminus would literally be the end of the line for many of the citizens of Sydney. Working with the stonemason Henry Apperley, Duckett's brief was to embellish the Gothic building in keeping with the dignity of the occasion and elaborate carvings of angels, cherubs, gargoyles, flowers, sycamore, apples and pomegranates were carved out of the sandstone. The two main embellishments were of angels on each side the northern arch – one of the angels held a scroll representing the Judgement Book and the other held a trumpet representing Resurrection. The summer of 1867 may have been a success for Duckett in terms

The Angels of Rookwood

of his growing reputation but the season had been excessively hot even for Australia and his health declined accordingly, so that Henry Apperley carved much of the work under Duckett's instruction. The two angels came to be known as The *Angel of Death* and the *Angel of Mercy* but it was not to be known by mourners that they would be harbingers of doom for their sculptor just as much as for their loved ones. There was something deeply disturbing in the nature of Thomas Duckett's commission for symbols of death on Haslem Creek Receiving Station and for those inclined to supernatural explanations of events it provided a rich source of wonder.

The train into Rookwood

The Final Blow

Duckett had confided to a friend in Sydney that although he worked to the best of his ability it was never his intention to stay in Australia but his one aim was to return home with his health intact. However, it appeared that his long voyage to the other side of the world had at best staved off his symptoms for a time and in November, 1867, his disease resurfaced with a vengeance. But there was far worse to come in December of the same year when he was given the devastating news that Lizzie had died leaving Lucia and the baby she had safely delivered without a mother. Duckett's state of mind at this time does not bear thinking about but from that time onward he embarked on an onerous workload, working at a frantic pace and filling the precious hours of days that were already numbered. In January, 1868, Duckett was commissioned to design and execute a series of eleven 10 ft by 5 ft illuminated transparencies in honour of the visit to Australia of Queen Victoria's second son, Prince Alfred. Working at a prodigious rate, Duckett produced one completed portrait each day until the work was completed on the 1st of February; six of the original sketches survive and include portraits of Captain Cook, Sir Walter Raleigh, Christopher Columbus, Galileo, James Watt and Sir Henry Davy.

Thomas Duckett Junior

The transparencies were Thomas Duckett's final work and it was just a matter of weeks before he died in the house of Mr Grafton Ross, Sydney, on Sunday 26th April, 1868, aged just 29. In the relatively short time he had been there, Duckett had made many friends in Australia and it was one of his friends and admirers of his work who wrote his obituary in the *Sunday Morning Herald* of May 1st, 1868, praising the quality of his portrait busts, his sculptures at Haslem Creek Receiving Station and his transparencies. His obituarist reserved a special mention for Duckett's compositions of children *"for which he entertained a strong sympathy"* and *"the tenderness of his feelings for the little people."* It's not difficult to surmise that Duckett's *"tenderness for the little people"* was engendered by thoughts of his own children in England, one of which he knew only briefly and the youngest that he never saw at all.

Blessed with good health, there is no telling to what heights Thomas Duckett would have reached as an artist and sculptor but in the long run his quest to throw off the scourge of tuberculosis transcended all else and he is more remarkable for his heroic struggle than for anything else. Sadly, he was never known by a Dickens or a Rossetti or a Gaskell whose works were full to the brim of pathos, but had they known him his epic striving to be creative despite the shackles of his illness would undoubtedly have earned him a place in the pantheon of artistic and literary immortals.

Thomas Duckett is buried in Rookwood Cemetery, Haslem Creek, Sydney, Australia. Very little of his work has survived with the greater part being sketches in archives which are rarely visited.

The bizarre concept of a steam train stacked with coffins and mourners travelling through Sydney and outwards to Rookwood Cemetery became a common sight from its inception in 1867 until the line finished in 1948.

A Family of Sculptors

The Father

*"If people knew how hard I worked to get my mastery,
it wouldn't seem so wonderful at all."*

– Michelangelo

William Spence (179? – 1849)

The Early Years

Although most sources place William Spence's birth at 1793, the 1841 census has his age as 43 in which case he was born in 1797. Given that Spence's first known marble bust was sculpted in 1811, this would make him a child prodigy, which is unlikely but not impossible. Compounding the problem is that in an article written in 1939, *The Liverpool Post and Echo* gave William's date of birth as 1796 and to make things even more complicated his death certificate states unequivocally that he was buried on July 10th, 1849, at the age of 52, in the churchyard of St Anne's (Richmond), Cazneau Street, the same Church where he was married – again placing his date of birth as 1797.

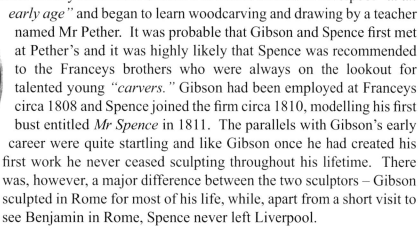

Medallion of Canning, 1824

What is certain is that William Spence was born in Chester and his early career closely resembled Gibson's in that he arrived in Liverpool *"at an early age"* and began to learn woodcarving and drawing by a teacher named Mr Pether. It was probable that Gibson and Spence first met at Pether's and it was highly likely that Spence was recommended to the Franceys brothers who were always on the lookout for talented young *"carvers."* Gibson had been employed at Franceys circa 1808 and Spence joined the firm circa 1810, modelling his first bust entitled *Mr Spence* in 1811. The parallels with Gibson's early career were quite startling and like Gibson once he had created his first work he never ceased sculpting throughout his lifetime. There was, however, a major difference between the two sculptors – Gibson sculpted in Rome for most of his life, while, apart from a short visit to see Benjamin in Rome, Spence never left Liverpool.

Spence exhibited in 1812 at the Liverpool Academy with only his second statue, entitled *Young Hymen* and a drawing of *Centaurs Pursuing Dante,* and thereafter exhibited for the remainder of his life. Again in a similar scenario to the career of John Gibson, William Roscoe became a patron of Spence and commissioned a bust of himself which was shown at the Liverpool

Academy in 1813 and just as he would do with Gibson, Roscoe advised Spence to go to Rome, the acknowledged home of classical sculpture.

The Liverpool Academy whose full title was *The Academy of the Liverpool Royal Institution*, was formed at the beginning of the 1800s by Liverpool notables interested in art and sculpture – William Roscoe was foremost among members. There were financial difficulties involved in finding suitable headquarters for the Academy and exhibits were first shown in Marble Street Gothic Rooms and a room on the top floor of The Union News Rooms, until the group finally settled in Colquitt Street in a building which is still standing.

Roscoe must have felt a pang of envy when he watched his young protégés make their way to places such as Rome and Venice as unlike many of his friends and contemporaries Roscoe never left England and for him it remained a fabled Shangri-La of the art world. However, on this occasion, Roscoe's advice was ignored and Spence chose to remain in the relative obscurity of Liverpool, a decision which possibly prevented him from reaching his full potential as a sculptor but from which he benefited in other ways, as shall be seen. In 1814, Spence sculpted subjects as disparate as a bust of *The Duke of Wellington* and *Tom Cribb in an Attitude of Boxing*. At first glance, the choice of Tom Cribb, a bare knuckle fighter from Bristol, seems an unlikely subject for Spence whose passion was for neo-classical subjects, but on closer examination it was a good choice from a financial perspective. As champion boxer of England, Cribb was a household name and in common with other prize fighters, was subsidised and managed by an aristocratic and upper class sportsman, the most famous being Lord Byron. Cribb's statue would have been attractive to both aristocratic boxing fans and the many thousands of working-class followers of the sport; marble statues were of course out of the range of the man in the street but there were many reproductions of the famous fighter made out of porcelain which was more affordable. Whether Spence was commissioned to sculpt a statue of Cribb or if the boxer ever posed for his statue is unknown.

Royal Academy, Colquitt Street

Great Responsibilities

In September, 1819, Thomas and Samuel Franceys went their separate ways and the *London Gazette* formally noted that *"The partnership heretofore consisting between us the undersigned as marble masons and builders is this day dissolved by mutual consent."* Although the whole story will never be known of why the two brothers parted company, there is a sense that there was some bad feeling involved, made more so by the pronouncement that *"All debts due to or owing the late said concern will be received and paid by Mr Samuel Healey, Accountant, Castle Street."* To all intents and purposes, it appeared that Franceys Marble Works had run its course and was about to close, but once again although it can never be proved, there is the distinct impression that Spence was the saviour of the firm when he offered to take the place of Samuel and in 1819 the firm was renamed Franceys and Spence. It is no coincidence that from that time onwards the partnership flourished and it was undoubtedly Spence's sheer energy and industry which was the driving force; Spence's output of marble busts, portrait medallions, neo-classical sculptures, carvings for pediments and not least a multitude of massive memorial stones speaks of a man with a huge workload prepared to undertake any commission and bent on making a success of his business. Gibson had always complained that many of his sculptures carried out on behalf of his employers were signed *"made by Franceys"* but Spence's work is invariably marked beneath a plinth *"William Spence, Fecit Liverpool."* Although Spence employed assistants to complete many of his sculptures, there's no doubting the fact that many of the commissions were of a mundane nature and earning money took precedence over art works that Spence preferred to work on. He did in fact turn to sculptures of his own design whenever the opportunity arose and these were usually classical themes of his own design. James Allanson Picton (1832 – 1910) remarked on Spence's frustrations in his *"Memorials of Liverpool"* – *"Although necessarily absorbed in the mere manufacture of marble as a trade, he snatched every leisure moment he could steal for a loving devotion to art as such."*

Detail from Robert Roughsedge memorial (1831) at St Nicholas' Church showing Spence's penchant for neo-classicism. Roughsedge it will be recalled was Henry Park's great friend

Spence may well have been naturally conscientious but there was another motivation for his hard work when on the 3rd January,1820 he married the 19 year old Elizabeth Evans at St Anne's Church (now demolished) in Cazneau Street and they soon began a family – Benjamin Evans Spence was born in Chester in 1822 (baptized in 1823 at St Peter's Church, Church Street), followed by Margaret (1826), James (1828), John (1829), Thomas (1830), Eleanore (1836), Mary (1838) and finally Clara who was born in 1840.

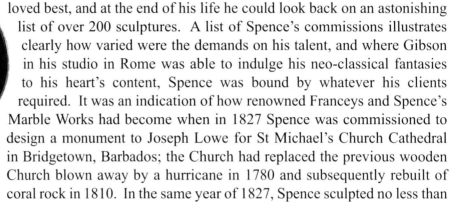

Medallion of Huskisson, 1831

From that time onward, Spence's story is one of unrelieved toil at the work he loved best, and at the end of his life he could look back on an astonishing list of over 200 sculptures. A list of Spence's commissions illustrates clearly how varied were the demands on his talent, and where Gibson in his studio in Rome was able to indulge his neo-classical fantasies to his heart's content, Spence was bound by whatever his clients required. It was an indication of how renowned Franceys and Spence's Marble Works had become when in 1827 Spence was commissioned to design a monument to Joseph Lowe for St Michael's Church Cathedral in Bridgetown, Barbados; the Church had replaced the previous wooden Church blown away by a hurricane in 1780 and subsequently rebuilt of coral rock in 1810. In the same year of 1827, Spence sculpted no less than six busts of Liverpool worthies, including one of the architect John Foster who also ordered a statue of his dog. Despite his oppressive workload Spence unfailingly exhibited work of his own choosing each year at the Liverpool Academy and on two rare occasions he showed *Caractacus before Caesar* and *Aristides Showing the Shell to the Vates* at the Westminster Hall Exhibitions inspiring widely varying critiques.

In 1828, Spence had the honour to be chosen as Master of Drawing from the Antique in the Liverpool Academy Schools (he would later be Treasurer of the Academy in 1845) and in May 1829, Samuel Franceys passed away and was buried in the Wesleyan Chapel in Brunswick Street. Thomas Franceys would continue in business with Spence until 1844.

A Present for a President

In the early years of the 1800s William Roscoe's fame was such that it was almost obligatory for his friends to request marble busts of the great man. Roscoe ordered several busts for himself which Gibson sculpted and Spence made a bas-relief medallion of Roscoe for his patron, Benjamin Hick (1790 – 1842), Member of Parliament for Bolton of Mitton Hall, Blackburn. As well as being a great patron of the arts, Hick was deeply involved in the burgeoning railway system and as a major shareholder in the Bolton and Leigh Railway was present at the opening ceremony in 1828 when the locomotive *The Lancashire Witch* was the main focus of attention. Yet another bust of Roscoe made by Spence in 1813 was exhibited at the Liverpool Academy and was notable for being far more realistic than Gibson's idealized version of his patron; it was perhaps for this reason that the bust was chosen by the firm to be reproduced in porcelain at the Herculaneum Pottery Works. The Marble Works had a place set aside to exhibit their wares and showcase the extent of the work they could undertake and the warts-and-all bust of Roscoe was placed on display among the other works of art for sale.

Bust of Roscoe

What is also certain is that Franceys Marble Works was frequented by the upper classes of Liverpool and the surrounding areas, on the lookout for statues for their great houses or ordering custom-made sculptures of their families or ornate friezes for fireplaces and so on. Browsing among the displays one day in 1820, was no less a figure than the American Consulate to Liverpool, James Maury (1746 – 1840), whose home was just a stone's throw away in Rodney Street (the house is still standing with a plaque on the front recalling Maury's tenure). The American War of Independence which had begun in 1775 had ended officially with the signing of the Treaty of Paris in 1783 and the American Constitution was drawn up in 1787. As such, the war was still a recent memory in 1820, and it was only in January of that same year that George III had passed away, along with his legacy of losing the American colonies during his reign. George IV who had been Prince Regent for many years acceded to the throne in the same year. One of the most potent and recognizable documents in history, The Declaration of Independence, was drafted in July, 1776, during the war with Great Britain, and of all the now renowned members of the committee dedicated to independence,

Thomas Jefferson (1743 – 1826) was chosen to compose the original draft. Jefferson who is now immortalised as one of the Founding Fathers of American Independence was also a great friend of William Roscoe and the two men had exchanged letters since 1805 when Roscoe sent Jefferson a copy of his book *The Life and Pontificate of Leo X* – Jefferson responded that the book would *"stand worthily on the shelf with The Life of Lorenzo de Medici"* also by Roscoe, and he would later receive Roscoe's *A Catalogue of Plants in the Botanic Garden at Liverpool* (1808). Roscoe's original Botanic Gardens were built in Crown Street in 1807 and are recalled today by the numerous street names pertaining to the gardens – Myrtle Street, Vine Street, Mulberry Street, Grove Street and Olive Street among others. It was indicative of the speed that Liverpool was extending outwards that within two decades the plants within the gardens were choking from the smog produced by myriads of coal-fires and in 1830 Roscoe moved the Botanic Gardens to a new site in the rustic countryside of Wavertree. Roscoe's name is always associated with the Abolition of the slave-trade which came about in 1807 but prior to that date many of Roscoe's friends and associates had been slave-traders – a fact which could easily be construed as hypocrisy on Roscoe's part but is simply proof of how endemic the slave-trade was among the aristocracy of Liverpool. Roscoe's great friendship with Thomas Jefferson was also proof that the practise of slavery in America remained as widespread as ever and would remain so until the American Civil War; Jefferson's home at Monticello, Virginia, was a plantation which maintained several hundred slaves although Jefferson himself paradoxically was said to oppose slavery. How Jefferson equated the axiom written into the Constitution that *"all men are created equal"* with his role as plantation owner is a mystery known only to himself.

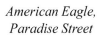

American Eagle,
Paradise Street

Just three years after the Treaty of Paris and the official ending of the American War of Independence, James Maury had the great distinction of being appointed the first American

Ambassador to England by the fledgling nations first President, George Washington. The Embassy, opened in 1790, was situated near to The Old Dock in Paradise Street, at the very heart of Liverpool's maritime empire in a street which was dear to sailor's hearts around the world. And it was there amidst the prostitutes and land-sharks, rowdy taverns and boisterous sailors that James Maury had his office. Today the American Eagle which was probably taken from an American sailing ship stands proudly above the old Embassy as it has done for two centuries. Maury's tenure as Ambassador lasted from 1790 to 1829 but in 1820 when he was wandering amongst the bric-a-brac in Franceys and Spence's Marble Works he was well entrenched in his role and a great friend of America's 3rd President, Thomas Jefferson. Maury had been a classmate of Jefferson and he knew that Roscoe was also a friend of the President so that when he spied a porcelain bust of Roscoe, after Spence's original marble, he bought it as a present for Jefferson and shipped it off to Monticello with the message, *"In passing a porcelain Warehouse the other day, I was so struck with a correct likeness of Wm Roscoe in a small Bust that I thought it would be pleasing to you to have the opportunity of giving it a place in your collection at Monticello."* Jefferson subsequently wrote to Roscoe that he would receive it *"with great pleasure and thankfulness and shall arrange it in honorable file with those of some cherished characters"* – and true to his word Jefferson gave the bust pride of place in his home at Monticello where it can still be seen to this day.

The Old Dock and Custom House 1843 by Herdman

A Mansion in Wigan

The Neptune Fountain

In 1831, Franceys and Spence accepted a new challenge when they were commissioned to sculpt a large fountain of Neptune surrounded by horses rampant within an octagonal stone basin with a waterlily frieze. The Neptune Fountain was designed by Meyrick Bankes II (1811 – 1881) of Winstanley Hall, who probably contributed to its later decline with his profligacy in embellishing his family home with statues and decorative artwork wherever he thought fit. Winstanley Hall near to Wigan dates from 1560 and was originally built for the Winstanley family who sold it soon afterwards to James Bankes, a London goldsmith and banker. The house was at that time a magnificent mansion with an Elizabethan frontage, a huge courtyard and extensive gardens. Several generations of the Bankes' family lived in the house until in the 1960s the cost of maintenance became too much and they abandoned their ancestral home which very soon fell into disrepair and decay. The sculpture of Neptune was a complete departure for Spence in that it was made of bronze and larger than anything he had ever done before. But Spence completed the work successfully and the fountain, with the water pouring from the horses mouths, was still working when the Bankes' abandoned the house. The statue soon went the same way as the house and began to fall prey to vandalism and neglect – however, both house and statue today are the subject of several campaigns to see them restored to their former glories.

Spence carried out several other commissions for the Bankes' family – notably a group called *Charity* which is a monument to Meyrick Bankes placed within St Aidan's Church, Billinge.

Another memorial can be found in Upholland Church to the Reverend John Bird whose daughter married Meyrick Bankes; an example of how one commission led to another.

Portrait of a Sculptor

In 1841, William Huggins painted a fine portrait of Spence in his studio surrounded by the tools of his trade, his dog at his side and a tiny bust of Huggins by his elbow. Although it was written at a much later time, Picton's description of Spence complements the portrait to perfection; *"Modest and gentle in his outward demeanour, he was in character and conduct one of the kindest and most unselfish beings it has ever been my lot to meet. He was never so happy as in his workshop surrounded by his assistants, the sharp click of the chisel in his ears, the modelling tools in his hands, clad in a long grey duffel coat, his curling hair flowing over his shoulders. Here he would chat merrily with his friends, working assiduously all the time, his eye lighting up with pleasure as tidings came from time to time of his son's progress in Rome."*

Portrait of Spence by William Huggins.
Walker Art Gallery

In Memoriam

It's a sad fact that over 165 years after his death, most of William Spence's sculptures have been lost or are untraced and of the small percentage that have survived most of them are the memorials which were of secondary importance to his neo-classical sculptures. It is not difficult to discern why the memorials have survived the passing of the years – most of them have taken sanctuary in Churches and Cathedrals around the country where their cloistered existence and extraordinary size and weight have ensured their longevity. What is more difficult to ascertain is why the greater part and arguably the more valuable part of Spence's work is now quantified as *"untraced."* Most of Spence's sculptures would have been decorative additions to mansion houses or sold to wealthy aristocrats and it can only be assumed that with the demise of the great estates the sculptures were sold on, with perhaps a small proportion being broken or lost in transit. Despite his lack of interest in funerary memorials Spence still produced work of the highest quality and in many cases found the urge to embellish the marbles with neo-classical motifs irresistible, making distinctive works of art of the stones. Quite apart from their aesthetic merits, the memorials are often extraordinarily moving accounts of life and death, revealing something of the ephemeral quality of life during the Victorian era; there are too many to show every plaque sculpted by Spence but a selection below illustrates both the many ways that death came early in the Victorian era and the many ways in which Spence memorialised them.

Joseph Brandreth (1746 – 1815)

The memorial to Joseph. P. Brandreth is one of Spence's earliest memorials and is also one of his finest. In a world which immortalizes Generals far more than Physicians, Joseph Brandreth is one of the unsung heroes of the city of Liverpool. Born in Ormskirk, Brandreth became one of the leading physicians of his day and was a loyal friend of Henry Park. He was a personal physician to the Duke of Gloucester and Lord Derby but his finest achievement was the establishment of the Liverpool Dispensary which stood in Church Street next door to the original Athenaeum building, now the haunt of shoppers in the department stores which now stand on the site.

The Dispensary opened in 1781 and was a place where the less well-off could obtain advice and treatment for the many ailments they suffered – another Dispensary opened later in James Street and a third in Ormskirk which is still standing and replicates the design of the Liverpool Dispensary. Brandreth was also present when William Huskisson met with his tragic accident at Parkside and accompanied by two other eminent surgeons, Dr Southey and Dr Hunter did his best for the dying man. Brandreth

The Dispensary Church Street had a plaque above the door by the Liverpool sculptor John Deare

later wrote a letter of the account in a letter to Mrs Gaskell of Thorne's House, Wakefield, and another in an article for the *Cornhill Magazine*. Spence's memorial to Brandreth appropriately named *The Good Samaritan* was commissioned by his wife Catharine, exhibited at the Academy in 1827 before being placed within the Dispensary itself and later found its way to Ormskirk Church where it can be seen today. Outside the Church, the gravestone to Brandreth is sited against the Church wall. A later version of *The Good Samaritan* dedicated to Dr Wainwright was placed in St George's Church (the Iron Church), Heyworth Street, Everton, in 1841, where it is today sadly neglected and in need of restoration. In the graveyard of the same Church is the tomb of one of Brandreth's surgeons, Dr George Beaumont, who worked at the Liverpool Dispensary.

The Good Samaritan in Ormskirk Church

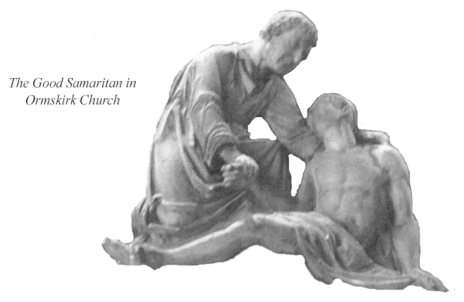

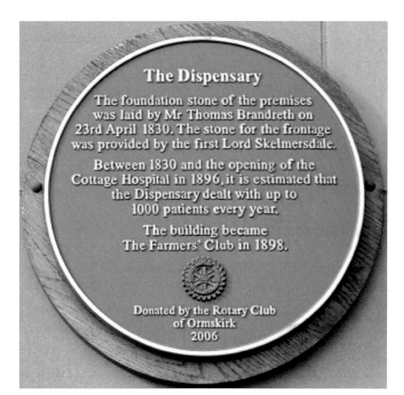

Plaque above the Dispensary, Ormskirk

*John Bibby Memorial,
All Hallows*

John Bibby (1775 – 1840)

John Bibby was born near Ormskirk and worked in Liverpool at a ship's iron merchant producing anchors and chains. In 1801, Bibby diversified into ship broking at Duke's Dock, taking a small share in a 60 ton ship called *Dove* and in 1805 he married Mary Margaret Mellard, whose sizeable dowry enabled Bibby to form the firm of John Bibby and Co. By the 1830s the firm was flourishing with a fleet of 18 ships trading across the globe and John and Mary's marriage had also flourished producing 4 sons and 2 daughters. Mary died at an early age and John Bibby never remarried preferring to concentrate on bringing his sons into the family business. On the 16th July, 1840, Bibby was walking to his home called Mount Pleasant on Linacre Marsh, north of what is now Aintree race course, and following what was deemed to be a random theft he was thrown into a ditch where he drowned. The robbers were never found and following the tragedy Bibby's sons took over the firm which flourishes to this day. Bibby's memorial can be found in an alcove in All Hallows Church, Allerton, with several motifs signifying something of his life; an anchor for the sea, a beehive for industry and wings carrying an hourglass for the speed at which life passes. There's also a profile of Bibby underneath which is carved '*Spence, Fecit Liverpool.*'

John Gore

*John Gore Memorial,
the Oratory*

The memorial to John Gore in the Cathedral Oratory is to the grandson of the better known John Gore whose tale is yet another in the long litany of poignant Georgian and Victorian tragedies. John Gore's volumes of books called *Gore's Advertiser* were a precursor to the later census and were filled to the brim with street names, house numbers, the names of house tenants and the work they did. It all sounds quite boring until you pick up one of Gore's books to find that they are painstakingly researched histories of Liverpool streets and they tell a tale of Liverpool when ostlers, ladies' maids, coachmen, butlers, chimney-sweeps, resurrection men, rivermen, rope makers and scavengers were common occupations. The amount of work that it took to produce just one of Gore's volumes is staggering and the books are still referred to today by historians in awe of their size and accuracy. The *Advertiser* was begun in 1765 by John Gore who was later helped in his monumental task by his only son Johnson Gore, until in 1832 Johnson died prematurely. A hearbroken John Gore was unable to carry on after the sudden death of his son and he himself died soon afterwards when the *Advertiser* was taken over by the Mawdsleys.

Henry Faithwaite Leigh (1756 – 1833)

Henry Faithwaite Leigh of Colquitt Street was prominent in the foundation of St Nicholas' Pro-Cathedral on Brownlow Hill and also the Catholic School and Chapel adjoining the building. The memorial which includes the names of his son George Leigh and his mother-in-law Catherine Pulford is sited within the Oratory, St James' Churchyard. The memorial was rescued from demolition in 1973 when it was purchased from Mander's Demolition Company of Romford Essex for £100.

A lancer at the battle of Aliwal

William Henry Swetenham (1819 – 1846)

The memorial to Henry Swetenham can be found in St Marys Church, Astbury in Cheshire and recalls the Sikh Wars in the Punjab. The now almost forgotten Battle of Aliwal (spelt various ways) was one of the bloodiest and fiercely fought battles in that war, pitting 12,000 British and Bengali troops against 30,000 Sikhs and 67 cannon. The XVI Lancers played a major part in the battle and distinguished themselves in routing the Sikh cavalry force before going on to attack the Sikh infantry which formed squares. Forming squares had long been a traditional defence against cavalry famously adopted by the British at Waterloo when Ney's cavalry were blown into tatters as they circled the British squares which remained steady. The situations were reversed at Aliwal with the Sikhs forming squares to repel the British cavalry epitomised by a Sergeant Newsome who shouted *"Hullo boys, here goes for death or a commission"* as he leapt his horse into a Sikh square, attempting to take a Sikh colour. Newsome was killed by 19 bayonet wounds but his charge opened the way for others to follow and all the Sikh squares were broken, leaving the field open to a British victory. Newsome wasn't the only cavalryman killed on that day of the 28th January, 1846, and of the 300 Lancers alive that morning, 144 of them died during the battle, including Lieutenant William Henry Swetenham.

Henry Swetenham Memorial

IN MEMORY OF
HENRY DONNITHORNE SWETENHAM.

Milborne Kemeys-Tynte (1824 – 1845)

If William Swetenham was unfortunate to die at such a young age at least he lost his life in one of the most glorious cavalry charges in history, winning glory and the respect of his fellow cavalrymen. The same cannot be said of Milborne Kemeys Tynte of the Royal Irish Regiment of Dragoon Guards who died in Tipperary, Ireland, aged just 21 when his horse fell on him and killed him. Kemeys-Tynte's memorial is on the wall of St Edward's Church, Goathurst.

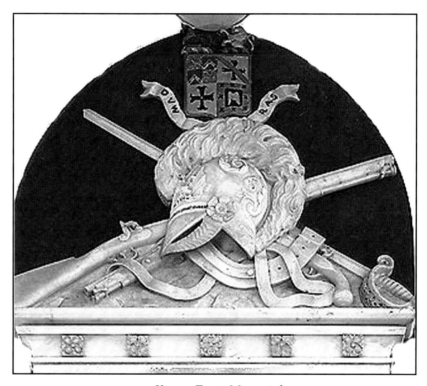

Kemys Tynte Memorial

There's no escaping the Georgian and Victorian tragedies which seemed to play such a part in the lives of so many people in that era. The penchant for families to have large numbers of children may well have been an antidote for the high child mortality but the vast numbers of illnesses lying in wait were neither respecters of rank or of age. Ailments which today would be eminently treatable were then virtual death sentences with men and women being carried off suddenly with cholera or lingering on for years with tuberculosis. Although the loss of loved ones was no less tragic than at any other time, the Victorians became so inured to the numerous diseases over which they had no control, that they regarded it as something almost preordained; the Gregg memorial in Derry is typical of the age. There's no doubt that the everyday tragedies entered into popular culture and either consciously or subconsciously much of what was on offer was suffused in sentimentality and pathos. In the theatre plays were inevitably tragedies with sobbing maidens which was a common motif, paintings were of tragic heroines bidding soldier lovers farewell, and novels by Dickens, Hardy and Kingsley were merely reflections of everyday life. Poetry in particular was full of flowery verse and cloying sentimentality as if to compensate for the realities of everyday life and it was only in late Victorian times that a different view of life began to emerge and imagination took flight with the novels of H.G.Wells, Kipling, Conan Doyle et al. There were at least two sculptors from Franceys Marble Works whose lives were blighted by illness and although William Spence appeared to have remained hale and hearty during his lifetime, the same could not be said of his son, Benjamin.

Gregg Memorial

In 1860, *The London Illustrated News* printed a retrospective article on William Spence accompanied by a sketch of the sculptor as an older man and in the same year James Allanson Picton described the Marble Works after Spence's death in the following manner. *"There is nothing in the building to look at of the slightest interest either internally or externally. Two or three dingy shops in front with a labyrinth of mean sheds and workrooms behind form about as unattractive picture as the eye could dwell upon; yet these poor feeble remains were once irradiated with the light of genius, enterprise and art."*

Willliam Spence was remembered in the Illustrated London News, 1860

A Family of Sculptors

Benjamin Evans Spence (1822 – 1866)

"All children are artists.
The problem is how to remain an artist when they grow up."

– Pablo Picasso

His Father's Son

Born on the 12th November, 1822, Benjamin Evans Spence was baptized on the 1st January, 1823, at St Peter's Church, Church Street, a Liverpool landmark from 1704 until its demolition in 1922; the gardens of the Church lingered on into the 1960s but all that remains today is a brass cross set in the pavement signifying where the Church once stood. Benjamin Evans Spence is often referred to as Benjamin Edward Spence but the former is the correct name with *"Evans"* after his mother's maiden name. The young Spence would have been familiar with the paraphernalia of his father's workplace at Franceys yard from a very early age and no doubt as a child played among the jumbled pieces of marble. By the time he came to enrol in the Liverpool Academy Schools on 1st May, 1838, aged 15, Benjamin was already adept as a stone-carver and showing every sign that he had inherited his father's talent. At the age of 18 Benjamin was still living at the family home in Brownlow Street with his occupation listed as *"sculptor"* on the 1841 census returns, and although in all probability he helped his father in the Marble Works from time to time, he was still attending the Academy producing little more than several busts which he exhibited – one was of a fellow student and another was the almost obligatory head and shoulders of William Roscoe. Several years passed in this way, until at the age of 22, Benjamin suddenly came to prominence with a sculpture in clay which surpassed by far all his previous efforts; *The Death of the Duke of York at Agincourt* was an ambitious sculpture by any standards and was good enough to be exhibited at The Westminster Hall Exhibition of 1844 where it won general acclaim before being transferred to the Royal Manchester Institution where it was awarded the 1846 Silver Medal. One year later Benjamin repeated his previous year's success with a statue of *Ulysses* also in clay. Both statues are now lost but they were in all probability part of the reason why John Gibson wrote to William Spence inviting Benjamin to study in his studio on the Via della Fontanella. Gibson had left for Rome in 1817, long before Benjamin was born, and following an apprenticeship under the great Canova had established himself as an acclaimed sculptor with a clientele which began with members of the wealthy intelligentsia and led onto the Royal

Benjamin Spence in later life

Family itself. Gibson's studio was a place of pilgrimage for those on the Grand Tour, his visitors were a virtual who's-who of the British establishment and he was in a position to pick and choose his commissions; his invitation to Benjamin was a great honour and the young sculptor took the opportunity which his father had declined at the same age.

Crossing The Road

Benjamin set out for Rome early in 1846 and was set to work in Gibson's studio with a life-size group entitled *Hector and Andromache* which he began to model in clay. It was only a matter of weeks before Gibson found he was unimpressed with Benjamin's modelling and the older man was not slow in telling him so. Gibson outlined his first impressions of Spence in a letter dated 23rd June, 1846, to his Liverpool friend, John Crouchley.

"I left Mr Ben (Gibson's brother) and Mr Spence at my studio, Spence had begun a group, life-size of Hector and Andromache but he is sadly behindhand in art, he should begin a regular ABC study of the figure from the antique and then from nature and in two years to do something of his own. Like all those who know nothing of art he is very rapid – he was surprised when I told him that Wyatt and myself after making many small models for the same figure, the best we hid out of sight for one year and at the end of a year we brought it out and if we liked it we executed it large, if not, we broke it up, we made a model three feet and from that one, by scale, we made the large one, spending months upon the clay, he said to me in England they do not go about it in such a roundabout way. All this you must keep to yourself – young Spence seems to me a very good young man but I do not think he has a genius for art."

It was a withering put down for the aspiring sculptor and resulted in his quickly moving out of Gibson's studio and into the studio of Richard James Wyatt (1795 – 1850) which was directly across the road. Gibson was not an unkind man in any way, just the opposite in fact, but he may well have found the youthful Spence's speedy approach to modelling the very antithesis to his own learning process at the same age; Gibson had spent many tedious hours over many years studying human anatomy and found it difficult to understand how Spence was able to model figures without that laborious background and it is probable that Spence rebelled at being instructed to follow such a strict regime.

As so often happens, the move to Wyatt's studio proved a blessing in disguise not least because Gibson was evangelical about neo-classical sculpture and if the break had not occurred sooner then it would certainly have done so later; Spence always sculpted in a classical style but his subjects were often of non-classical origin which would never have suited the pedantic Gibson. Wyatt and Gibson had been great friends since Wyatt arrived in Rome in 1820, three years after Gibson and there was no ill-feeling between any of the three sculptors. In fact, as time went by Spence grew very fond of Gibson and Wyatt and they formed the nucleus of a large American and English colony of artists and sculptors.

Lavinia

Benjamin settled into life in Rome in much the same way as Gibson and Wyatt and many others had done before him, breakfasting at the nearby Caffé Greco at No.16 Via Condotti (the Café is still there today), chatting about their various projects and picking up their correspondence. In his leisure time Spence of course sought out the art works scattered throughout Rome remarking that within the famous fresco in the Sistine Chapel. Michelangelo had *"stolen the very figure of Adam"* and that *"notwithstanding all Flaxman's beauty, Thorvaldsen beat him hollow."* Bertel Thorvaldsen (1770 – 1844) and John Gibson had both been students of the great Antonio Canova (1757 – 1822) and had remained firm friends until Thorvaldsen returned to his native Copenhagen in 1838. It must have been a sobering thought for the youthful Benjamin to find that Canova had died in the year that he himself was born and by now he would have realised that his illustrious companions had received their training from the finest sculptor in Italy. He would also have been inspired by their very presence and it was indicative of how Benjamin had found his feet when he moved into his own studio on the Via degli Incurabile which was always a sign that an artist was confident of his own talents. The studio which was just a few streets away actually belonged to Wyatt who had purchased it and never moved in. Spence's first sculpture as an independent artist was *Lavinia*, a tragic heroine of the long pastoral poem *The Seasons* by the Scottish poet James Thompson (1700 – 1748). Lavinia represented Autumn and in an allegory of how summer turns to autumn she falls *"from ease and affluence into the depths of poverty."* In its day Thompson's poem was incredibly popular but although most of them will never have heard of *The Seasons*, Promenaders recognize him for having written the lyrics to *"Rule Brittania."* Judging *by Lavinia*, Spence had benefited greatly under the easy-going tutelage of Wyatt and following its exhibition at the Academy of Art, the prestigious Art Journal gave its verdict, stating that the statue *"was beautifully wrought and happily conceived"* and *"the statue is altogether a work that does great credit to so young a hand."* The comments by the Art Journal would have gratified not only the sculptor but Samuel Holme (1800 – 1871) the man who had commissioned it in the first place. Holme was a Liverpool businessman who had made his fortune in railway construction with premises on Mount Pleasant, between Benson Street and Roscoe Street, just a stone's throw from where Spence had begun work with his father. Holme became Lord Mayor of Liverpool in 1852.

Lavinia from The British Art Journal 1849

Highland Mary

Despite all its faults and immense chasms dividing the rich from the poor, Victorian England was notable for the patriotism of its citizens which extended across the whole spectrum of society. For the well-heeled gentry who travelled to Rome as part of the Grand Tour there was a certain patriotism attached to visiting the studios of British sculptors where they turned up unannounced and were welcomed with open arms. The studios of Gibson and Wyatt and many others in the colony of sculptors regularly received captains of industry, politicians, bankers and even Royalty on occasion and it was rare for any of them to take their leave without buying or commissioning a work of art for their mansion houses. Spence's success with the statue of *Lavinia* ensured he would also begin to receive visitors, and in 1849, Thomas Brassey (1805 – 1879) the renowned railway engineer, commissioned a statue of *Ophelia*. On the 17th January, 1849, Gibson's brother *"Mr Ben"* wrote to John Crouchley that *"Spence is going well with his statue of Ophelia – he continues to show much talent."*

Spence's wife Rosina – pen and ink drawing by Gibson

The 1850s was an auspicious decade for Spence, beginning with his marriage to Rosina Letitia Gower (1827 - ?), the daughter of George W. Gower, the British consul at Leghorn (now Livorno). The couple moved into a palazzo overlooking the Trevi Fountain but the happy event was tempered by an unexpected tragedy within the colony of sculptors; on the morning of the 28th of May, 1850, Spence paid a visit to Wyatt's studio where he found his mentor and friend gasping out his life in agony on the floor. It was later concluded that Wyatt had neglected a cold which had turned into a throat infection which went on to block his airway. Wyatt had long been a favourite of Queen Victoria and there were several unfinished works in his studio commissioned for the Royal Household; Spence completed the statues and they were forwarded to their destination, while Gibson carved a medallion memorial for his friend's headstone which can still be found in the English Cemetery, Rome.

As the shock of Wyatt's death subsided Spence returned to his own work and began a period which would see him move away from classical statues in order to sculpt subjects which were immediately recognizable to the Victorian public; whether Spence deliberately chose romantic Victorian icons for financial reasons is open to conjecture but the sculptures that he carved proved more popular than he could have ever imagined.

Highland Mary

In 1852, Spence carved the statue which would establish his reputation in Victorian society and inspire many repetitions and copies – the statue was that of the tragic heroine known as Highland Mary, whose story struck a chord with the Victorian public for not being taken from some literary theme but from real life. The poems of Robert Burns (1759 – 1796) had long been favourites of Scottish and English readers and although those Georgian and Victorian literati would have been loath to admit it, Burns' poetry was made more piquant by his scandalous lifestyle which was often of more interest. However, a louche lifestyle was one thing but a poignant love story was another and the tragedy of the poor Scottish maiden touched the Victorian public, exemplifying the fleeting quality of life they all knew so well. Burns first met Mary Campbell (1763 – 1786) in church at Tarbolton and soon immortalized her in poems in praise of her charms. Although the details are sketchy the couple fell in love and in May, 1786, they were married in an informal and traditional manner on the banks of the river Ayr, in which part of the ceremony was to exchange Bibles, which is the reason why Mary is always portrayed holding a Bible. Mary then travelled to the West Highlands to arrange matters with her family and friends, returning by sea from Campbeltown with her father to Greenock in the autumn when she was to be reunited with her lover. However, Mary's brother had contracted typhus and while nursing him she also contracted the disease and passed away without ever seeing Burns again. Mary is buried at Greenock where a monument marks her last resting place and the rumour persists that there are also the remains of a tiny child whose premature birth was the true cause of her death at the age of 23. Whatever the truth of the matter, the heartbreaking story of Mary Campbell still resonated with the Victorian public when in 1852 Spence's first *Highland Mary* was sculpted for Charles Meigh of Grove House, his palatial mansion at Shelton in the Potteries, and such was the popularity of the statue that it was soon mass-produced as a miniature Parian ware figure. In 1853, Spence received the ultimate accolade for *Highland*

Mary when Prince Albert commissioned a replica for Victoria's birthday after reading an article by a critic of the Art Journal who had described the original as he had seen it in Rome.

"A plaid is cast over her head, falling around the figure in heavy folds, arranged with the nicest skill. I complimented Mr Spence on his good fortune in having achieved so Scotch (sic) a physiognomy in classic Rome. His reply was, he had studied from many faces."

Queen Victoria's birthday present was presented to her in 1854 at Osborne House and was later placed in the Guard Room at Buckingham Palace.

Replicas of *Highland Mary* are commonly seen today in various galleries around the country with one which attracts a great deal of attention in the Walker Art Gallery, originally commissioned by Spence's great patron John Naylor and another in Sefton Park Palmhouse which is fondly remembered by an older generation who have known the statue since they were children.

Patrons

Devereux Plantagenet Cockburn memorial, Rome

Early in the 1850s, Spence was commissioned to sculpt one of only three known memorial sculptures that he ever undertook; the memorial was of Devereux Plantagenet Cockburn, an erstwhile cavalryman in the Royal Scots Greys, 2nd Dragoons. Spence carved a life size statue of Cockburn reclining atop a massive plinth, a Bible in his hand with his favourite dog beside him, and the wording on the plinth chosen by his parents was a heart-rending reminder of how they had desperately tried to fend off his death from tuberculosis.

"First born son of Sir W.S.R. Cockburn. Bart.N.S. of far off Britain. Of deep and unpretending piety; of rare mental and corporeal endowments. He was beloved by all who knew him. And most precious to his parents and family, who had sought his health in many foreign climes, he departed this life in Rome on the 3rd May, 1850, aged 21 years."

The memorial can be seen today in the English Cemetery, Rome, a harsh reminder of how the dreaded tuberculosis was a respecter of neither age nor class. The advice of physicians to seek out warmer climates rarely cured the disease but only served to prolong it. John Gibson's beloved brother, Benjamin, died the following year in August, 1851, after many years of struggling with the same disease.

In 1854, Spence sculpted a statue entitled *Liverpool* which was housed in the rebuilt Crystal Palace; Sir Joseph Paxton's original Crystal Palace was erected in Hyde Park for the Great Exhibition of 1851 and rebuilt in 1854 at Sydenham until it was destroyed by fire in 1936. It is probable that *Liverpool* was destroyed at this time, along with a marble bust by Spence of *Queen Victoria* and another of *Joseph Paxton*.

In 1856, Spence was commissioned by a committee of the friends and admirers of the Reverend Jonathan Brooks for a statue to be placed alongside the pantheon of Liverpool worthies in the Great Hall of St George's Hall. Evidently, the committee were less steadfast than the Reverend when they altered the agreed sum for the statue from £1,800 to £1,200, leaving Spence somewhat aggrieved at his treatment. Following a great deal of disagreement among the committee, the only one who emerged from the fiasco with his integrity intact was Spence who upheld his side of the bargain, completed the statue, and accepted the reduced sum. The statue itself was acclaimed as a fine work of art but many people believed that although Brooks himself may have been a fine man, his achievements never merited a place among the Roscoes and Stephensons of the town – Sir James Allanson Picton was foremost among the critics of the siting of the statue.

In common with all of the British sculptors. Spence entertained prospective patrons and clients with lavish dinner parties, escorted them around the sights of Rome and finally introduced them to examples of his own work in his studio. It is quite probable that Spence came into contact with John Naylor in this way and began an association which would find him working on commissions for the Naylor family throughout the mid 1850s and many years to come. *The Finding of Moses* and the portrait figures of John Naylor's wife, Georgiana, with their two sons Rowland and Christopher are complex groupings of disparate figures, large and small, which are breathtakingly bold and arguably Spence's finest work. Both statues have been in storage for many years – the greater story can be found in a later chapter.

Uncertain Days

One of the more unlikely patrons of John Gibson and Benjamin Spence was a man named Joshua Frey Josephson (1815 – 1892) who was born in Hamburg to Jacob Josephson and his wife Emma Wilson who had three children from a previous marriage. One month after his birth Joshua was christened at St Matthew's Church, Bethnal Green, London following the whole family's conversion from Judaism to Christianity. Joshua was still an infant when his father, Jacob, was convicted of forgery and in May 1818 was sentenced to transportation to Sydney, Australia, sailing soon afterwards on the *Neptune*. On the 12th September, 1820, Jacob's family, including the now five year old Joshua, boarded a ship called *Morley* and followed him out to Australia.

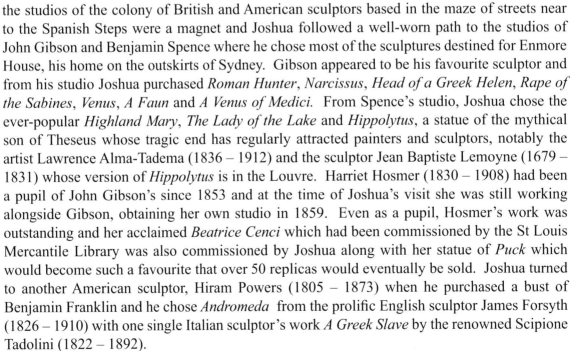

Hippolytus.
New South Wales

Australia was obviously to Joshua's liking and by the age of 20 he had become an accomplished pianist, flautist and singer and by 1834 he was teaching music and performing in concerts. In 1838, Joshua married Louisa Jane Davies in Sydney and in 1844 he was admitted as a solicitor, advancing to the New South Wales bar in 1855. Joshua's star was still in the ascendancy in 1848 when he became a Justice of the Peace and in the same year was appointed mayor.

In the ensuing years, there seemed to be no end to Joshua's ambitions when he invested in real estate, played a part in establishing the Sydney Dry Dock Company, the Hunter River Railway Company and the Sydney Insurance Company. It goes without saying that Joshua's business dealings made him a wealthy man, and in 1847, still in his early thirties, he began to show an interest in the Fine Arts founding The Society for the Promotion of the Fine Arts which presented Sydney's first public art exhibition at the Australian Library.

In a surprising departure from his life in Australia, in February, 1856, Joshua took his family back to England, ostensibly to take time out to partake of The Grand Tour. Whether he felt it was some kind of challenge to work as a barrister in London is difficult to say but he did work at that profession briefly in April 1859. However, Joshua did take The Grand Tour and it was between the years 1857 and 1860 that he began the collection of statues and paintings that were later bequeathed to the New South Wales Art Gallery. For anyone interested in sculpture the studios of the colony of British and American sculptors based in the maze of streets near to the Spanish Steps were a magnet and Joshua followed a well-worn path to the studios of John Gibson and Benjamin Spence where he chose most of the sculptures destined for Enmore House, his home on the outskirts of Sydney. Gibson appeared to be his favourite sculptor and from his studio Joshua purchased *Roman Hunter*, *Narcissus*, *Head of a Greek Helen*, *Rape of the Sabines*, *Venus*, *A Faun* and *A Venus of Medici*. From Spence's studio, Joshua chose the ever-popular *Highland Mary*, *The Lady of the Lake* and *Hippolytus*, a statue of the mythical son of Theseus whose tragic end has regularly attracted painters and sculptors, notably the artist Lawrence Alma-Tadema (1836 – 1912) and the sculptor Jean Baptiste Lemoyne (1679 – 1831) whose version of *Hippolytus* is in the Louvre. Harriet Hosmer (1830 – 1908) had been a pupil of John Gibson's since 1853 and at the time of Joshua's visit she was still working alongside Gibson, obtaining her own studio in 1859. Even as a pupil, Hosmer's work was outstanding and her acclaimed *Beatrice Cenci* which had been commissioned by the St Louis Mercantile Library was also commissioned by Joshua along with her statue of *Puck* which would become such a favourite that over 50 replicas would eventually be sold. Joshua turned to another American sculptor, Hiram Powers (1805 – 1873) when he purchased a bust of Benjamin Franklin and he chose *Andromeda* from the prolific English sculptor James Forsyth (1826 – 1910) with one single Italian sculptor's work *A Greek Slave* by the renowned Scipione Tadolini (1822 – 1892).

Joshua returned to Sydney in September, 1861, and would enjoy his sculpture gallery for the rest of his days, firstly at Enmore House which was demolished in 1883 and finally at St Killians, Woolabra. Joshua's wife, Louisa, had been at his side throughout his many business ventures and in the 25 years they were married she had borne him 12 children. Although Louisa's death in 1863 must of necessity have been a tremendous shock, Joshua was still only in his late 40s and in 1868 he married for a second time to Katerina Frederica Schiller and they went on to have a child together. When Katerina died in 1884, Joshua was approaching 70 but true to the last to his unusual lifestyle, at the venerable age of 76 he married for a third time in 1891 to Elizabeth Geraldine Brenan. Although Joshua's overwhelming zest for everything that life had to offer had never wavered, in the same year that he had married for the final time he came to the realization that his life was coming to an end and he began the procedure of transferring his works of art to New South Wales Art Gallery which had only been in existence since its inception in 1880. The mechanics of Joshua's intention to sell part of his collection and bequeath the remainder were a tedious and slow process of letters back and forth outlining the details. However, the process was too tiresome for Joshua and his impatience was there for all to see when on the 29th December,1891, he asked the trustees of the gallery to *"make your valuation without delay"* and wrote the poignant line *" my days are now few and uncertain."* On the 2nd January, 1892, Joshua wrote again to the trustees of the gallery who had apparently asked for some kind of written provenance for the statues and he replied somewhat testily that *"a large amount of literary correspondence took place between the artists and myself but during a course of 30 years it would be difficult to find it now."* Joshua died on the 26th January, 1892, without seeing the transaction completed and it was only later in that year that the statues were removed to the New South Wales Art Gallery where they form the nucleus of the collection to this day.

The Angel of The North

The Angel's Whisper in Sefton Park Palm House

In 1857, Spence chose to sculpt another romantic theme and created a statue which vied with the evergreen *Highland Mary* in its subsequent popularity. There are several interpretations of *The Angel's Whisper* but Spence's statue takes its interpretation from the Irish belief that when a baby smiles in its sleep it is being visited by an angel, epitomised by Samuel Lover's (1797 – 1868) poem of the same name. *The Angel's Whisper* was commissioned by Spence's patron James Smith of Seaforth in 1863 and bequeathed to the Walker Art Gallery in 1892 by his son James Barkeley Smith. The statue was transferred to the Palm House in Sefton Park in 1898 where over the years the angel has suffered the indignity of losing her wings but remains a firm favourite of an older generation who remember the statue from their own childhood. The replica of *Highland Mary* stands nearby and after all these years it is difficult to tell which is the more popular, the Scottish maiden captured taking her marriage vows for all eternity or the Irish angel bending over a sleeping infant.

A replica of the statue was purchased by Liverpool businessman Henry Robertson Sandbach (1807 – 1895) for his manor house Hafodunos in Llangernwy, North Wales, and its popularity later inspired several more replicas; the art critic William Bell Scott wrote as part of his critique of the statue – *"He (Spence) departed from the classic subject and having that inventive fancy that belonged more to the painter rather than the sculptor he endeavoured to produce groups and single figures of a new and popular character."* Henry Sandbach was an avid collector of John Gibson's work and filled his home with portrait medallions, busts, statues and bas-reliefs, most of them by Gibson. Originally Henry Sandbach had collected his treasures accompanied by his wife Margaret (1812 – 1852) who was the grand-daughter of William Roscoe and a devotee of Gibson but following her early death at the age of 40 Sandbach demolished the old house and built a magnificent mansion on the site designed by Sir George Gilbert Scott. In 1857 Sandbach remarried and continued to travel to Rome for statuary for the remainder of his long life. Following his death in 1895, Hafodunos began a slow process of decay until in 1933 the Sandbach family sold the house and disposed of the artworks that Henry had collected so assiduously – many of the treasures were sold to the National Museum of Wales, Cardiff, and others were purchased by the Walker Art Gallery where at both galleries the greater part of John Gibson's work can be seen today. *The Angel's Whisper* from Hafodunos was purchased in 1969 for Syon Lodge Ltd, and later auctioned at Christie's in 1993 it was purchased by the Musée D'Orsay, Paris, and exhibited in the Louvre, having the distinction of being the single sculpture by an English sculptor among the collected works in the Louvre. The angel in the Louvre has retained her wings and the statue is so pristine that it appears to have been sculpted only yesterday but although The Angel in the Louvre is well received by an appreciative public from around the world, she has never earned half the affection of the battered and worn angel in Sefton Park Palmhouse.

The Lady of the Lake

Queen Victoria led the way in favouring British sculptors in Rome and had collected sculptures by Wyatt and Gibson and many others but in 1859 it was to Spence that she turned for a reciprocal birthday gift for Prince Albert in recognition of his gift to her of *Highland Mary* five years earlier. The sculpture that Victoria chose was the *The Lady of the Lake* taken from Sir Walter Scott's 1810 poem of the same name which formed a perfect companion piece to *Highland Mary* – given that Victoria loved Scotland the sculpture was as much a present to herself as much as Albert. Both of the sculptures are in an arrangement of statues within the Guard's Room in Buckingham Palace adjacent to Gibson's once tinted statue of *Queen Victoria*, Emil Wolff's *Prince Albert* and Mary Thornycroft's *Princess Louise*.

The Final Years

In 1860, true to his penchant for alternating the neo-classical with literary heroines, Spence carved a statue of *Psyche at the Well* based upon Apuleis' story of Cupid and Psyche where Venus has set Psyche the seemingly impossible task of filling a vessel from a River Styx which is surrounded by impenetrable rocks and guarded by dragons. There were two versions with the one represented here presented to the Walker Art Gallery in 1907 where it can be seen today. Curiously, the wings on Psyche have similar markings to several unrelated statues within the gallery.

In 1862, Spence returned to his romance with Scottish heroines and on this occasion created a sculpture entitled *Jeanie Deans Before Queen Caroline*. Jeanie Deans was on a par with Spence's *Highland Mary* with the major difference being that Jeanie was a fictional character from within the pages of Sir Walter Scott's popular novel *Heart of Midlothian* written in 1818. It's difficult today to comprehend today just how sensational the character was in Victorian times, particularly in Scotland where it was as if Jeanie had stepped out of the pages of Scott's novel and into the hearts of its readers – at the time it seemed as if Jeanie Deans was everywhere with locomotives and steamships and public houses named after her. Largely forgotten today, Jeanie Deans was according to Scott based upon a real person, and as a model of both moral and religious rectitude she appealed to a Victorian public which viewed both fiction and real life in terms of black and white. The novel is unusual in that it is centred around an infanticide which Scott claimed was true and a highlight of the book is Jeanie's epic barefoot walk from Edinburgh to London to plead with Queen Caroline for her sister Effie who is accused of the murder of her own child. Spence's inspiration for the sculpture may have been taken from a painting by Charles Robert Leslie (1794 – 1859) showing Jeanie pleading with Queen Caroline in Kew Garden. Although the sculpture was exhibited at the International Exhibition of 1862 in a cavernous glasshouse similar to the Crystal Palace and was obviously of great interest at the time, it is yet another of Spence's sculptures which has been lost and can only ever live in the imagination.

Contemporary drawing of Jeanie Deans

But time was running out for Spence and the ubiquitous tuberculosis which had been plaguing him for years became worse during the 1860s. John Gibson knew that his friend was dying and in July, 1865, accompanied by another great friend, the Welsh artist Penry Williams, he spent a week with Spence at the home of his father-in-law, George W. Gower at Leghorn. However, in a strange twist of fate, on the 9th January, 1866, Gibson suffered a stroke and despite being nursed by Letitia Spence and his pupil Mary Charlotte Lloyd, he died on the 27th January. Doubtless Gibson had fully expected to carve Spence's memorial just as he had done so for Wyatt but in a strange reversal of fortune it was Spence who carved Gibson's headstone instead. The cameo medallion of Gibson's head in profile above a eulogy by Lord Lytton was Spence's final sculpture and can still be seen in the English Cemetery, Rome. Spence lasted only a further few months and died in the house of George Gower in October, 1866 aged just 43. He is buried in the now unkempt English Cemetery in Livorno.

In Memoriam

Psyche at the Well. Walker Art Gallery

For some unfathomable reason the Victorian critics were never kind to Benjamin Evans Spence. They never eulogized over even his finest sculptures and they seemed perplexed by his ability to switch from neo-classical sculptures to those of characters from popular literature which they frowned upon. The critics of the day were purists who regarded anything which deviated from classicism with suspicion and in many ways it was their high-handed and snobbish attitude which possibly influenced galleries to neglect the works of Spence in favour of other sculptors – it is in fact not too much of an exaggeration to state that their blinkered pedantry has been one reason why so much of Spence's work has been lost. The kindest of the critics was The Art Journal which published several engravings of Spence's sculptures, but even that well-respected journal was patronising towards Spence stating in his obituary that he was *"A man of gentle bearing, affable and of kindly heart"* and damning him with the faint praise of *"Mr Spence, though not a great sculptor, maintained a highly honourable position among the artists of our time."*

Although the self-styled experts of the establishment may have been influenced by the judgements laid down by the critics, people in general have always made their own minds up about what they consider to be *"good"* and in a strange paradox, are less easily fooled. The intelligentsia may have sniped at *Highland Mary* and sneered at the sheer sentimentality of *The Angel's Whisper* but when the Victorian public were allowed to eventually see them on display they took them to their hearts and it is no coincidence that it is these statues and their replicas which have survived while those the critics frowned upon have not. Queen Victoria took little notice of the critics, and both her and Prince Albert bought sculpture which they liked as opposed to sculpture that was chosen for them, and at the same time most of Wyatt's and Gibson's and Spence's patrons were never influenced by anything other than their own judgement.

The Marine Venus.
Hereford Town Hall

Apart from the fact that Spence has the honour of having had two sculptures on display in Buckingham Palace for over 150 years and is the sole English sculptor to have a sculpture on display in the Louvre, *Highland Mary* and *The Angel's Whisper* have been favourite sculptures in both Sefton Park Palmhouse and The Walker Art Gallery for many years, making it inexplicable as to why his work is so under-rated; there is more than a suspicion that the mid-Victorian critics' assessments have lingered on and a reappraisal of Spence's work is long overdue. It is also inexplicable how so many of Spence's sculptures have seemingly vanished off the face of the earth and it is to be hoped that although not on public display, they are at least safe in the hands of collectors.

In June 1870, many of Spence's works were placed for auction at Christie's Auction House in London, selling at ridiculously low prices, and the same year his wife Rosina donated the plaster casts from Spence's studio of *The Lady of the Lake, Jeanie Deans, Highland Mary, Lavinia, Rebecca, Boy and Kid, Ophelia, Flora MacDonald, The Angel's Whisper, Hector and Andromache, Oberon and Titania* and *The Finding of Moses* to the City of Liverpool. When the casts arrived from Rome in 1870, Sir James Allanson Picton wrote to Rosina thanking her for her gifts to the city and stated that *"they* (the casts) *may remain here to hand down to future generations."* Unfortunately, Picton's hopes were never realised and only *The Lady of the Lake, Jeanie Deans and Highland Mary* have survived albeit in storage in a very poor condition. Six of the statues were later sited within sheltered niches behind the Corinthian Columns of The Picton Reading Rooms on William Brown Street where they remained until 1921 when they were subject to wanton vandalism by demonstrators demanding *"Work or Full Maintenance"* and three of the figures were destroyed. Many of the demonstrators were ex-servicemen who had served in the First World War and at one point they occupied the Walker Art Gallery itself until the police dealt with them in brutal fashion and the steps of the Walker ran red with blood. In the circumstances it was difficult not to sympathise with the demonstrators and in retrospect it was fortunate that the three plaster casts were the only casualties.

It's a strange fact that of all the statues and works of art the trio of Gibson, Wyatt and Spence produced in Rome for over half a century not one has remained in that city and every sculpture that each produced was purchased by patrons from Great Britain and across the world. As established favourites of the art establishment most of Wyatt's and Gibson's work has survived the years and can be found in galleries and mansion houses across the country while much of Spence's work is lost.

****

Flora from the British Art Journal.

Although the facts about them are sketchy, Benjamin Spence and Rosina Letitia had three children – the first was William Gibson Spence (1855 – 1933) who was born in Rome on the 31st March, 1855, with his middle name an obvious reference to Benjamin's high regard for John Gibson. Educated at Exeter College, William Gibson Spence was something which his father had never been which was an avid sportsman, excelling in rugby, track and field, cycling, angling and shooting. A man of many parts, William Gibson Spence was also an accomplished musician and had travelled a great deal before becoming the oldest member of London Police Reserve; it was on duty during the First World War he was injured by a bomb blast during an air raid on London. Spence was also a great lover of plants and animals and had firm views about the role of women in society including his own axiom that women should never attend funerals as *"it was man's work"* which explains why his sons Mr W.H.G. Spence and Mr Harold. E. Spence attended but there were no women present at his interment in 1933. Spence had lived at 75 Thicket Road, Anerley, for the final 30 years of his life, a house which again recalled his father being named *Roma*, and in a final note, it is noticeable that as times changed William Gibson Spence lived to the age of 78, nearly twice that of his father.

There is very little known about the Spence's daughter, Maria Lena Spence apart from the fact that she married her cousin William Lewes Gower.

Benjamin Edgar Spence (1864 – 1903) was born on the 27th September, 1864, and baptized soon afterwards in Rome. There is little known of his life apart from his harrowing death detailed on a spidery, handwritten note by a Captain Bury which reads:

"Captain Bury on Dear Spence born at? father's house Mr G H Gower of Leghorn and dear Ben died at Mombasa Hospital from Blackwater Fever caught on his ship on the Victoria Nyami Lake where the Foreign Office had sent him to guard the land, he is buried in the Cemetery at Mombasa (Mbazaki), and had just received permission to return home to England. Everyone who knew him loved him and regretted his death, he was so good and unselfish."

****

There is very little known of Benjamin's eight siblings – there is however some information on his brother John C. Spence who was born in 1829 and originally worked for the Duke of Argyll at Inverary Castle where a son Harry was born. At some stage, John attended the Mechanics' Institute in Montreal which taught young men French, arithmetic and drawing and by 1854/55 John Spence had graduated to teaching landscape and ornamental drawing. John had evidently inherited some of his father's talent for art and became quite renowned for being Montreal's first stained glass decorator with three of his windows above the organ loft in the Church of St John the Evangelist (1861) and another three above the altar at Holy

Trinity in Iron Hill. As time went by and John's sons grew older they worked with him in what became a family firm. There is some evidence that some of John's family eventually moved to western Montana in the 1890s and family tradition has it that whoever they were, they homesteaded on a hill outside Troy, Montana, living in a log cabin, the ruins of which can still be seen. Today there are Spences scattered across America claiming descent from William Spence and proud to be descended from the two sculptors from Liverpool.

List of Works

Name	Date	Location
Busts		
Liverpool Academy Student	1838	Unknown
Liverpool Academy Gentleman	1839	Unknown
Unidentified Lady	1840	Unknown
Unidentified Subject	1843	Unknown
Unidentified Child	1844	Unknown
Unidentified Gentleman	1844	Unknown
Charles Holland	1849	Given to the Royal Academy
George Smith, model	1849	Unknown
Peter Bancroft	1863	Unknown
Sir Joseph Paxton	1865	Chatsworth House
Sir Joseph Paxton replica	1865	Crystal Palace - destroyed in fire 1933
Thomas Brassey	undated	Unknown
Mrs Thomas Brassey	undated	Unknown
Unidentified Gentleman	undated	Sold at Christies, July 1993
Unidentified Lady	undated	Coll.B. Dawkins (Cardiff)
Venus (two)	undated	Unknown
Funerary Monuments		
Devereux Plantagenet Cockburn	1851	Sculpture, English Cemetery, Rome
Lieutenant James Marshall	1855	St Peter's Church, Leeds
Julia Josephine Muspratt	1857	St Marys Church, Flint
John Gibson	1866	English Cemetery, Rome
Statues		
The Death of the Duke of York at Agincourt	1844	Unknown
Ulysses	1845	Unknown
Children of Mr A Holmes	1846	Unknown
Mabel Atkinson	1848	Unknown
Parting of Hector and Andromache	1848	Unknown
Lavinia	1849	Originally for Samuel Holmes - now lost
Ophelia	1850	Originally for Thomas Brassey - now lost
Highland Mary	1852	Charles Meigh - Grove House
Highland Mary replica	1852	Picton Library, Liverpool
Highland Mary replica	1852	Sefton Park Palmhouse, Liverpool
Highland Mary replica - exhibited at the French Exhibition, Paris, in 1855	1852	New South Wales Art Gallery
Innocence (the Dove)	1853	Unknown
Georgiana Naylor and her Children	1854	Originally Leighton Hall now in storage At Walker Art Gallery
Dora and Margaret	1854	Originally Leighton hall now Sudley, Mossley Hill

Liverpool	1854	Probably destroyed in Crystal Palace fire 1933
Venus and Cupid	1855	Richard Naylor - Hooton Hall
Venus and Cupid	1855	Philadelphia Museum of Art
Rev. Jonathan Brooks	1856	St George's Hall, Liverpool
Girl at the Fountain	1857	Unknown
Psyche	1857	Unknown
Spring, Summer, Autumn, Winter	1857	Unknown
The Angel's Whisper	1857	Originally for James Metcalfe Smith - donated by his son James Barkely Smith to Liverpool City Council and placed in Sefton Park Palmhouse
The Angel's Whisper replica	1857	Henry Robertson Sandbach of Hafodunos - bought in 1969 by Syon Lodge - auctioned at Christie's in 1993 and purchased by the Louvre Museum
Bacchus	1860	Unknown
Psyche at the Well	1860	Walker Art Gallery, Liverpool
The Lady of the Lake	1861	Buckingham Palace
Hippolytus	1862	New South Wales Art Gallery
Jeanie Deans before Queen Caroline	1862	Exhibited at the International Exhibition 1862 - now lost
The Finding of Moses	1862	Walker Art Gallery - damaged and in storage
Flora MacDonald	1865	Donated to Stanley Palm House 1929 by George Audley. The Palm House fell into disrepair in the 1980s and in 1986 it was sold to a private company, The statue was subsequently destroyed by vandals.
Marine Venus	1865	Hereford Town Hall
Boy With a Bird's Nest statuette	undated	Unknown
Boy with a Flute statuette	undated	Unknown
Sabrina	1865	Exhibited at Leeds National Exhibition of Works of Art 1868 by James Metcalfe Smith. Sold at Christie's in June 1870 for 210 guineas.
Oberon and Titania	1866	Victoria and Albert Museum
Miscellaneous		
Three Unidentified Gentlemen	1841	Unknown
Shepherd and Dog	1844	Unknown
Icarus -Bronze Fountain	1855	Originally Leighton Hall now in Powys Town Hall
Flora	Circa 1855	Probably destroyed in Crystal Palace fire 1933

Slaves and Sculptures

The Forgotten Statues of Leighton Hall

The Inheritors

It's not clear when and how Benjamin Spence came to meet John Naylor (1813 - 1889) but it is highly likely to have been at Spence's studio in Rome in the early 1850s when Naylor would have been aged 37 and probably taking the Grand Tour. What is clear, however, is that John Naylor became an immediate admirer of Spence's work and his association with the sculptor would produce some of Spence's finest sculptures. John Naylor's brother, Richard Christopher Naylor, also liked Spence's work and by 1855 had commissioned the neo-classical *Venus and Cupid* for his vast mansion and gardens at Hooton Hall. Richard Naylor had purchased Hooton Hall for £6.6 million in today's money and spent a further £4 million on building an orangery, a polo field, a heronry and a racecourse on what was then one of the largest estates in England. The extent of Richard Naylor's riches could be measured also by the building of St Paul's Church, near to Hooton Hall, which he funded entirely at his own expense. As an avid yachtsman Richard Naylor was greatly upset when the building of the Manchester Ship Canal in 1875 cut him off from access to his beloved yacht and he promptly decamped to his other estate in Nottinghamshire leaving the estate to manage for itself. When the First World War began in 1914, the park was almost custom-built for aircraft and the house made a perfect barracks – accordingly, the whole site was requisitioned by the army for the duration of the war. The military occupants of the house were less than ideal tenants and as early as 1932 the mansion house on which Richard Naylor had lavished so much care had deteriorated to such a degree that it was demolished. The parkland remained as an airfield until 1957 when the land was given over to the Vauxhall car plant, Ellesmere Port, where it began production in the 1960s and has been there ever since. There's little left of Richard Naylor's inheritance which he so carelessly threw to one side and his real legacy is St Paul's Church which is still standing today as a testament to the no-expenses-spared lifestyle he once knew.

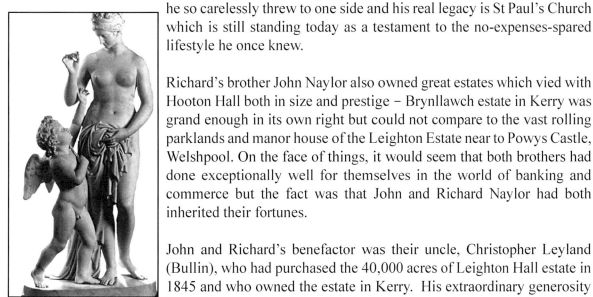

Venus and Cupid

Richard's brother John Naylor also owned great estates which vied with Hooton Hall both in size and prestige – Brynllawch estate in Kerry was grand enough in its own right but could not compare to the vast rolling parklands and manor house of the Leighton Estate near to Powys Castle, Welshpool. On the face of things, it would seem that both brothers had done exceptionally well for themselves in the world of banking and commerce but the fact was that John and Richard Naylor had both inherited their fortunes.

John and Richard's benefactor was their uncle, Christopher Leyland (Bullin), who had purchased the 40,000 acres of Leighton Hall estate in 1845 and who owned the estate in Kerry. His extraordinary generosity began in 1846 when following the marriage of John Naylor to Georgiana

Edwards on the 20th August,1846, he gave the newlyweds the whole of the newly acquired Leighton Hall estate as a wedding present. In addition to this John was also given the estate in Kerry. But Christopher's largesse did not end there and in 1847 he gave each brother the staggering sum of £100,000 which in today's money is about £8 million sterling. Perhaps the reason why Christopher Leyland found it so easy to part with such incredible sums of money is that he also had inherited his wealth; how one family came to be in possession of riches beyond the dreams of avarice at a time when most of the population of Liverpool lived in abject poverty is a complex tale of good fortune, buccaneering enterprise and the ruthless business acumen of one man, Thomas Leyland, whose story began in the middle of the 18th century.

Thomas Leyland – A Georgian Upbringing

Thomas Leyland (1752 - 1827) was born in Knowsley but spent most of his life close to the source of his wealth on Liverpool waterfront where he was said to have boasted of three ambitions:

1) To make a fortune – which he achieved several times over.

2) To become Lord Mayor of Liverpool – which he did on three occasions.

3) To found a dynasty – because he never had children it is generally believed that this was the one ambition Leyland left unfulfilled. However, as possibly the most important of his three wishes, Leyland did go on to form a dynasty, although it was more tailored to circumstance and pragmatism than to bloodline.

Whatever else he may have been, Thomas Leyland was a hard-working opportunist who had an extraordinary talent for making money, acquiring over a lifetime far more wealth than he could ever have spent and becoming one of the wealthiest men in England.

Fowler's Court off Chapel Street, 1798. Liverpool Record Office

George III (1738 - 1820) had been King of England for 14 years when Thomas Leyland was born and he would remain King for most of Leyland's lifetime. America was still a British colony until Thomas was 24 years of age when the American Revolutionary War of 1776 changed the fate of North America forever, and he was still only 37 in 1789 at the beginning of the French Revolution when the guillotining of Louis XVI sent shock waves throughout Europe. There was no doubting that Thomas lived in interesting times and in 1805 he would have exulted with the rest of the nation over victory at Trafalgar while mourning the death of Nelson at the hands of a French sniper. And Thomas would have watched with interest the unfolding of the Napoleonic era from its beginnings on the streets of Paris to its end at St Helena in 1821 with the death of Napoleon.

Thomas Leyland's Liverpool was still awaking from centuries of slumber during its medieval past when Thomas was born and with a population of around 20,000 people never extended much further than the original seven streets. Thomas would see enormous changes to the city within his lifetime and the legacy of Georgian architecture we value so much today seemingly sprang up around him as brand new buildings; Rodney Street (1784), The Union News Room (1800), the Lyceum (1802), Canning Street, Gambier Terrace and Percy Street were just a few of the buildings that Thomas Leyland would have known. In Thomas's twilight years the city maintained a population of 118,000 people, had expanded outwards as far as Abercromby Square (1820) and was on the cusp of an industrial era which Thomas would have never envisaged in his wildest dreams.

Hanover Street 1857 – W.G.Herdman

The Liverpool which Thomas Leyland would have taken most interest in was the waterfront where Thomas Steers Old Dock (1815) was the beginning of the end for the Pool which ran through the centre of the old town almost bisecting it into two districts. The Old Dock would be closed just one year before the death of Thomas Leyland but for most of his lifetime he would have been familiar with rowdy Paradise Street and the dock which was almost a canal into the city centre. Salthouse Dock which was built in 1753 one year after Thomas's birth, Canning Dock (1737), Coburg Dock (1840), Clarence Dock (1840), Queen's Dock (1785) and George's Dock (1771) which preceded all of them would have all been familiar to Thomas Leyland – but his life was over before he could witness the exponential expansion of the dock system north to Seaforth and the greatest dock of them all, the Albert Dock, built in 1845.

Although the great buildings and the expansion of the dock system were a source of great pride to the citizens of Liverpool and the forest of masts on the river was proof of its booming commerce, many of the ships had Liverpool owners whose condemnation by various humanitarian groups was at first a whisper which later grew into a crescendo. Over many years it has since become axiomatic that the whole edifice of Liverpool's prosperity was built upon the slave-trade and Thomas Leyland was one of its foremost proponents.

How Fortunes are Made

Thomas Leyland

Thomas Leyland first worked for Edward Bridge and Company, a firm of Coopers of Cooper's Row, before moving on to the service of an Irish merchant named Gerald Dillon. Dillon's offices were at the bottom end of Water Street where he supervised the carriage of basic foodstuffs such as oats, peas, wheat, oatmeal, bacon, lard etc for the Irish Trade. At the age of 22, Leyland borrowed £500 (£50,000 today) from three friends, investing the money into the business and becoming a partner in the process. In 1776, after two years of working in partnership, Leyland and Dillon had an incredible stroke of good fortune when they won the State Lottery worth £20,000 (over £2 million today) after staking £7 on winning - even their stake was a huge amount of money at over £750 by today's values, illustrating clearly the lengths to which Leyland was prepared to go to make his fortune. *Williamson's Advertiser* of the 27th December, 1776, stated: *"No 52,717 drawn on Saturday last a prize of £20,000 is the property of Messrs Dillon and Leyland, merchants of this town."* They must have had a fine Christmas that year. In May, 1777, aged just 25, Leyland married Ellen Bridge, his first employer's daughter at St Thomas' Church, near to Cleveland Square (now demolished) and shortly afterwards Ellen's father, Edward Bridge died leaving his wife to continue running their business, Ellen's mother lasted only a few more years after the death of her husband and in 1782, Leyland and his wife inherited one third of the estate.

Leyland's sister Margaret had married a Staffordshire Ware merchant named Christopher Bullin, an event which would have repercussions far into the future and right up to the present day. In the short term, Bullin had the misfortune to become bankrupt in 1778, and once again Leyland profited from situations not of his own making when he acquired Bullin's former premises.

Privateering during the 1700s was for many shipowners a way of life and for a man who was out to make his fortune it was almost inevitable that Thomas Leyland would be attracted to such a lucrative business. A privateer was a ship which was authorized by the government to attack and take the ships of other nations during wartime and since Great Britain was almost in a permanent state of war with France there had been a war of attrition on the high seas between the two countries since anyone could remember. Both countries issued Letters of Marque (Lettres de Marque) which was in effect government licenced commerce raiding and both sides took full advantage of the situation. The American Revolutionary Wars and rivalry with Dutch and Spanish fleets at various times ensured that it was a rare occasion when privateers were not allowed to operate and volumes have been written about the exploits of Liverpool privateers and their battles at sea, taking and losing *"prizes"* which were shared by everyone involved from owners to seamen. Thomas Leyland was still a young man of 27 when he entered into the world of privateering with a one-sixteenth share in a ship called *Enterprize* shortly becoming half owner. In 1780, Leyland dissolved his six year partner ship with Gerald Dillon and formed Thomas Leyland and Company, in partnership with his nephew Richard Bullin and William Molyneux.

At around this time, in the absence of children of his own Thomas Leyland transferred his dynastic ambitions to his nearest relatives and a knowledge of the sons and daughters of those relatives is integral to the understanding of what became of his fortune. The situation is made complicated by many of the Christian names being the same – nevertheless introductions to Leyland's sisters and nephews are essential to an understanding of what followed.

The above mentioned partner of Leyland, Richard Bullin, along with his brother Christopher, were the sons of Margaret Leyland and Christopher Bullin whose bankruptcy has already been mentioned. Margaret and Christopher also had a daughter named Dorothy who married John Naylor of Hartford Hill in 1809 and went on to have four children of their own – Thomas, Richard Christopher, John and Elisabeth Mary. All of these names will appear and reappear throughout the following narrative but genealogy is complex at the best of times so I will leave it there for the time being and proceed with Thomas Leyland's irresistible rise to fame and fortune. Genealogy is not my best subject and the following layout is more for my own benefit than anything else.

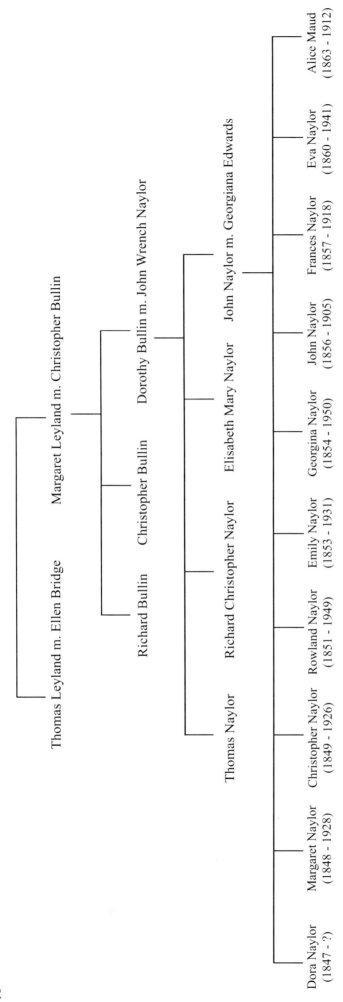

The Slave Ships

Although privateering could be incredibly lucrative it was at the same time highly risky and the partnership of Leyland, Bullin and Molyneux ensured their profits mainly by trading. A growing number of ships carried olive oil, sherry, ox-beef, pork, butter, herrings, hides and so on, selling them in various ports and countries around the globe. In a world where profits counted for everything, it was almost inevitable that Leyland would enter into the slave-trade and a combination of trading, privateering and slaving would in the years to come earn Leyland, who was already rich, the fortune that he had wished for in his youth. In 1789 Leyland was in partnership with David Tuohy running a slave ship named *Kitty* and from 1793 to 1795 Leyland owned a ship called *La Convention* which was a French prize judging by its name. A few years later Leyland purchased a ship which for obvious reasons he named *The Lottery* – in the year 1798 the ship made a profit of £12,000 which is nearly 1 million pounds at today's rates. Leyland was never content to rest on his laurels and as the money poured into the company coffers he reinvested in more ships so that in the year 1799 alone *The Earl of Liverpool* captained by Charles Watt picked up 353 slaves from the coast of Angola, *Louisa* captained by William Brown took on board 465 slaves from the coast of Bonny, *The Lottery* captained by Roger Leathom took 460 slaves also from Bonny and the seemingly indestructible *Enterprize* captained by John Heron picked up 363 slaves also from Angola. If 1799 was representative of the numbers of slaves being transported to America and the West Indies each year, and there was no reason to believe otherwise, then the company had become fabulously rich, although trading in human misery never seemed to be a consideration. An incident which took place in the same year of 1799 was indicative of the manner in which the Africans were thought of as mere commodities; on a second trip by *The Earl of Liverpool* this time carrying a cargo of 315 slaves to Jamaica, Captain Watt came across a ship named *John* owned by J. Bolton carrying 402 slaves and captained by Joseph Hinsley when the two ships became becalmed 3000 miles off the Jamaican coast. The two Captains realised that the price of their slaves would be lower if they both landed at the same time so they agreed that the *John* would land first, Hinsley would sell his slaves allowing a percentage of the profit to Charles Watt while the *The Earl of Liverpool* stood out at sea for ten days. When the *The Earl of Liverpool* finally landed in Kingston harbour the slaves were sold at an inflated price, the two Captains profited from the trick they had played and they eventually sailed for Liverpool with holds full to the brim with rum and sugar to be sold on for evermore profits. In the meantime, as if that were not enough, all captains were instructed to capture *"prizes"* whenever the opportunity arose. In 1802, *The Lottery* and the *Enterprize* delivered 412 slaves between them and those voyages alone in present values made a profit of £1.7 million and in 1803 the *Enterprize* under Captain Cesar Lawson took on board a cargo of male slaves only for the Spanish market with the standard instruction to capture *"prizes"* whenever he was able.

In the latter days of the slave triangle, all the Liverpool shipowners knew that abolition would soon put an end to the most profitable trade they had ever known and in common with many other owners Leyland and Company kept their ships at sea in order to extract the last drop of profit from the slave-trade. Leyland's slaver *Fortune* made as many voyages as possible between 1805 and 1807 and both *The Lottery* and the *Enterprize* were still sailing in 1807 until legislation finally put a stop to one of the greatest diasporas in human history.

The Lord Mayor's Chain

The surviving records show that from 1780 to 1800 alone Thomas Leyland had a vested interest in 69 voyages involving the transport of slaves, and the ships noted above are just a fraction of Leyland's income from privateering, trading and the slave-trade. Although knowledge of Leyland's career as a shipowner is quite extensive and the profits run into breathtaking amounts of money the full extent of his career and profits is an unknown quantity due to a fire during the 2nd World War which destroyed half of his log books and documents.

In 1798, Leyland became Lord Mayor of Liverpool for the first time (the 2nd was 1814 and the 3rd 1820) and formed a link in the chain of 21 Lord Mayors of Liverpool from 1787 to 1807 who were all involved in the slave-trade. But the slave-trade was not confined to Lord Mayors alone and prior to Leyland's election, in the year 1787 out of 41 members of Liverpool City Council no less than 37 were involved in the Trade in one way or another. Given the wealth and mansion houses of the slave -traders and shipowners of Liverpool, it was difficult to argue with the actor, George Cooke, on the stage of The Theatre Royal, Williamson Square, 1772, whose barbed riposte to his barracking audience *"I have not come here to be insulted by a set of wretches, every brick in whose infernal town is cemented with an African's blood"* was more pointed than many anti-slavery speeches in Parliament.

However, the ramifications of the slave-trade never ended there and it is no exaggeration to state that the centuries of trafficking Africans across the world by English, French, Dutch and Spanish ships changed the landscape of North America forever. The slave-traders of the 1700s had no conception of what they were doing in terms of demographics and the millions of Africans they sold into bondage changed the landscape of America forever; there is an argument to be made that their greed and avarice went some way to the deaths of thousands on the battlefields of The American Civil War.

A Sea Change

In the early years of the 1800s the slave shipowners knew that there was no stopping the groundswell of Abolition and many of them were involved in violent reprisals – the confirmed Abolitionist, Thomas Clarkson (1760 - 1846), was attacked on the Pier Head one evening and narrowly escaped being thrown into the river, and William Roscoe came in for some rough treatment while travelling in his coach along Castle Street. Thomas Leyland, however, was nothing if not a pragmatist, and as early as 1802 began to diversify his business affairs in anticipation of the slave-trade Act which came into force in 1807. There was some irony in the fact that Leyland's choice of a fresh career was into the eminently respectable world of banking as opposed to the tenebrous world of the slave-traders and it was a strange metamorphosis when he became a senior partner in a banking business on the corner of Castle Street and Dale Street. The business had run into difficulties and Leyland's new partners were glad of his financial input and business acumen; the company was then renamed Leyland, Clarkes and Roscoe. For a man who was vehemently opposed to the slave-trade and was still working alongside William Wilberforce (1759 - 1833) and Thomas Clarkson towards its end, William Roscoe had many business associates involved in slavery – a circumstance which could easily be construed as hypocrisy on Roscoe's part. However, the reality was that the slave-trade was so endemic throughout the city and there were so many people involved at every level it would have been almost impossible for Roscoe to avoid coming into contact with them on a daily basis. Leyland's first venture into banking met with a setback when Clarke died in 1805 at the age of 52, and one year later in November, 1806, William Roscoe was elected to parliament, following which Leyland resigned from the partnership. There have been several reasons put forward as to why Leyland resigned – being associated with Roscoe so close to Abolition would have placed Leyland in a difficult position was one reason. However, it is also possible that Leyland became wary of Roscoe's abilities as a banker when Royal customers withdrew their accounts and if this reason is the reason why he left then Leyland's prescience would prove correct when Roscoe went bankrupt in 1820.

In the same way that he had anticipated the end of the slave-trade by entering into banking, in 1802, Leyland also purchased the vast Walton Hall estate from a fellow slave-trader named John Atherton who had purchased the estate from its previous owner as early as 1746. The estate included the monumental mansion which was situated to the rear of the present day bowling greens with the entrance through a set of ornamental gates at the bottom of what is now Haggerston Road. There seemed to be no end to Leyland's acquisitions as Haggerston Road was subsequently named after another estate he owned in Northumberland. And as if that was not enough, Walton Hall estate also encompassed Harbreck House which was built circa 1740. Harbreck House was once the home of William Sparling – the same Sparling whose infamous duel in 1804 had caused such a scandal. Also the home of two Lord Mayors, Harbreck House was purchased in 1858 by Henry Lafone, a shipowner and blockade-runner during the American Civil War, and following its demolition is now the site of Fazakerley Hospital.

Walton Hall Mansion

Thomas Leyland's house in York Street today

Thomas Leyland was typically undismayed by the relative failure of his first venture into the banking business and was confident that he had learnt enough to start into business on his own account and on 10th January, 1807, the year that the slave-trade ended, the firm of Leyland and Bullin opened for business. The building on the corner of York Street and Henry Street that Leyland used for his premises is still standing today – little changed from its appearance 200 years ago and surrounded by cobbled roads, the area still retains an indefinable air of yesteryear and it takes only a little imagination to envision horse-drawn drays and ladies in crinolines peopling the streets. The Phoenix Foundry was to the rear of Leyland's premises and the owner at that down York Street where he lived for over 60 years. Fawcett had a huge influence in the running of the Phoenix Foundry which made virtually anything of an engineering nature, until his death at the age of 82 in 1844. A few years later, Robert Berthon Preston (1820 - 1860) inherited the factory which incorporated the renowned Fawcett name into Fawcett, Preston and Company. Robert Preston and his wife Eleanor Leonora Preston (1833 - 1891) married in Windermere in 1850, followed by a trip to Rome where they visited the studio of John Gibson which is when the couple commissioned the statue which would eventually become the *The Tinted Venus* – the statue's first home was in the Preston's home at No.10 Abercromby Square. The Prestons also met Benjamin Spence on their trip to Rome and commissioned some family groups in marble which have unfortunately become lost. Leyland's partner in his new business was of course Richard Bullin who was later joined by his brother Christopher and in 1809 the firm's name was changed to Leyland and Bullins. On 5th February, 1816, Leyland and Bullins moved to a new premises in King Street which would later prove unfortunate in that this would be the place where many of Leyland's voluminous files were lost during the May Blitz of 1941, while despite being near to the waterfront, York Street was left unscathed. In the otherwise dry *"A Hundred Years of Joint Stock Banking"* by Crick and Wadsworth there is a charming description of the offices in King Street which draws back the curtains on the past for a brief glimpse of the Liverpool of yesteryear.

"In King Street, Liverpool, there stands today an old building, blackened with age and the smoke of steamers, whose story runs back for more than a hundred years. Around it, where formerly hummed the business of a thriving port, are warehouses and chandlers shops – the centre of business has moved north-westward. Within easy reach are the Customs House and the Docks. On the door, as a sign of adopted modernity, are the words "Midland Bank Limited" but inside are the desks and stools of a counting house, rather than the fittings of a modern bank. The ancient safes, one of them operated well-like by an old-fashioned pump handle, another protected by an iron door filled with sand, still stand as a tribute to the ingenuity of the locksmith and safe-maker of a hundred years ago. The Manager's parlour is a relic of olden times, with its handsome mahogany table, horse-hair couch and wooden gun case, its portraits of Leyland and Bullin, and its model of a three-masted schooner."

Contemporary sketch of Thomas Leyland's house in York Street

The Inheritance

Thomas Leyland was 75 years of age when he died on the 29th May, 1827, leaving a sum of over £40,000,000 by today's estimate. There was also Walton Hall estate where Ellen Leyland lived until her own death in 1839, and various other properties, which went up to make a vast fortune inherited by Leyland's nephews Richard and Christopher Bullin. One of the terms of Thomas Leyland's Will was that each time his fortune changed hands the eldest inheritor should adopt the name of Leyland and its coat of arms and it was by this means that Thomas Leyland fulfilled his third ambition to form a dynasty. Richard Bullin, who had also followed in his uncle's footsteps by becoming Lord Mayor of Liverpool in 1821, was the first of his nephews to take the Leyland name and with his brother Christopher continued the family business. Richard died childless in 1844 and Christopher took on the mantle of the Leyland name until he died, also childless, in 1849.

Although the sums of money and estates that Christopher Bullin (Leyland) gave to his nephews in 1845 and 1847, the year that he retired, were handsome gifts by any standards, placed against the context of Thomas Leyland's fabled wealth they seemed quite modest. However, Christopher's gifts were simply anticipating the passing of the baton to his own nephews as he was approaching his own twilight years. When Christopher died Thomas Naylor was the nephew who adopted the Leyland name and fulfilled his great uncle's dynastic dreams by also becoming Thomas Leyland. If John and Christopher Naylor were wealthy prior to Christopher Bullin's death, then after his demise, they could both be described as having fabulous riches – nevertheless, both brothers continued in the banking business until Richard Christopher Naylor retired in 1852 and John took on a new partner. John Naylor ensured that his sister, Elisabeth Mary and her husband Lieutenant General William George Gold were cared for, by purchasing the rebuilt Garthmyl Hall near to Leighton Hall. Now a listed building, Garthmyl was a handsome manor house within extensive grounds and gardens. John also purchased more land at Leighton Hall, the estate in Kerry and several other sites which he planned to extend but his real love was Leighton Hall on which he lavished most attention.

Leighton Hall

Leighton Hall in its heyday

John Naylor was born on the 25th April, 1813, in Mount Pleasant and was just 3 years of age when his father died in 1816. His mother, Dorothy, then moved to her brother Christopher's house in Liverpool taking with her Thomas, John, Richard Christopher and Elisabeth Mary. Although the death of her husband after only 7 years of marriage must have been a terrible shock, Dorothy was fortunate in having a rich family to fall back on – others in her situation at that time would have had every chance of ending their days in the workhouse. John Naylor was 13 years of age when he went to Eton where he stayed from 1826 to 1832, moving on to Trinity College, Cambridge for a further three years. He first entered into the banking business in 1844 when Richard died. On the 20th August, 1846, well-educated with a fine future ahead of him, aged 33, John Naylor married Georgiana Edwards (1819 - 1909), the daughter of John Edwards of Ness Strange, Shropshire. They spent their honeymoon at Corndavon Lodge near to Balmoral Castle and on their return went to live in Liscard Manor, Wallasey.

John and Georgiana Naylor

The Naylors moved into Liscard Manor while the old manor house of Leighton Hall was demolished and the new mansion built to John Naylor's specifications was being built between 1850 and 1856 and it was there that the first of their 10 children, Dora, Margaret, Christopher and Rowland were born. John Naylor employed a Liverpool architect Mr W. H. Gee to supervise the demolition of the old Tudor mansion and design the new house along with the attendant stables, kennels and farm buildings, and just as his brother, Christopher, had done at Hooton Hall, John Naylor also instructed the architect to design a Church on the site. The interior of the house was designed by the renowned Pugin (1812 - 1852) whose Christian names of Augustus Welby Northmore were as grandiose as his famous designs. Pugin designed many Gothic Churches in several different countries but was always known for his interior designs for The Palace of Westminster and comparisons have been made with Westminster's great hall and the hall he designed for Leighton Hall. Pugin must have designed Leighton Hall long before the building was completed, as in February, 1852, while travelling by train with his son, he suffered a complete mental breakdown and was admitted to Bedlam Hospital before being taken to his home in Ramsgate by his wife where he died in September, 1852. It is quite reasonable to believe that John Naylor originally wanted Pugin to design his Church but in the event the hard-working Gee was the architect for the Gothic Church which stood overlooking the whole estate and in accordance with all his other building works, John Naylor's Church was spared no expense with its Minton tiles and expensive brass fittings throughout the interior. The foundation stone was laid in 1851 and it is astonishing to record that the building was completed by 1853.

When Naylor turned his attentions to the estate gardens and farmland he employed a student of the great Sir Joseph Paxton (1803 - 1856) to oversee the alterations which included a Corn Mill, a Saw Mill, a Smithy, a Wheelwright, a Dovecote and a Fowl House which was more sumptuous than most families could afford. Naylor also introduced groundbreaking schemes to the farm with some of them quite startling in their ambition; the water-powered turbine generated electricity while a gasworks supplied heat and light but Naylor's funicular railway which carried manure from the farm to a storage unit at the top of Moel y Mab was undoubtedly the most innovative. No expense was spared on the new Leighton Hall estate and John Naylor lavished a great deal of care on the mansion house and estate in equal measure, at one stage alarming Georgiana at the growing expenditure which at one stage included kangaroos and bison in the parkland. The Leighton estate was just a few fields away from the majestic Powys Castle and its ornate gardens and there was some rivalry between the two historic estates as to which had the finest gardens and best managed farmland.

In the years when the British Empire was painting the map of the world pink, the great Victorian mansion houses of England were busy importing rare plants from around the world. Displayed in grand custom-built conservatories, plants from the tropics such as the great lily-pads of Victoria amazonica amazed a Victorian audience with pictures of children sitting on the giant leaves. Many garden treasures of today were imported during the Victorian era and for the most part have enhanced English gardens immensely, but there are some notable exceptions such as Japanese Knotweed which has proven almost impossible to eradicate and will break through concrete and tarmac with no difficulty whatsoever. After improving his gardens by creating a cascade and a small lake, John Naylor followed the fashion for importing plants which in his case were mainly North American trees for his arboretum, which included Redwood, Sequoia, Swamp cypress, Douglas Fir and many others which were highly prized at that time and can still be seen today in many of the great houses of England. Among John Naylor's collection were Monterey cypress and Nootka cypress which grow thousands of miles apart in the wild but grown in close proximity in Leighton Hall arboretum the two trees unexpectedly interbred – the resulting hybrid produced one of the most maligned plants in England. Delighted at creating his own unique tree, Naylor called his hybrid Cupressocyparis Leylandii or Leyland cypress and his gift to horticulture, the notorious Leylandii, has been plaguing English gardens ever since.

The Statues of Leighton Hall

With the mansion house and its palatial interior completed, John Naylor followed the fashion for adding oil-paintings and sculptures to embellish the already ornate surroundings. *Highland Mary* was purchased in 1852 and many wealthy householders went on to have busts made of family members, but Naylor was ever the innovator and he favoured full size statues of his family in groups which were best described *as tableaux vivants,* displaying his family in informal poses as they were in life.

Georgiana, Rowland and Christopher

The statue of *Georgiana, Rowland and Christopher* was commissioned in 1854 and was sculpted in Rome with the inscription *'B.E.Spence fecit Roma'* carved into the base and shows Georgiana seated with her sons at her knee. The three figures are dressed in the neo-classical style which came in for a great deal of criticism at the time with critics complaining that politicians such as John Gibson's *Huskisson* looked ridiculous dressed as Roman senators. However, Georgiana's dress is not greatly dissimilar to the Victorian fashion and the children's garb does not look out of place at all – the resulting *tableau* was a pleasing study of John Naylor's wife and children which took pride of place in Leighton Hall.

A sculpture of the Naylors' two daughters, Dora and Margaret, was completed soon after the sculpture of *Georgiana and her Sons*. The sculpture of the two girls was to the same scale as the larger group and portrayed them studying the Bible together. Spence sculpted the girls in neo-classical dress in the same style as the larger sculpture and it forms an unmistakable companion-piece to the original family group.

Dora and Margaret as they were displayed in Leighton Hall

Although Benjamin Spence excelled at the difficult art of groups of figures within one sculpture, after his portraits of the Naylors he reverted back to single statues for several years – he was in all probability fulfilling prior commissions. However, around the year 1860, Spence returned once again to a group sculpture which turned out to be one of his finest works. It is not clear whether the sculpture was commissioned by John Naylor but Spence rarely carved religious figures and with a background suggesting that the family were devout Christians, it may well have been commissioned by Naylor. On the other hand, John Naylor may well have seen the sculpture on display at the International Exhibition of 1862 in London and purchased it at that time. Whichever was the case, the sculpture finally ended up in Leighton Hall. The sculpture was originally called *Pharoah's Daughter* but altered later to *The Finding of Moses,* taken from the famous Biblical story from the Book of Exodus. For those who have forgotten their Sunday school teachings and their horror at the Pharoah's decree (probably Rameses II) that all Hebrew newborn babies were to be murdered, the story centres around the newborn child of Yocheved, Moses' mother. Unwilling to meekly accept the Pharoah's decree, Yocheved hides her baby for three months until the day when the soldiers are about to arrive, when she hides the baby in a basket in the bulrushes. The Pharoah's daughter finds the baby in the rushes and is immediately approached by the baby's sister, Miriam, offering to find a nurse for the baby – the Pharoah's daughter agrees and Miriam proposes Yocheved who then looks after her own baby. The sculpture by Spence has a kneeling slave holding the baby up to the Pharoah's daughter who is musing what to do about the situation – at her side, with a hand on her shoulder is a noblewoman. The sculpture is a powerful tableau of a critical juncture in the story and for once Spence has taken a departure from neo-classical themes and clothed his figures in Egyptian dress.

John Naylor commissioned one other statue from Spence which meant that for the first time the sculptor would be working in bronze – it was a challenge his father had faced years before and for the same reason which was the centrepiece of a fountain. On this occasion, it was the figure of Icarus falling to earth after his wings have been melted by the sun and formed the centrepiece of the fountain in the centre of the serpentine lake where it could be seen from the windows of the mansion house.

The End of an Era

John Naylor put his heart and soul into Leighton Hall estate; it was there that he lived in luxurious surroundings within the mansion and indulged his passion for his trees and gardens, and it was there that his children were brought up in what can only be described as an idyllic childhood. There was a great deal of irony in the fact that Thomas Leyland's dreams of having children had remained unfulfilled, while his nephews produced a large family whose lifestyle was in the main due to his dynamic business dealings. John Naylor had never relinquished his interests in the banking business and in 1879, aged 66 and probably verging on retirement, he introduced Christopher, Rowland and John to the family business. John Naylor died on the 13th July 1889 and in 1895 the Head Office was transferred to 36 Castle Street amalgamating with the North and South Wales Bank in 1901. In 1908 the bank was absorbed by the Midland bank and eventually became the HSBC as it stands today – it's interesting to speculate as to how many of the present day's HSBC employees are aware that their anodyne counting-houses and stolidly respectable employment has its origins in the slave-trade.

The Finding of Moses statue by Spence

Changing Fortunes

With the slave-trade years long passed into history and the Victorian era coming to its end, as the world entered into the 20th century the fortunes of the Naylor clan also began to change as the family scattered and went their own ways. The millions of pounds that Thomas Leyland had so energetically accrued, slowly but surely ebbed away as the Golden Age of the Leyland heritage slipped inexorably into the past as surely as the Victorian age.

Dora, the small child who can still be seen studying so assiduously at her sister Margaret's side in the marble tableau at Sudley, grew up to marry Edmund Charles Drummond, an Admiral in the Royal Navy. The marriage took place in 1872 and the couple were blessed with one son and one daughter until in 1878 Dora died aged just 31; in an age where high child mortality was accepted as a normal way of life the Naylor family were exceptionally long-lived, and it was just a pity that poor Dora drew the short straw and became the exception that proved the rule. Margaret also married and in the strange way that these things sometimes work lived to the grand age of 80.

John Naylor the third son of the Naylors was born in 1856 at the same time as the statues of his brothers and sisters were being installed in the mansion house. He went to Eton in 1874 and remained in the family banking business throughout his life. Circa 1890, John married Magdalene, the daughter of Archibald Tod of The Grange, Woolton and the couple went to live in Elmwood, a huge mansion house in Dowsefield Lane, Woolton. John Lived in Elmwood until his death in 1905 and Magdalene was still living there in 1911 – the house was demolished in the 1930s but the Lodge is still standing on the corner of Dowsefield Lane and Yew Tree Road.

Rowland Edward Naylor also went to Eton and remained in banking in Warwickshire where he married in 1875 and had one daughter. Rowland was the longest-lived of the Naylor children, dying in 1949, at the age of 98; it seemed remarkable that his statue, sculpted in 1854, as a little boy sitting on his mother's lap, was still in the same place it had occupied for nearly a century and would remain so for years after Rowland's death.

Christopher John Naylor who was the other child in the sculpture, seemed to have inherited something of his ancestor's buccaneering spirit and lived a far more adventurous life than his brothers. Christopher was aged 13 when he entered the Britannia Royal Naval College and two years later aged just 15 he must have been incredibly proud to sail as a midshipman on the S.S. *Victoria*, the flagship of the British Mediterranean Fleet. Service in the Pacific was followed by a term aboard the aptly named wooden screw frigate *Liverpool* until his final posting in command of a gunboat in the South China Seas. All in all, it was quite an honour to have served in the Royal Navy when Great Britain really did *"rule the waves"* but Christopher retired from the service as early as 1872 aged just 23, which was perhaps prompted by his courtship of Everhilda Elizabeth Creyke (1851 - 1890) the girl he married in 1874. The couple moved to Trelystan, close to Leighton Hall where Christopher, who had evidently inherited his father's passion for forestry, took a great interest in the arboricultural work on the estate. When John Naylor senior died in 1889, as the eldest son, it was incumbent upon Christopher to follow Thomas Leyland's instructions and take on the name of Leyland, which he changed by royal licence. It must have been a devastating blow for Christopher, who was now head of the family, to suffer the deaths of not only his wife, Everhilda but also one of his two daughters, just after the death of his father. It was perhaps this trilogy of tragedy that decided Christopher to leave Leighton Hall to the rest of the family and take his surviving daughter, Joan, to live with him at Haggerston Hall, Northumberland. Three years later in 1892, Christopher married again in York Minster to Helen Dora Cayley (1860 - 1940), a union which would later produce three sons and 3 daughters.

Christopher had also inherited his father's leaning toward embracing the latest technology and in 1894, he became a Director of Parson's Marine Steam Turbine Company and shared in financing the turbine-powered *Turbinia* which could outdistance any ship in the Royal Navy. Christopher had the honour to captain the revolutionary ship at Queen Victoria's Diamond Jubilee fleet review at Spithead in 1897 and later impressed naval officers at the 1900 Universal Exhibition in Paris in a demonstration for the French Navy.

Christopher was as passionate about Haggerston Hall as his father had been about Leighton Hall and he began a programme of alterations, refurbishments and innovations just as John

Naylor had done. In the mansion house itself, Christopher used a Parson's turbine engine for heating and lighting and built an observatory, while the nearby courtyard had on one side kennels and what was then a radical technological advance - a garage. The gardens were littered with greenhouses, a palm house, lakes, temples, terraces, Italianate pleasure gardens, statuary and the obligatory arboretum while further into the parkland was a menagerie of cattle, deer, ostrich and even bears. In 1911, disaster struck when a major fire destroyed much of the house but Christopher returned to the task with renewed energy and the house was rebuilt better than before. The Leylandii of which John Naylor had been so proud may never have moved from Leighton Hall if it had not been for Christopher who took some seedlings to Haggerston where he produced several cultivars of his own which resulted in praise from the Royal Horticultural Society and the plant being named officially Cupressocyparis Leylandii in 1938. Nobody could have anticipated that the Leylandii which was universally acclaimed in 1938 would in a few short years turn out to be the scourge of horticulturalists throughout the country.

When Haggerston Hall was requisitioned during the 2nd World War, Christopher and his family moved to the Mead, Beal, Northumberland and it was there that he died in 1926. Haggerston Hall is today a holiday camp – apart from one or two Gothic features which survive there's little left today to tell that there ever was a Haggerston Hall.

The House of Wonders

It doesn't take much imagination to visualise the vast rooms of John Naylor's massive mansion house ringing with the cries of small children at play or the numerous domestic servants dodging out of their way as they went about their interminable chores. The vibrant environment was in the main down to the energy and drive of John Naylor who spent nearly half a century in the cultivation and enhancement of Leighton Hall; and it was his initiative which had transformed the moribund estate into a showpiece of technological advancement and his enthusiasm which had turned the mansion house into a treasury of paintings, furniture and sculpture.

When John Naylor passed away the heart went out of Leighton Hall estate and began a slow but inexorable spiral of decline in which the works of art he had collected so assiduously were removed in a strange process which took longer than it had taken to accumulate them. There is a sense that Georgiana may have had a point when she was so concerned about the inordinate amounts of money her husband was lavishing on his beloved estate, not to mention his private yacht *Sabrina*, because it was not long after his death that she sold four of the Turner paintings to the National Gallery. However, Georgiana painted for a hobby and before the Turners were sold she made a point of copying them and hanging the copies onto the exact places that they had occupied. It was a clear indication that Georgiana had sold the paintings reluctantly and that she valued them almost as much as John had done but significantly, by hanging them in exactly the same place John had placed them, she was respecting his memory. As time went by and Georgiana passed away in 1909, her sons and daughters (and later grandchildren) sold John Naylor's collection piecemeal and in 1926 two more Turners, *The Harbour at Dieppe* and *Cologne* were auctioned at Christie's for £42,000 and are now in the Frith collection. This process was to continue for years to come.

In 1931, John Naylor's grandson sold the mansion house itself and in 1950 the house was sold on to William Rupert Davies (1879 - 1967). Davies was born in Welshpool and had lived in America for many years where he was active in politics eventually becoming a member of the Senate. On his retirement, Senator Davies returned to Wales and purchasing Leighton Hall he lived in the mansion house for the next 17 years. Senator Davies' son was the author Robertson Davies (1913 - 1995) and after visiting his father in his Welsh homeland he left a vivid account of his memories of Leighton Hall. Brought up in America, Senator Davies' mansion in Wales was quite a novelty to Robertson Davies and he remembered the house with humour and affection describing it as *"grandiose, pretentious, absurd and yet congenial, lovable and delightful, as so many Victorian things were."* Both father and son knew about Georgiana's copies of the Turner paintings as they had fallen off the wall when Senator Davies first entered the house, causing no little damage as they crashed down.

From Robertson's description, it is apparent that much of John Naylor's stamp remained on the house and most of his art collection still remained. It seemed that there was some arrangement whereby the art treasures which included paintings by Landseer, Delaroche, Turner and Ansdell would remain the property of the Naylor family, as every so often one of them would arrive to claim one of the pictures. As Robertson Davies put it, *"There were other pictures, huge in dimension, that remained in place until some unspecified time when the Naylor descendants would come and take them away. (But where? In what ordinary dwelling could such monsters hang?).* Davies described in detail *The Temptation of Christ* which is indeed a huge picture with *"the Fiend portrayed naked, but decently vague where the Victorians demanded vagueness"* which was painted in 1854 by Ary Scheffer (1795 - 1858) and is now in the Victorian room in the Walker Art Gallery. Davies also mentioned *Napoleon Crossing the Alps* by Delaroche and the more than life-size portraits of Georgiana and John Naylor, painted by Sir Francis Grant in 1857 - Davies' description of the portraits is a little mocking when he describes them as *"she, large and bonny and he, slight and looking rather like Mendelssohn disguised as a wealthy ship-owner."*

From Robertson Davies' description of the artworks within the house, nearly everything is dated circa 1855 or thereabouts, and it tells a tale of a John Naylor who cannot wait to adorn his brand new mansion house with his collected treasures like a child arranging his toys. Davies recalls also that *"wherever it was possible to carve a monogram in oak, linked J's and an N in the most gnarled Gothic script were to be seen"* and he states that the Great Hall where many of the art treasures were to be found *"was 3 stories high with 20 stained-glass windows and a floor area which held 125 people easily."* One of the main features of the Great Hall is what Davies refers to as *"an altar to gluttony"* which was in fact a massive sideboard carved in Germany which John Naylor purchased in 1851 at the Great Exhibition. The gigantic sideboard was so large that according to Davies it even dominated the room of the Great Hall and contained life-size carvings of fruit, flowers, meat and game, and had 4 full-size wooden hounds chained to each corner by wooden chains which were made in such a way that the hounds could be moved into any position. Senator Davies disliked the sideboard so much that he had it dismantled and removed to a stable. In addition to the carved edibles and wooden hounds there were carvings of 4 fat, lifelike children representing the Four Seasons and during the dismantling of the sideboard, Robertson Davies rescued the figure of Autumn and took it back with him on his return to America. His final words on the amazing sideboard were *"It was awesome; it was a triumph of the woodcarver's craft; it was monstrous."* And it was John Naylor's.

The Temptation of Christ.
Walker Art Gallery

Another wonder which entranced Robertson Davies was a fine hall clock, the face of which was in the hall but the workings were at the top of a spiral staircase. The bronze and ormolu workings recorded the seconds, the hours, the days of the week, the months, the seasons and the signs of the Zodiac. The clock also struck the hours and played Welsh, English and Scottish national songs and hymns when a hidden cord was pulled – Senator Davies delighted in amusing his grandchildren by secretly pulling the cord and making music appear as if by magic.

Robertson Davies also noticed the statues of *Georgiana and Her Two Sons* which he described in detail right down to the inscription *"B.E.Spence fecit Roma 1855 under the tassels of Mrs Naylor's cushion"* and of the smaller statue sited immediately opposite he describes *"the small female Naylors reading the Lord's Prayer from a marble book."*

It was strange that Robertson Davies omitted to mention *The Finding of Moses* tableau – it could hardly be missed, but stranger still was that for over a century the statues of Georgiana and her first 4 children remained in the house and neither Christopher, Rowland, Dora or Margaret had thought to place them in their own extensive properties as part of their heritage.

Moving Statues

Little by little, the landscape of Leighton Hall, which John Naylor had so loving crafted, was changed in ways he would never have approved of and in the 1950s the statue of Icarus was removed and has found its way to the home of Powys County Council.

In 1967, Senator Davies died – an event which seemed to be the catalyst for the removal of many more of the remaining artworks. It is probable that there was some arrangement whereby Senator Davies lived in the mansion but the Naylor family still owned the artworks – although if that is the case then it did not stop the Senator from dismantling the gargantuan sideboard. Many more of the paintings were removed at this time including the full size portraits of Georgiana and John Naylor painted by Sir Francis Grant in 1857, now in the custody of the Walker Art Gallery. It was only by chance that the long-forgotten statues by Spence were commented on by an official of the Walker Art Gallery as he wandered through the house assessing other artworks which resulted in a letter to the Walker Art Gallery from representatives of John M. Naylor, informing officials that they could have the statues providing they removed them at their own expense. It was, therefore in this way that in 1967 the Walker Art Gallery acquired the statues of *Georgiana and Her Two Children* and its companion-piece *Dora and Margaret*. The two statues were displayed for many years in the erstwhile home of the Holt family in Sudley, Mossley Hill, where they were admired for what they were but by a public who knew nothing of the Naylor family. The statue of Georgiana was removed circa 2010 and is now in storage, leaving *Dora and Margaret* at the bottom of the staircase, endlessly poring over their marble Bible.

For some indiscernible reason, *The Finding of Moses* has been universally neglected since its first showing at The International Exhibition of 1862, and having been transported to Leighton Hall immediately afterwards has been seen by very few people apart from the Naylor family. However, in 1967, it was agreed to be taken by the Walker along with the other statues and for admirers of Spence's sculptures, hopes were high that for the first time in over a century, his *opus magnum* would be seen by a larger audience. But hopes were to be dashed before the statue ever reached the Walker Art Gallery when workers found that the group could not get through the doors of Leighton Hall and the astonishing decision was taken to take the statue to pieces. It was hardly credible that anyone could contemplate removing the figure next to the Pharoah's daughter but worse was to come when parts were sawn off the arms of the Pharoah's daughter. The dismantled tableau was in a sorry state when it reached the Walker and has remained that way ever since, languishing in the cobwebbed dungeons of the Walker Art Gallery awaiting restoration by a Conservation Centre which has itself been dismantled. Carved in Rome in 1860, exhibited in London in 1862, hidden away in Leighton Hall until 1967 and with an indeterminate sentence in the bowels of the Walker, Benjamin Spence's tableau has been seen by only a privileged few, but would undoubtedly be a major asset to any sculpture gallery in the world. There are some questions which remain to be answered in respect of the sanctioned vandalism of the *The Finding of Moses* – the first is that if the statue was worthy of moving to the Walker Art Gallery then how could anyone allow its dismantling (imagine the uproar if Michelangelo's grown-up *Moses* in the Vatican had been taken to pieces for any reason), the second question would it not have made more sense to widen the doorway from the house, but the real question is how did the statue get into the Great Hall in the first place? The photograph of the Pharoah's daughter overleaf shows a disembodied hand remaining on her shoulder where the statue of Miriam has been removed.

*The statue of
Moses dismantled.
The disjointed hand of the Pharoah's
daughter can be seen resting on the
Pharoah's shoulder*

*The interior of Leighton Hall.
The Temptation of Christ can be seen on the far wall*

*Spence's Icarus in the lake at
Leighton Hall*

The Brownlow Hill Bohemians

"At any rate, they were strange fellows, these bohemians. They lounged around doing nothing and told you they were working; they were frightfully miserable and yet would tell you that they were perfectly happy. They had more troubles than others but seemed to bear them better, as if they fed on suffering."

– Dezső Kosztolányi, Skylark

Williamson's tunnels entrance by Herdman. Liverpool Record Office

Cornelius Henderson (1799 - 1852)

In the first quarter of the 19th Century, Brownlow Hill seemed to be something of a Bohemian quarter with an astonishing number of artists and sculptors living in close proximity to each other, attracted no doubt by low rents and not least the semi-rural aspect of the area. Even the classy mansions of Mount Pleasant had more than their share of artists – the architect John Foster lived there, as did W.G. Herdman, whose pictures of old Liverpool are unsurpassed and Richard Andsell who is of national importance today; Samuel Williamson who left a legacy of local landscape paintings lived in Ranelagh Street next door to Peter Jackson, patron of the arts and future MP and originator of Birkenhead; and in the more downmarket streets of Brownlow Hill itself there were the sculptors that worked in Franceys Marble Works; the sculptor Edwin Lyon (1806 - 1853) was born in Russell Street into an artistic family who later moved to 2 Rupert Street with their business premises at 91 Brownlow Hill. In 1824 Lyon was living at No.70

139

George III
by Cornelius Henderson

Pleasant Street and would have known William Spence and Gibson very well until he moved in the opposite direction from the usual destination of Rome and travelled to New Orleans. There were many more but nobody would record aspiring artists who fell by the wayside and returned to the drudgery of everyday jobs and even talented portrait painters such as Cornelius Henderson are little known today. Henderson who was born the son of a shoemaker and amateur landscape painter in a small house adjacent to the gates of Lancaster Castle on the 9th October, 1799, first appeared in Liverpool living at No.7 Brownlow Hill between 1825 and 1827, moving next door to No.8 Brownlow Hill in 1829. Henderson evidently found work as a portrait artist, painting William Roscoe in 1826 and Joseph Williamson in 1828. Henderson was a great friend of the man they called The Mole of Edge Hill, Joseph Williamson (1769 - 1840), whose eccentricities have become the stuff of legend. By 1832, Henderson had moved closer to his friend's home in Mason Street, living for a short time in Smithdown Lane, but in 1834 he moved into No.10 Mason Street, across the road from Williamson, where he lived for the rest of his life. Williamson was fond of building peculiar houses which he designed himself, and set about designing a house for Henderson which was meant to be a dwelling place and an atelier but in typical Williamson style he had ordered his contractors to build massive windows, none of which had natural overhead light, a deep basement and three huge rooms one on top of the other. Unfortunately Williamson had neglected to put in any domestic conveniences or a kitchen and when Henderson refused to live there he berated his friend with the words *"Don't tell me such rubbish that a better light can be got from a poking skylight than from such windows as these of mine"* it was a measure of Williamson's regard for the artist that he soon cooled down and took no offence. The house itself remained empty for the length of its existence and was still standing in 1920 as the nearest house to Grinfield Street. *The Liverpool Mercury* wrote a wonderfully evocative passage called *"A Soirée at Edge Hill,"* Friday March 1, 1839.

"On Friday evening last Mr Henderson's portrait galleries in Mason Street, Edge Hill, were thrown open to the admiring gaze of his numerous friends. The extensive premises having been previously lighted up with gas, in the most brilliant style, gave a coup d'oeil to the splendid collection of paintings tastefully arranged for the occasion. Dancing and singing were kept up to an early hour by a company of nearly eighty persons; and never before did Edge Hill present such a gay and happy assemblage of friends; displaying wit, beauty, taste, elegance and fashion. The refreshments included every delicacy of the season. The health of the worthy

Joseph Williamson

and respectable proprietor, Mr Williamson, 'monarch of the place' was drunk with great enthusiasm."

Unfortunately, by the following year, the wonderfully eccentric Mole had reached his inevitable *"three-score-and-ten"* and true to his erratic style to the last, just a few days before his death he amended his will to leave tracts of farmland and tenements in Roswen, Wigton Parish, Cumberland, to his housekeeper, Elizabeth Walton, along with his books, pictures and clothes. His friend Henderson was left an annuity of £100 per annum to be paid in two portions each year. Cornelius Henderson had lost his first wife, also named Elizabeth, in 1836 and a few months after Williamson's death in 1840 he married Elizabeth Walton. Little is known of Henderson after this but his loyalty to Williamson remained firmly in place when in 1958 James Stonehouse gave an explanation to the Lancashire and Cheshire Historical Society as to why he withdrew a paper on Joseph Williamson, explaining that he had been threatened with a libel action by the painter.

The Rembrandt of Liverpool - William Daniels (1813 - 1880)

Conflicting Accounts

Unlike many of his contemporaries whose lives are little-known and information is sketchy at best (Cornelius Henderson being a perfect example) a great deal is known about William Daniels probably because his stormy nature drew just as much attention as his paintings. Because so much has been written about Daniels, in particular a touching contemporary piece in the *Liverpool Lantern* I was for a long time reluctant to add to the numerous obituaries and writings; however, the very fact that there is so much material to research makes it a challenge of a different kind – and so, I have added a little to one account, subtracted a little from another and added a sprinkling of my own researches to hopefully arrive at a coherent modern sketch of an artist whose way of life is as fascinating as his work.

The *Liverpool Lantern's* sometimes rambling account of Daniels' life by H.T. Kemball, the editor of the paper, is an outstanding essay; clever, concise, witty and above all an affectionate account of a man that he knew for over 35 years. However, it has to be said that as a long-standing friend of Daniels, Kemball was understandably reluctant to be overcritical of his friend's erratic behaviour usually brought about by his excessive drinking and others have not always been so generous

in their praise. If the *Lantern* biography can be faulted at all it is in the absence of dates which makes it difficult to relate events chronologically which is reflected in my own text when more often than not I have no idea when events occurred and have *"guesstimated."* Other obituaries and letters are generally informative with one or two plainly incorrect but none of them approach the *Lantern's* quaint account of the painter's life and it is surprising to note that the worst of them all is within the pages of *The Liverpool Mercury. The Liverpool Mercury* is renowned to this day as a source of stories of Liverpool history but William Daniels' obituary, written soon after the artist's death by William Tirebuck, is an example of the very worst of Victorian journalism – the flowery sentences and purple prose are more an exercise in unnecessary verbosity and it is quite obvious that Tirebuck is more concerned in extolling his own dubious virtues as a writer rather than the life of his subject. The following sentence is just one small portion of an article which was called *"tall writing"* by a slightly embarrassed *Mercury:*

"Our lisping pens about his tomb are yearnings after that full speech of silence which is his, our hieroglyphics but outward and visible signs of that inward emotion found in the blank where he once stood and worked, while many knew not and few heeded."

Even the Victorians must have stood aghast when they tried to decipher Tirebuck's nonsensical ramblings in their morning papers. Luckily there are far more prosaic reminiscences which are a far cry from *"lisping pens"* and *"speeches of silence".*

The Liverpool Mercury offices are still standing in 16 Wood Street. Now a night-club the offices were built circa 1800 and the *Mercury* began in 1811. The building is a tribute to the Georgian bricklayers and looks like it will last for another 200 years. The sculptures of Mercury and a cornerstone of a Liver Bird with the word *"Libertas"* are reminders of the time when the offices belonged to the foremost newspaper in the city.

The Early Years

When William Daniels was born in Gascoyne Street off Vauxhall Road on the 9th of May, 1813, the name Vauxhall Road had only been in existence since 1796 – prior to that it had been called Pinfold Lane after the *"pinfold"* or cattle enclosure which once stood there. Although biographers and essayists of Daniels have described Vauxhall Road as *"notorious"* they were describing the area as they knew it in the latter years of the 19th century, but when the Daniels family settled there at the turn of the century Gascoyne Street was part of a bucolic landscape of pleasant gardens and country dwellings and not at all *"notorious."* In the year that William was born the Leeds and Liverpool Canal was extended for ¾ of a mile until it ended at the bottom of Gascoyne Street and when William was nine years of age in 1821, Princes Dock was opened to admit its first ship, a Liverpool built East Indiaman named the *"May"* with cheering crowds forming a backdrop to the momentous occasion (the canal extension was later filled in and returned to its original ending at the Eldonian centre). Prior to the building of Princes Dock the north shore was just that – a sandy beach with grassy sand dunes, fisherman's boats and the odd cottage dotted here and there, and in the distance to the rear of the river the heights of Everton Brow could be seen. It was in fact the extension of the canal and the building of the new dock which were the beginnings of the industrialisation of the area so that it could later be described accurately as being *"notorious."* The canal and docks were a magnet for manufacturing industries and a white-lead factory on the canal, Eccles Moroccan Leather factory, Forrester's Foundry and an alkali works were the forerunners of a host of factories which were the beginning of the end of the sylvan countryside that William Daniels knew; James Allanson Picton summed it up in a few pointed words *"wherever they* (factories) *are established, verdure, foliage and amenities take their flight."*

The North Shore 1830

Although it's only a minor matter, there is some reason to believe that William Daniels was in fact born William Daniel without the s; Daniel was forever trying to convince people of his real name and despite his growing frustration and attempts to educate people it has remained as Daniels with an s.

William's father, Samuel Daniels, was a tall, powerful and handsome ex-soldier who had married a girl working as a barmaid in a public house in the city; they eventually had five children of which William was the second. Samuel had set himself up as a brick-maker, a business in which the whole family were expected to play a part, and William was put to work in the brickfields as soon as he was able to hold a brick; in later life, Daniels maintained that his well-known fondness for drink stemmed from his days in the brickfields. *"When I was a little boy my father who was a brick-maker he used to make me get up between 4 and 5 o'clock in the morning and look after the (?) of the bricks and made me take some whisky to keep out the cold. Is it any wonder I cannot leave off now."* A century later, Maurice Utrillo, *"The Artist of Montmartre"* made a similar claim for his alcoholism when he blamed his grandmother for giving him wine as a baby to make him sleep. Whether Daniels' theory was correct or not it is a strange fact that it was those same bleak brickfields which also gave him his chance in life when a fortuitous encounter with one of the leading lights in the Liverpool art world chanced to pass by. The *Daily Post* of June 1908 reminisced that *"on wet days he* (Daniels) *amused himself by modelling subjects in clay. One of those subjects was a little fat man who frequently*

The Savoyard by Mosses

walked past the brickfields." The *"little fat man"* was Alexander Mosses, art master at the Royal Institution and a member of the Royal Academy who daily walked past the brickfields on the north shore accompanied by a friend who was as thin and lanky as Mosses was stubby. Evidently, the young Daniels believed the odd couple to be a suitable subject for a clay model which Mosses immediately recognized as showing a great deal of latent talent at such a young age. William had previously used a pocket knife to make a house and *"mill"* for keeping mice, constructed tiny windmills and made a Noah's Ark with tiny animal figures which fitted into the interior – William's mother was so proud of this model that she placed it on the mantelpiece in the family home. Mosses was shown all of William's creations in clay which had made him a local celebrity and persuaded Daniels' father that it would be advantageous for the young boy to study at the Royal Institution, Colquitt Street (still standing today), on days when he could take his leave from the brickworks, and to his great credit William's father agreed.

It is possible that Alexander Mosses (1793 - 1837) saw something of himself in the young Daniels as his father was also a tradesman working in Brownlow Hill and he had also shown an aptitude for drawing at an early age, becoming over the years an accomplished portrait painter. Although it made him a good living, in some ways Mosses' ability to paint high quality portraits of Liverpool worthies worked to his detriment as it took up so much of his energy he had little time left for painting in other genres. Paintings such as *A View of Birkenhead Priory* painted in 1811, *Christ's Agony in the Garden, The Expulsion from Paradise* and *The Savoyards* were proof of his talents in other fields than portraiture but such was the excellence of his portraits he was constantly in demand. Paintings such the full length portrait of Thomas Branker, mayor of Liverpool, Reverend John Yates, Dr Rutter and many others were highly acclaimed but being restricted to local gentry they were of only passing interest to London art critics and while Mosses' subjects may have been celebrities in their day, they are little known today. In 1828 Mosses was living at No.12 Benson Street, which runs parallel with Bold Street, in a house where he had his workshop – the house is still standing today as an end house which has survived the wholesale demolition of Benson Street. Destined to die young, Mosses would almost certainly have been familiar with the sculptors in Franceys Marble Works when he later lived at No.18 Pleasant Street, where he died on 14th July, 1837, aged just 44, leaving a widow and 2 sons.

The young Daniels' talent shone brightly in the drawing classes at the Royal Institution and he soon won First Prize for a black and white drawing of *The Dying Gladiator* which Mosses took and framed for himself. In those days it was common for working people to wear wooden clogs and when the day of the prize-giving came around Daniels realised that clattering up to the podium would be an ordeal and was only saved from his embarrassment at the last minute by a sympathetic fellow-pupil who lent him his shoes.

Following his tutelage at the Royal Institution, Mosses then took on Daniels as an apprentice in his wood engraving and painting workshop in Benson

No.12 Benson Street on the left

Street; it was an employment which would grow increasingly dismal as Mosses' philanthropy gradually changed into jealousy and brought out his worst traits. It was jealousy which caused Mosses, the master, to teach his apprentice the intricacies of engraving but refused to allow him *"the secrets of the brush"* which was of greater importance to Daniels. However, the compulsion to paint was overwhelming and Daniels worked at home in the evenings by the light of flickering candles and it was said that those variances of light and shadow had a major influence on his future paintings; there's no doubting that chiaroscuro effects are a hallmark of Daniels' work but whether they were truly influenced by his candlelit labours or his own nature which was as chiaroscuro as his art, is open to debate. In later years, as he became better known, Daniels was labelled *"The Rembrandt of Liverpool"* by the influential Victorian art critic John Ruskin, whose judgements from on high were unassailable – Oscar Wilde proclaimed of Ruskin *"To you the gods gave eloquence such as they have given none other."* Eloquent or not, Ruskin's private life was as disreputable as Wilde's and his judgement was not always correct, and William Daniels' paintings are more Caravaggio than Rembrandt.

Light and Shade

Working in his dimly lit home was hardly the best environment in which to produce quality paintings, but making it work to his advantage, Daniels took to painting portraits which he sold for 5 shillings each, and aged 17 exhibited his work for the first time at the Liverpool Academy Exhibition to the embarrassment of Mosses who was mortified at comparisons with his own work. By this time, the once open-handed and philanthropic Mosses had altered completely and in a mean-minded gesture he attempted to claim Daniels' candlelight paintings as his own property, ignoring completely the hypocrisy attendant in his request. On another occasion, a fellow apprentice, a little older than Daniels, had him cleaning brushes and other menial tasks, until Daniels rebelled at being treated like a slave and a fight followed between the two apprentices. Daniels won the fight but received a cut on his hand from a painter's knife which remained with him until his dying day. Daniels made his way home where Mosses found him and he was encouraged to return to work on the understanding that he would slave no more on the older apprentice.

Daniels entered into his apprenticeship around 1826 which at that time would have been from the age of 14 to the age of 21 and was far stricter than an apprenticeship today, stipulating that the apprentice must be sober at all times, never fall foul of the law, dress in an appropriate manner and obey the master at all times. Written and signed by master and apprentice, the indentures were a legally binding document which could lead to prosecution if flaunted in any serious manner. An indentured apprenticeship was not to be taken lightly and it is no coincidence that it was only on completion of his apprenticeship, circa 1831, that Daniels began to express himself freely; Daniels always saw himself as a free spirit and wearing earrings to go with his flamboyant clothes was just the beginning of a life style which would become increasingly wild.

The Hunted Slaves by Andsell

One of Daniels' friends at this period of his life was Richard Andsell R.A. (1815 - 1885) who attended the Liverpool Academy in 1836. Following the death of his father when he was quite young, Andsell attended The Bluecoat School for Orphans. Andsell went to live in London after he married in 1847, where he painted the stunning *The Hunted Slaves,* a painting which is so gripping in intensity that it stopped people in their tracks when it was displayed in the Walker Art Gallery – the picture is fittingly now in the Slavery Museum, Albert Dock. The American Civil War was an obvious inspiration for *The Hunted Slaves* and it was no coincidence that the painting is dated 1861 and inspired by a poem *The Dismal Swamp* by Henry Wadsworth Longfellow. While *The Hunted Slaves* is a favourite in Liverpool, Andsell's painting of *The Fight for the Standard at the Battle of Waterloo* is just as iconic in Edinburgh where it is displayed in Edinburgh Castle alongside the now faded standard which is in the painting. Sergeant Charles Ewart is shown capturing the Standard from a French Lancer and the hero of the Scots Greys is revered in Edinburgh where The Ensign Ewart public house is just one of many homages to him. Richard Andsell's paintings of rugged landscapes and animals made him a favourite in Victorian times and he is one of the few Liverpool painters who have been nationally recognized. There's little doubt that Daniels could and would have achieved the same fame but for several catastrophic errors of judgement undoubtedly fuelled by drink.

Light and shade would remain a hallmark of Daniel's paintings throughout his lifetime and he often expressed the wish that he *"should like to go on a painting tour in Hell for the sake of the light and shade."* The juxtapositions of light and shade which fascinated him so much were not just a feature of Daniels' paintings but characteristics which applied to every facet of his life – just one example being boisterous bouts of heavy drinking among dubious acquaintances in the evenings interspersed with serious studies of Shakespeare, Milton, Byron and Gray during the daylight hours. Daniels' love of literature was something which never left him and in his lifetime he expanded his reading to include Homer, Virgil, Cervantes et al, and went on to study mathematics, ancient and modern history, poetry and geography. Unfortunately, his love of drinking was also something which never left him and was the cause of his increasing erratic behaviour as the years went by.

The Path of True Love...

Daniels met the lady who was to become his wife circa 1838 when he was aged 25 and the picaresque adventures which featured in all aspects of his life were very much to the fore in his courtship of Mary Owen. Daniels had met Mary at the home of a mutual friend and true to his passionate nature had fallen in love with her at first sight. Evidently, Daniels' courting of Mary was successful, and having asked her hand in marriage, he one day purchased the engagement ring and was returning along Lime Street with a song in his heart and the jewel in his pocket when he came across a group of ruffians outside one of the many pubs on the street. The hooligans who were in process of defacing the freshly painted wall of the pub began to throw insults at the young painter and finally threw an oyster shell which struck Daniels beneath one eye. This was too much for Daniels who by this time had

The Brigand, 1837

grown into a powerfully built man, 6 foot tall in his stockinged feet, accustomed to sparring with the boxing fraternity and afraid of nobody, and he proceeded to give the thugs a good hiding. The matter might have ended there, but for the arrival of a Constable who immediately assumed that because the ruffians were being badly beaten that Daniels was the aggressor and *"with numerous assistants and infinite difficulty conveyed the painter to the Bridewell."* Luckily for Daniels, a man named Tyndall Atkinson had been passing by, witnessed the whole thing and recognized the painter from a gathering they had both attended. Atkinson, who was a man of good standing and well known in the town followed Daniels to the Bridewell and secured his release on the understanding that he appeared next morning before the magistrate.

However, fate was not finished with Daniels on that particular day and finally reaching the home of his beloved Mary in Grosvenor Street, he found a Mr Parry there in the process of persuading Mary to attend the theatre with him that very night. It was inevitable that the meeting would end in a fight and before long Daniels was raining blows down upon the would-be interloper. Parry was a river pilot and no weakling but Daniels' wrath was too much for him and he retreated into a back room where he dropped out of a window and straight into a water-butt and was left to make his way home dripping wet – no doubt reflecting that artists were generally thought to be sensitive souls and not usually given to throwing punches in such a professional manner.

William Daniels' and Mary Owen's wedding was never fated to run smoothly and in the months preceding the great day, Daniels, who lived a day to day existence began to realise that there was no money to pay for the celebrations. He began to earn money the only way he knew how, by painting portraits, and received a request to paint the Lord of a Manor in one of the great houses in Wales. Daniels' lodgings were in the small village where *"a bonny, plump, rosy Welsh lassie"* fell for the romantic young artist whose handsome looks she found irresistible and she ran after him unashamedly. Unfortunately for all concerned, the Welsh girl was already promised to another man who turned out to be none other than the gamekeeper of the Welsh Lord Daniels was painting. Although the bonny Welsh maiden did her level best to attract the attractive painter Daniels was indifferent to her charms, but when the Welsh gamekeeper became jealous and insisted on settling the matter with his fists Daniels was not one to back down. The fight was arranged in a saw-pit one dark night with the gamekeeper's supporters holding lanterns and creating a flickering chiaroscuro setting which could have well been a subject for a fine painting by the artist. The gamekeeper eventually lost the fight and gained two black eyes and the whole party retreated to The Goat Inn where Daniels treated the beaten swain and his followers to a round of drinks. The following day the gamekeeper had a pre-arranged interview with his master and Daniels skilfully painted out his black eyes.

Eventually, Daniels returned to Liverpool, where despite the money earned in Wales one week before his wedding, he was still short of money and painting a picture of Mary dressed as a Gypsy pedlar he took it round to Sir Joshua Walmsley who then lived in Mount Pleasant. Walmsley was an admirer of Daniels work and reputedly bought the picture *"before the paint was dry"* and forever after called it *"The Wedding Ring"* picture.

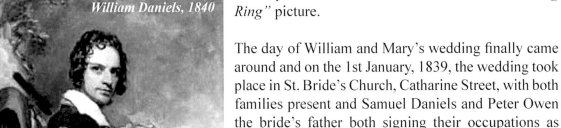

William Daniels, 1840

The day of William and Mary's wedding finally came around and on the 1st January, 1839, the wedding took place in St. Bride's Church, Catharine Street, with both families present and Samuel Daniels and Peter Owen the bride's father both signing their occupations as labourers. There had, however, been one final bizarre interlude which was presumably kept secret from the bride hours before the ceremony, the Welsh girl that Daniels thought he had left behind forever turned up on his doorstep in Brownlow Hill with a final entreaty to favour her instead. One of Daniels greatest friends was the fellow student who had lent him his shoes over 12 years previously and it was Ryland who came to his rescue once again when he escorted the besotted girl around Liverpool, showed her the sights and saw her safely on her way back to Wales where she eventually married the poor gamekeeper. Strangely the newlyweds began their married life, not in bustling Liverpool where the nightlife and patrons were in good supply, but in Runcorn in a house in Clarence Terrace.

A Cottage in the Country

Despite his rugged good looks and flamboyant manner Daniels was no ladies' man and was completely faithful to Mary throughout their married lives; the only love affair he ever confessed to was with his clay pipes which he smoked from morning till night, permanently suffused in a fog of fragrant tobacco smoke. Daniels often spoke in glowing terms of the joys of smoking which he argued was more of a pleasure than drinking although he practised both vices to excess. Sometime early in their marriage William and Mary moved to a Bootle which is today difficult to imagine and seems more of a dreamscape than a landscape – it was a picturesque land of meadows, hedgerows and woodlands where *"on Derby Road gigantic ash and willow trees completely over-canopied the way."* Even when Daniels lived there the idyllic scenery and the tiny villages were beginning to be encroached upon, until by the end of the century it was completely covered in layers of concrete, nondescript houses and ugly warehouses. The Daniels' tiny cottage was near to Mersey View and close to the shoreline where in 1824 William Spurston Miller, a Liverpool solicitor, built a magnificent folly called Miller's Castle which was a mansion complete with castellated turrets. The mansion reached down to the

Girl by a Pedestal 1846

shoreline of the Mersey and was flanked by two narrow steles stretching skywards which were navigating points for ships entering the river – they could be seen at a later date at the front of St George's Hall on Lime Street. Daniels painted a scene of domestic bliss here called *Washing the Baby* showing Mary washing their first child, Mary Ann. Those who saw it said the picture was magnificent and in his usual offhand manner with his own work Daniels sold it to a wealthy timber merchant. Daniels' family was enlisted once again in a picture called *Beggars* in which Daniels' son played a beggar along with the now older Mary Ann while Mary nursed her youngest child Penelope, all under a bridge in Islington – a picture which was sold to the same merchant.

Two of Daniels' early works are regularly on show in the Walker Art Gallery – a portrait simply called *Joseph Mayer (1803-1886)* the great Liverpool antiquarian, was painted in 1843 when the artist was 31 years of age and reveals that Daniels had attracted other wealthy patrons.

149

The subject of the painting, Joseph Mayer, is shown in his personal museum, seated in a chair once owned by William Roscoe and admiring a vase. The room is full to the brim with Mayer's curiosities which later formed the nucleus of Liverpool Museum's collection including the vase which is still on show. Beneath the chair Daniels painted one of Mayer's dogs, a subject which Richard Andsell chose to paint for Mayer − the two paintings are very often exhibited side by side but it's rare that anyone notices that the dogs belong to the same owner.

In 1844, Daniels painted *A Girl on a Pedestal* which is also an exhibit in the Walker Art Gallery − once again Mary Ann was the subject of the painting only on this occasion she was aged about 11 years old.

Portrait of Joseph Mayer, 1843

Customers and Not Patrons

Joshua Walmsley, 1846

Daniels had several strange foibles – one of which was a dislike of people with a fair complexion and another was a dislike of the word *"patron"* preferring the word *"customer"*. But the fact was, that no matter how he chose to interpret it, Daniels had several patrons who recognized quality when they saw it and commissioned and purchased his pictures over many years. One of Daniels' most ardent admirers was Sir Joshua Walmsley (1794 - 1871) who was a friend to the artist for many years, not only buying his paintings but attempting on many occasions to further his career, sometimes with disastrous results. Sir Joshua was well acquainted with Daniels' weakness for drink and his sometimes erratic behaviour but never wavered in his liking of the man; Sir Joshua's son wrote of his father that *"the outstanding trait in his character was in trying to educate an unfortunate man from trouble – whether worthy or unworthy did not matter in the least."* If that statement is true and there's no reason to believe that it isn't then Daniels proved to be his greatest challenge and as his patron and friend he certainly worked hard on his behalf – to what extent he succeeded is a moot point.

Joshua Walmsley was born in Wood Street/Concert Street and made his way in the world as a merchant, businessman and politician, eventually becoming mayor of Liverpool in 1839. Walmsley first lived in one of the mansions in Mount Pleasant until he later became the last owner of Wavertree Hall which was fast falling into dereliction, standing next to Botanic Park in Wavertree Park until its demolition in 1840. As a friend of George Stephenson and Henry Booth, Walmsley attended the opening ceremony of the first passenger railway in the world at Edge Hill on 15th September, 1830, and invited Daniels as his guest where he met Stephenson and later painted his portrait as well as that of Walmsley himself. In later life, Walmsley, his wife and four children went to live in his ornate mansion in Bournemouth. Walmsley's children travelled widely particularly Joshua born in 1819 who had many adventures in Zululand when Shaka ruled supreme – each in their own way found their way home and they are all buried in a marble tomb in St Mary's Church, Edge Hill, which stands proudly among the building rubble, as glittering today as it was when it was first carved.

A Gleaner 1850 posed by Mary, Daniels' eldest daughter

Unfinished Paintings

The peculiar anecdotes which are an inescapable part of William Daniels' life fall thick and fast from this time onwards and reveal a complex personality full of contradictory traits – always unpredictable, sometimes grave and serious, sometimes studious, often combative and sometimes impulsive to his own detriment – on the other hand, Daniels was always generous to a fault (usually his own), always courteous, often light-hearted and ready for a joke and loyal to his friends; light and shade were always a mark of Daniels' make-up. However, there were numerous occasions when the subjects of his paintings annoyed him so much that his reaction was to abruptly end any further work and the portraits usually ended half done. In an early instance of his impulsive nature Daniels heard that the great violinist Nicolò Paganini (1782 - 1840) was in town for a short time and staying at the home of a lady in south Liverpool. Coincidentally, Daniels was working on a portrait of the lady and saw it as an entrée into meeting the renowned musician; besides being a great lover of music Daniels was aware that a portrait of Paganini would be a great coup in his career. The lady in question was, it seems, extremely pious, and had already rebuked Paganini for playing his violin on the Sabbath to which the Italian virtuoso had replied *"Why if the Sabbath is so holy does nothing have to be done at all, why does Providence permit the little birds to sing on that day"* and went on to quote similar examples of joy in the natural world on a Sabbath. Paganini's skilful defence fell on deaf ears and unmoved by either his debating skills or his violin playing the lady further refused to allow his portrait to be painted on a Sunday which was the only day available to Paginini and to Daniels – as a result Daniels never met Paganini but continued to paint the portrait of the lady who had thwarted his ambitions. Daniels had given his subject strict instructions not to look at her portrait before it was finished but when he arrived for a sitting one day he noticed that the lady's dress was multi-coloured with paint from his palette and realized that she had been peeking at the picture – the artist left the house, never to return, with the painting unfinished and himself unpaid.

The Colporteur

Another picture which remained unfinished was that of the popular Shakespearian actor Barry Sullivan – a picture around which a myth had grown that Daniels had lost his temper and put his fist through the canvas. The true story is that the editor of the *Lantern* and the great tragedian were one day (circa 1850) strolling in the Botanic Gardens, Wavertree Park, when they came across Daniels lost in contemplation of the vivid colours of the petals of a geranium. The resulting introductions led to Daniels undertaking a painting of Sullivan in the role of Hamlet. Things were going quite well until a friend of the thespian insisted on looking over the artist's shoulder. The results of this *faux pas* were fairly predictable and matters came to a head when Sullivan's friend commented *"He is not making you look very handsome Barry."* Daniels rose and said scornfully *"Flattery may be in your line sir, but it is not in mine"* whereupon Sullivan and his friend were banished from the studio and Daniels subsequently turned the painting to the wall and never touched it again. Some time later, Daniels cut the picture in half but damaged or not it was sold by a person unknown after lying in a pawnshop and declared a good likeness of Sullivan and a great picture despite being unfinished and damaged.

On another occasion, Daniels really did wreck one of his paintings; on his way along the drive of a mansion house to work on the portrait of the lady of the house he was met by her husband on horseback who berated Daniels for his tardiness in completing the picture. Daniels carried on walking and admitted to the house, he went to the canvas and deliberately put his foot through it – needless to say he was left unpaid.

Even Lady Walmsley, the wife of his patron, Sir Joshua Walmsley, was not immune to Daniels' whims and caprices and when he was commissioned to paint her full length portrait at their home in Wavertree Hall, it was only her husband's good natured approach that prevented a major clash between the painter and his subject. The canvas was a very large one and it seemed that much of the work required to be done in the artist's studio which led to Daniels' grumbling about carrying it back and forth – Sir Joshua solved the problem by putting his carriage at the disposal of the painter. The other problem which arose was a situation which all smokers will recognize and is more relevant today than it was then, which was Lady Walmsley's objections to Daniels' incessant smoking. The portrait was actually painted with Lady Walmsley posing on the steps leading down to the lawn and Daniels could see no harm in smoking seeing as it was outside, but she was adamant that he should not smoke either inside or outside. It was all too much for Daniels who might have done as he had before and left in high dudgeon but probably cognizant of how much he owed Sir Joshua Walmsley he completed the painting in his studio.

In the event, however, Daniels did eventually embarrass his patron, and rather than come into conflict with some average celebrity from Liverpool, he chose to do it in spectacular fashion and insult one of England's greatest heroes. Sir Joshua Walmsley was a very influential figure both in Liverpool and London and in his never-ending quest to further Daniel's career, he had obtained for him a commission with none other than the Duke of Wellington. Daniels must have known that it was a commission which would undoubtedly have earned him fame and fortune but in his own perverse way the painter spurned his greatest opportunity, and the quote from Shakespeare's Julius Caesar was never so apt: *"There is a tide in the affairs of men. Which, taken at the flood, leads on to fortune."* The painting was to be carried out at the home of the Duke at Apsley House and the initial meeting between Daniels and the Duke went well with some preliminary work completed successfully. Taking his leave, Daniels was instructed to return on the following day *"at 9 am prompt"* but according to the *Lantern* account arrived ten minutes late for the appointment. The conqueror of Napoleon was hardly likely to defer to a common artist, of which there were many in London who would have jumped at the opportunity Daniels had been given, and refused to see him. Daniels knew he had lost the chance to join an élite pantheon of artists which included Sir Thomas Lawrence, Goya and Thomas Phillips who have been immortalised by painting the Duke of Wellington and he undoubtedly knew that he could have produced a portrait as fine as any of them. Daniels regretted his behaviour for the rest of his days and often mourned his own incalcitrance when fame beckoned and he chose not to answer.

While the editor of the Lantern's version of events was true to some degree, Daniels was far later than ten minutes for his appointment with the Duke. He had in fact on the previous night become roaring drunk at his lodgings in the Strand, which unfortunately also happened to be a public house, and broken all the windows before retiring to bed to sleep it off. It was said that a commission to paint the Prince Consort ended up with similar results.

The Pugilist and the Painter

Jem Ward from painting

Although Daniels read the classics and listened to music he was generally described as having *"enormous physical strength"* and proved many times over that he was a born fighter. He was quite at home with the bare-knuckle boxers of the era as he was with any of the aristocrats that he painted and as a skilful boxer he sparred with champions of the day such as Mat Robinson, Tom Sayers, Jem Mace, who he painted, and Jem Ward, *"fearing never a pug who ever walked around to show his muscle."* Although Daniels painted both boxers, Daniels was most familiar with Jem Ward whose portrait he painted three times and whose chequered career is perhaps less known than his peers but no less illustrious.

Jem Ward (1800 - 1884) was born in Liverpool and having chosen the hard life of a bare-knuckle boxer for a career, nicknamed The Black Diamond, he began fighting from an early age. In 1822, he made the catastrophic mistake of accepting a bribe of £100 to lose a fight to the greatly inferior Bill Abbott and made such a hash of the proceedings that his cheating could hardly be missed. As a result, Ward earned the dubious distinction of becoming the first man in England to be disciplined by a professional sporting body and was banned from fighting by The Pugilistic Society. Undismayed, Ward carried on fighting at various venues across the country under assumed names until he was reinstated three years later in 1825 and promptly became Champion of England beating Tom Cannon at Stanfield Park.

In the greatest traditions of boxing, at a time when he should have cashed in on his newly won status, Ward fell into a life of dissipation, and two years later in 1827 he lost his title to Peter Crawley. However, in a strange turnaround Ward was reinstated as champion when Crawley refused a rematch and in 1828, he reinforced his position as Champion of England when he beat Jack Carter. Living a life of dissipation or not Jem Ward was still a formidable fighter and in 1831 he fought his last fight beating the Irish Champion Simon Byrne and retaining his title. Ward then announced his retirement after being challenged by James *"deaf 'un"* Burke but refused to relinquish the belt. After some persuasion, Ward then promised to hand over the championship belt to the winner of the fight between James Burke and Simon Byrne which took place in 1833. However, matters took a strange turn when Burke knocked out Byrne who unfortunately died of his injuries three days later and Burke was tried for murder. Burke was subsequently acquitted but Ward stubbornly refused to relinquish the belt until in 1839 he finally presented it to the Nottingham boxer, William Abednego Thompson, when he beat

James Burke. Thompson was so delighted to have won the title and receive the Championship Belt that on his return to Nottingham and his ecstatic fans he somersaulted into the crowd and ended up breaking his kneecap putting him out of action for two years. Sir Arthur Conan Doyle penned a rhyme about the boxer who is still revered in Nottingham:

You didn't know of Bendigo?
Well that knocks me out!
Who's your board schoolteacher?
What's he been about?
Chock a block with fairy tales;
Full of useless cram,
And never heard of Bendigo
The Pride of Nottingham

In later life Jem Ward became the proprietor of The Star Concert Hall which was built in 1866 and is now The Playhouse Theatre, Williamson Square, Liverpool. Ward retired to the York Hotel which was opposite the theatre on the corner with Tarleton Street. W.G. Herdman's print (above) shows The York Hotel with houses alongside. It was in his retirement that Ward continued his hobby of painting and under the tuition of William Daniels he showed enough talent to exhibit at the Walker Art Gallery and in London.

The above painting is called The Championship of England and America – Tom Sayers versus John. C. Heenan 1860 – a painting by Jem Ward. Ostensibly the first World Championship bout, the fight took place in a field in Hampshire where the two boxers fought for two and a half hours until the police stormed the ring and the fight was declared a draw. Charles Dickens, W.M.Thackeray, Lord Palmerston and The Prince of Wales all fled the illegal gathering

Richmond Row

Richmond Row, 1857, by Herdman. Liverpool Record Office

Dickensian buildings being slowly overtaken by industrialisation. The Three Loggerheads Pub is on the left with its humorous sign. Felicia Hemans stayed here aged 7 with her family who had fallen on hard times and were helped by the proprietor Mr Nicholson, one time mayor of Liverpool. Felicia was reputed to have begun her poetry writing here. Liverpool Record Office.

Circa 1860, Daniels was working out of a studio on Richmond Row, Everton, which had a set of steps with two plinths on each side with two lions *couchant* on top of each column. A friend of Daniels once sent him a letter from out of town with the only address being a sketch of the lions and a rhyme:

> *Good Postman, pause with this before*
> *Two lions couchant by a door*
> *In Richmond Row;*
> *Daniels in that lions den,*
> *AI of artists, he and men*
> *His like all Liverpool again*
> *May never know.*

Daniels was intrigued by the sketch and the rhyme and was amazed that he should be so well known that the letter found its destination. He kept the envelope for years, until the time that he was close to dying, when he sent it back to his friend.

Some of Daniels' finest pictures were painted in this studio including *Othello and Iago, Shylock* and *The Prisoner of Chillon* and this period is regarded as the pinnacle of his career, although it must be said that his consistent level of excellence makes any choice of his best work difficult. One of Daniels' patrons was a Mr Somerville and *Othello and Iago* was a commission ordered for a friend of Somerville's in Canada who gave the artist *carte blanche* to paint the picture any size he wished and any price he asked. In the end Daniels painted one of the largest pictures he had ever done and received the largest sum he ever received for a single picture which was £160, a princely sum in those days. The painting was duly sent to its owner in Canada and later sold on and is now untraced. *The Prisoner of Chillon* painted in 1864, was commissioned by Somerville himself and Daniels set the sum himself of only £40 for a picture which has been acknowledged by many as his greatest achievement. The subject of the painting was from a poem by Lord Byron published in 1816 which was in turn inspired by the martyred Bonivard locked up in the chateau of Chillon on Lac Leman where Byron was appalled by the man's suffering. Daniels was reputed to have spent many hours in the crypt of Chester Cathedral in order to capture the light effects in the painting which is now in the keeping of The Walker Art Gallery. *Shylock* was originally painted for a tavern sign above a public house called '*The Opera House'* in Williamson Square but its quality was outstanding and was subsequently purchased for a private gallery. The model for the painting was Daniels himself who enlarged his nose in the picture to conform with the perceived vision of the cruel face of Shylock.

The Prisoner of Chillon, 1862

Aristocrats and Publicans

Although Daniels' cavalier attitude towards pecuniary matters often left his family with no income, when times were hard the painter went without food in order that his wife and children should have more, but the reality of the situation was that Daniels should never have been in poverty at all. Sir Joshua Walmsley had been a patron of Daniels from his youth and apart from commissioning many paintings he introduced him to other influential patrons – not least Sir Humphry Davy and George Stephenson whose portraits he painted. Apart from his paintings over the years Daniels had a number of paying pupils as a further income – William Windus (1822 - 1907) who later became a member of the Pre-Raphaelites was the best known and always remembered Daniels as his first inspirational teacher. But painting always came first and there were many others who sought out the artist for family portraits and other subjects but two of his patrons stand out as especially faithful customers buying many paintings over the years at a fair price.

William Somerville had been an admirer of Daniels' work since he first arrived from Canada in 1857 and noticed some of his paintings for sale in a dealers in Clarence Street. Somerville was at pains to meet the artist himself and his enquiries led him inevitably to *"an inn nearly opposite to his former house that stands (stood) where the umbrageous grounds of Miller's Castle stand."* Somerville and Daniels became great friends with the former buying paintings off Daniels for many years afterwards for his homes in Leicester and Nottingham. A list of the paintings that he purchased is extensive but there were probably many more which have vanished into obscurity – apart from *The Prisoner of Chillon* there were *The Widow, The Brigand, The Image Maker, A Boy Blowing Bubbles, An Oyster Woman, The Sailor's Sweetheart, A Portrait of William Somerville, The Song of the Shirt, Faces in the Fire, A Portrait of Mr Friend, Picture of William, the Artist's Son, A Girl Selling Oranges, Medora, Doubt, Certainty* and *The Sailor's Daughter.* Many of the paintings had Daniels' wife and children as models – Bessie played the part of *The Sailor's Daughter* while Mary, his wife, played *A Girl Selling Oranges.* Even Daniels' servant girl was called into a different kind of service as *A Girl Peeling Potatoes.* Another painting which had young William begging under a bridge was acquired by Somerville and presented to Colonel Steble of Steble Fountain renown, at his home in the prestigious Sandfield Park. *The Widow* represented a young woman, modelled by Mary with a babe in her arms gazing soulfully at the miniature of an army officer – now lost, the painting was said to bring tears to the eyes of anyone who saw it.

William Dawbarn also became a great friend and patron of Daniels and often took him on trips outside Liverpool. In common with Somerville, Dawbarn collected Daniels' paintings throughout his lifetime for his mansion called Elmwood which stood just a short distance away from Jericho Lane going towards Aigburth Road. Dawbarn owned *The Irishman, A Fisherman, Family Portraits, 3 Religious Works, Macbeth, The Card Players, The Fisherman's Home, The Street Musician, A Sister of Charity, Ironing Day, Candle-Light* and one of Daniels' final paintings the acclaimed *The Nun* which was proof that the quality of his work had never diminished with age.

However, the light and dark theme which ran like a thread throughout Daniels' life also applied to his clients and customers and many of his commissions were carried out for publicans, brewers and bar-flies who regularly underpaid him or neglected to pay him at all. It was quite remarkable how Daniels would be on good terms with the aristocracy of the area, read the classics in his leisure time and carouse with the unsavoury customers of the taverns night after night. Not all of Daniels' pub commissions ended up in the hands of the unscrupulous. *The Friar of Orders Grey* now in the Williamson Art Gallery, Birkenhead, once hung inside the Clock Inn, London Road, while a picture of *Samuel Weller* was in Rigby's on Dale Street and several portraits of Jem Ward were in public houses in Williamson Square while one of the artist's greatest pictures *The Goldfish* was originally commissioned for The Opera Tavern in Williamson Square. *The Goldfish* which has a young girl gazing into a gold-fish bowl stands comparison with any of Daniels' other pictures and recognized as too good for a public house it was sold to a gallery, later finding a suitable home in the Ashmolean Museum, Oxford. Daniels painted another version of the picture in which a black cat is staring malevolently at the fish instead of the young girl and this picture was claimed to be immeasurably better than the original.

The Goldfish

However, there were others who took advantage of Daniels' largesse and realising the value of the pictures either sold them on or pawned them. It is worth noting that it was never any member of the aristocracy which cheated Daniels but his own working-class denizens of the taverns he frequented. It is also worth noting that Daniels' live-for-today philosophy was never taken advantage of by his upper-class patrons but it was his so-called friends in the taverns who preyed upon his diffidence when it came to money, so much so that on several occasions he narrowly escaped being sued for debts he may or may not have incurred. Dawbarn came to his rescue on one occasion while others sometimes purchased pictures which saved him from the courts but his come-day-go-day manner caught up with him when he was successfully sued by a publican he had been friends with for many years and in 1875 at the age of 63 he found himself in Walton Jail.

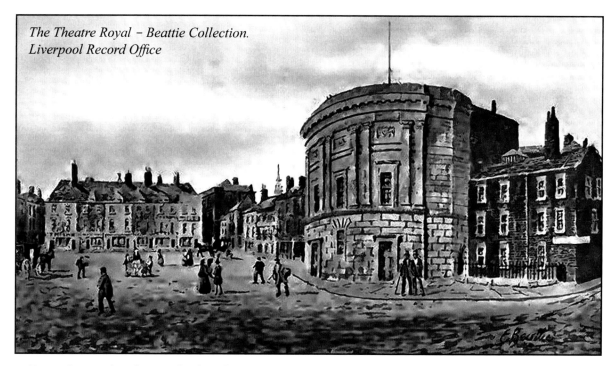

The Theatre Royal – Beattie Collection.
Liverpool Record Office

Daniels was familiar with The Theatre Royal in Williamson Square which opened for business in 1772. Sarah Siddons, Edmund Keane played there as did Julius Brutus Booth whose son, John Wilkes Booth would become infamous for the assassination of President Lincoln. George Frederick Cooke's famous ripost to his audience that "every brick in Liverpool is cemented with an African's blood" is today better known than any of his acting roles and Dickens gave readings there in 1847 and 1869. The building was later converted into a Cold Storage Unit until it was demolished during the architectural holocaust of the 1960s.

The Final Years

Daniels' sojourn in Walton never seemed to bother him overmuch and far from being an ordeal he turned it into an opportunity to carry on painting undisturbed. William Somerville visited him to see how his commissioned work *The Man at The Wheel* was proceeding which was then followed by *Castles in the Air* which Somerville also purchased and a third painting was completed called *Reading the News* before Daniels was released undismayed and unrepentant.

Daniels' last home was in No.85 Cresswell Street, at the foot of Everton Brow where he lived in a house which was a visual indictment of his careless ways with money. Whereas a man of his prodigious talent and energy could and should have been living in a home befitting a lifetime of hard work Daniels and his family were living in a house which was literally tumbling down. Built on the site of an old quarry the house was subsiding to such an extent that it was propped up with huge wooden beams, the floors were at a slant and the doors had been cut away at triangular angles in order to fit their frames. Unsurprisingly, Daniels loved the place and painted happily *"in a painting room which was as black as Erebus and thickly festooned with cobwebs which he would not allow to be removed. He loved the spiders and would not disestablish them."* And it was in this house that Daniels died, smoking his final pipe on

Charles Keane 1835.
Donated by Walmsley to the V and A

Wednesday 13th October, 1880, *"at 11.00 am, gazing at the glorious sunshine, with intellect unimpaired and in the very zenith of his art-power, in the sixty-eighth year of his age."*

Daniels' funeral in St James' Cemetery on the 18th May, 1880, was attended by a long cortege of his friends and admirers – several of them had been his pupils and others such as John Alexander Patterson McBride were artists in their own right. The hundreds of others who attended were members of the clergy, authors, musicians, merchants, actors and literati of Liverpool with who he had mixed freely and often drunk freely. Daniels' resting place was alongside Cyrus, another Cyrus, Emma and Samuel, four of his children who had evidently died before their father, in a grave near to Huskisson's monument which at that time still had John Gibson's marble statue within the mausoleum. Mary Owen Daniels for whose hand Daniels had fought for with such ardour over forty years previously, was present, his son William Daniels who he had painted in various guises was there, as were Mrs Priest (Penelope) and Mrs Fitzsimmons (Elizabeth or Bessie), his two married daughters he had painted many times as they grew up. Daniels' daughter Mary Ann who was once *A Gleaner* had moved to Boston in America and another son, Alexander, had settled in Canada.

William Daniels was reputed to have painted over 4,000 pictures during his lifetime; it is a staggering number and is possibly exaggerated but other long-lived artists are known to have painted far more and it is a fact that Daniels was an extremely prolific painter. The sad fact is that many of his paintings are today either lost or untraced – some were stolen, some sold at auction and some are undoubtedly scattered around the country gathering dust in the attics or basements of once proud mansion houses. Sir Joshua Walmsley knew the quality of Daniels' art and gifted 7 of his paintings to the Victoria and Albert Museum, Kensington, London, while the Walker Art Gallery has 23 paintings altogether. There are a number of paintings in other galleries around the country but overall they represent only a small percentage of the artist's work.

Not only have many of Daniels' paintings been lost but even his headstone has been mislaid during the civic vandalism of the 1960s when St James Cemetery was re-designed and many historic headstones were lost, misplaced or worse still broken.

The Man Who Loved Animals

William Huggins (1819 – 1884)

"Until one has loved an animal, a part of one's soul remains unawakened."

– Anatole France

William Huggins, a self-portrait

An Early Talent

H.C. Marillier's short biography of William Huggins begins *"William Huggins, whose fame as a painter (especially of animals) deserves to stand far higher than it has ever done."* Written in 1904, those words ring as true today as they did then, and if anything, Huggins and his paintings have become even more obscure especially in his home city of Liverpool where of all places, their value should be recognized. However, Huggins was an immensely prolific artist and over the years his paintings have spread far and wide, turning up regularly at the larger auction houses where they exchange hands at ever-increasing prices to private collectors, whose business acumen is often sharper than that of the establishment. Although Huggins specialised in painting animals, his self-portrait, his paintings of his wife and that of William Spence mark him out as an accomplished portrait painter, while his landscapes are second to none, and he excelled in every genre.

The very few biographies of Huggins invariably date his birth at 1820 but he was in fact born on the 13th May, 1819, in the parish of St Paul – the confusion has probably arisen because his baptism date is 28th May, 1820, just over 12 months later. Huggins' parents were Samuel and Elisabeth Huggins and his younger brother was the eminent architect Samuel Huggins (1811 - 1885). He also had three sisters, two of them, Anna and Sarah Huggins, became artists in their own right, exhibiting paintings of flowers, fruit, animals and landscapes – Anna exhibited a painting called *Dead Game* in the Liverpool Academy Exhibition of 1854. Although he never liked the appellation *"The Liverpool Landseer,"* going so far as to exclaim *"Landseer! if I had had Landseer through my hands for 6 months I could have made a man of him"* there is no doubt that Huggins' work was of similar quality. However, he was more of a natural successor to a Liverpool painter who had died 14 years before Huggins' birth, the renowned George Stubbs (1724 - 1806), with both artists painting that most difficult of subjects, the horse, to a degree of excellence rarely accomplished.

Huggin's talent for drawing became apparent at an early age and having enrolled in the Mechanics' Institute School of Arts, at the age of 15 he won a prize for an ambitious design called *Adam's Vision of the Death of Abel.* The Mechanics' Institute School of Arts later became The Liverpool Institute and is now LIPA (Liverpool Institute of Performing Arts) – the numbers of distinguished pupils from Huggins to Paul McCartney and John Lennon who have passed through its doors is quite considerable. By 1838, aged just18, Huggins painted *Lion and Lioness* for his patron John Elliot of Hoylake and began his lifetime passion for painting animals. It was a passion which led him to fill his house *"almost as full of pets as the famous Rossetti house in Cheyne Walk, London."* In common with most Victorians, Huggins was enchanted by exotic animals from India, South America and Africa and it is almost certain that *Lion and Lioness* was inspired by animals he had seen at a menagerie. John Elliott was a patron of Huggins for many years and in later years he showed the artist a picture he had purchased from him as a young man – it was proof of how prolific the elderly Huggins had been when he had no memory of the picture at all which was *Lion and Lioness.*

The Magnificent Showman

West Derby menagerie, 1851, by W.G.Herdman - Liverpool Record Office

For the average Victorian the British Empire was a source of never-ending wonder in which an intrepid vanguard of explorers brought back tales of fearsome gorillas, giraffes with necks which reached to the roof, giant crocodiles, man-eating tigers and many more exotic beasts which only served to whet the appetites of a public anxious to see them for themselves. The first giraffe seen in Europe caused a sensation in Paris in 1826 when more than 100,000

Parisians went to see Zarafa which had walked from Marseille to Paris in an epic journey which captured the imagination of the French public. Exotic animals had been kept in the Tower since medieval times – in 1686 a woman named Mary Jenkinson had actually stroked a lion's paw and had subsequently been mauled so badly that she died some days later – but the British Empire opened up a whole new world for the Victorian public and menageries became extremely popular.

There was a menagerie in Lime Street owned by a Mr Hilton (Hylton?) which opened in 1851; given that the menagerie lasted until at least 1938 it is quite surprising that little is known about a zoo which stood in the town centre for so many years; apart from an article by the *Daily Post* in 1938 which reported that two polar bears had escaped and were running wild in St James's Cemetery there is little to tell. It is possible that Huggins painted some of Hilton's animals but it is much more likely that the menagerie which attracted the young artist was that of Thomas Atkins which opened in 1833 on a 9 acre site between Farnworth Street and Butler Street off West Derby Road and lasted until 1863. Like most showmen Atkins was anxious to obtain ever stranger specimens to attract the public and his zoo boasted an animal called a ligon which was a hybrid between a lion and a tiger, and present day zoologists would have been fascinated to know that Atkins also exhibited a now extinct member of the zebra family called a quagga. Thomas Atkins had at one stage been a rival of another menagerie exhibitor, George Wombwell (1777 - 1850) who travelled around the country with an eclectic collection of animals which included elephants, giraffes, a gorilla, a hyena, kangaroos, leopards, lions, llamas, monkeys, ocelots, onagers, ostriches, panthers, a rhino, tigers, wildcats, zebras and anything else he could purchase from the ships bringing back animals from evermore remote parts of the globe. Wombwell was a consummate showman and in an incident at Bartholemew fair in London he upstaged Atkins in a comical and clever response to his rival's advertisement; Wombwell's elephant had died shortly before the Fair and Atkins took advantage of his rival's misfortune by erecting a sign outside his own exhibition which stated *"The Only Live Elephant in the Fair."* Wombwell promptly erected his own hoarding which stated *"The Only Dead Elephant in the Fair"* and the public flocked to poke and ponder at the only dead elephant they had ever seen.

When it came to showmanship George Wombwell was the unchallenged king of the menagerie exhibitors and travelled around the country exhibiting his exotic animals. Many of the animals were totally unsuited to the climate of England and whenever one died in the cold weather, Wombwell was undaunted by his loss

Lions by Huggins, Liverpool REcord Office

165

and sold the carcasses to medical schools or taxidermists. Born in Essex in 1777, Wombwell moved to London in 1800 where he worked as a shoemaker. However, the purchase of two boa constrictors from a ship in London Docks changed his life forever and was the beginning of his new life of fame and fortune; the two boas cost £75 which was a considerable sum in those days but Wombwell quickly recouped his money travelling from tavern to tavern exhibiting the two snakes and he retained an affection for the snake family forever afterwards. By 1810, Wombwell was travelling around the country exhibiting a host of animals to a Victorian audience in thrall to stories of the Dark Continent of Africa and Lost Worlds in South America. Stories of Wombwell and his adventures are legion and vary from his skill at breeding the first lion in England to arranging an animal fight in 1825 more fitting to an event in ancient Rome; Wombwell had named his newly-bred lion William after William Wallace but it was his docile pet lion named Nero that he first pitted against 6 bulldogs – Nero was reluctant to fight and was getting the worst of things until William entered the fray and the contest ended with the bulldogs badly mauled. Without doubt the contest was cruel but Wombwell's part in his lion baiting contest is placed into context when it is recalled that cock-fighting and dog fights were quite common at the time.

Always on the lookout to make the menagerie more thrilling, Wombwell introduced a new element into his exhibition, a lady called the *British Lion Queen*, who was a sensation among audiences especially since she was not named. Speculation was rife as to who the daring lady lion-tamer could be especially since she was reported to have been savaged by

*Wombwell's tomb guarded by Nero
in Highgate cemetery*

one of the lions and having been badly mauled was rescued in the nick of time by other trainers. In October 1847, the fame of Wombwell's travelling menagerie was such that Queen Victoria requested an exhibition at Windsor Castle so that the Royal family could acquaint themselves with the animals at close quarters. However, although she espoused the educational side of the show, the Queen was reluctant to allow the *Lion Queen* who had been identified as Ellen Chapman to perform her perilous tricks in front of the Royal Family and invited the 700 pupils of Eton instead, who were presumably immune to such vicarious thrills. Evidently the Queen was unable to resist seeing the *Lion Queen* putting her head in a lion's jaws and making the wild beasts perform tricks and ordered an evening performance for herself. The press, however, were a little more cynical concerning the deadly dangers faced by the *Lion Queen* and several journalists pointed out that the number of times the intrepid Queen of the lions had been nearly ripped to pieces by razor-sharp talons was becoming a little clichéd. Wombwell's menagerie exhibited twice more for Victoria and on one occasion Prince Albert sought Wombwell's advice as to why he thought the Royal dogs kept dying; Wombwell realised that the dogs were being poisoned by the water they were being given and a grateful Albert asked the showman how he could repay him, to which Wombwell replied *"what can you give the man who has everything."* But Albert was not to be denied and in the end Wombwell settled for the unusual gift of some oak timbers from the *Royal George* which had been partially salvaged in 1834, when divers accidentally discovered the remains of the *Mary Rose* lying nearby. As unconventional and pecuniary as ever, Wombwell had the timbers made into his own coffin which he exhibited in the menagerie for an additional fee.

Over the years, the menagerie which had begun with two boa constrictors became so large that it was split into three exhibitions which travelled around the country separately – one of the trio was a regular exhibitor at the annual Knott Fair in Manchester, near to Deansgate station where one of the star attractions was Pablo Fanque's Circus of *"Mr Kite"* fame. The eccentric, expansive and ebullient George Wombwell's life among the animals finally came to an end in mid-century and he was buried in his coffin of Royal George oak overlooked by a statue of a recumbent Nero, the lion who refused to fight.

In the Background

Most of Huggins' paintings of what were then exotic animals were drawn from Wombwell's menagerie which he followed around the country creating superb studies of the animals and inadvertently capturing the essence of Wombwell's exhibitions. While Wombwell's animals

Christian and the Lions

provided a wealth of material for Huggins, there was one element of the pictures that the showman was unable to provide which was the backgrounds. Huggins had no wish to paint the animals in the mundane and restrictive surroundings of the menagerie and painted them in *faux* backgrounds as if they were in their natural habitat. However, providing those backgrounds proved to be difficult since Huggins had never seen any of the big cats in their natural element but he found the answer was closer than he might have imagined; just as the Victorians were avid for the fauna of other lands, they were also enamoured of the strange and often bizarre flora from South America, Africa and Australia. Most of the large estates around the country had a stove-house or conservatory where the gardeners were required to cultivate the exotic orchids and tropical plants brought back by plant hunters and the larger estates such as Chatsworth sent out expeditions of their own gardeners. William Roscoe had gone one step further in 1802 when he built his own Botanic Gardens in the area which is now recalled by the street names of Myrtle Street, Grove Street, Mulberry Street, Almond Street, Laurel Street and Olive Street, with the entrance to the Botanic on Oxford Street. Roscoe built his Botanic Gardens at a time when the surroundings were out in the countryside but it was a measure of the speed of Liverpool's expansion that 25 years into the future the plants were being affected by the smoke from a myriad of chimneys as a sea of houses spread inexorably outward from the city centre. Roscoe was soon forced to search for another site and in the early 1830s moved further outwards to a rural site adjoining Wavertree Hall which would become Botanic Park in years to come. It was in the conservatory which housed Liverpool's famous orchid collection that Huggins found the backgrounds for his paintings which can be seen as the leaves of tropical plants arranged in such a way as to be what the painter imagined was a jungle clearing. Very often, Huggins took such a disinterest in the backgrounds to his paintings that he employed other artists to paint them in which allowed him to follow his passion for painting animals without such mundane distractions.

Tried Friends, 1852

Occasionally, Huggins felt compelled to return to classical or Biblical or literary themes and his paintings of subjects by Milton or Spenser proved just as powerful as his pictures of lions and leopards. But whether he was aware of it or it was something he did subconsciously, whatever he painted Huggins always managed to find some way of making animals part of the subject matter. *Christian and the Lions* painted in 1848 had more to do with the lions than it did with Christian, and at the same time the subject he chose from Shelley's epic poem *The Revolt of Islam* was a minor part of the poem but entitled *Fight Between an Eagle and a Snake*, Huggins' painting was again more about the animals than Islam. Even when Huggins was commissioned to paint portrait studies of local dignitaries he persuaded his subjects to allow their favourite animals into the picture and in the painting of Mr Cases (Cases Street) with his horse entititled *Tried Friends* (1852) most people are more fascinated with the horse than with Mr Cases – it is in fact a brilliant portrayal of Cases' horse and deserving of a painting in its own right.

As time went by, Huggins extended his animal subjects to take in domestic animals and produced a host of paintings of horses, donkeys, cattle and even pigeons. The backgrounds for his farm paintings are a far cry from the simulated jungles scenes of his lions and tigers and the far more realistic scenes of leafy woodlands and bubbling streams are the forerunners of his later interest in landscape art.

With the landscapes vying for attention with the farmyard animals it was clear that Huggins had changed his cavalier attitude to the backgrounds of his paintings and he extended his interest to create a technique which would make his paintings unique; Huggins began to paint on white millboard, on which he would sketch his subject in pencil, then glaze his pictures with transparent colours so that the white of the millboard showed through the painting creating a unique translucent effect.

It was a measure of Huggins' recognition in Liverpool that in 1847 he was elected an associate of the Liverpool Academy and in 1850 he was made a full member. However, Huggins left the Academy in 1856 during the infamous Pre-Raphaelite dispute and began exhibiting with a group of other secessionists at The Institute of Fine Arts.

Peculiar to Himself

While Huggins could never aspire to George Wombwell's flamboyant eccentricities, he did have his own brand of idiosyncrasies which have been noted with some affection by his contemporaries. The consensus of opinion was that Huggins was quite small in stature with florid, good-natured features – although he could be quite touchy and sensitive to remarks about his paintings even when they were complimentary. Huggins who was reported to resemble the great J.M.W.Turner, also dressed shabbily, never went anywhere without a large gamp over his elbow and wore an old-fashioned stock around his neck *"round which he had a habit of rolling his chin in a manner peculiar to himself."* Huggins was also a fair guitar player and one of his models, many years in the future, recalled how he would sing and play for her whenever she grew tired – *"to this day, I believe that the tune of 'T'were Vain to Tell Thee All I Feel' would bring back the little man with his long, light brown hair, his quiet attitudes and his impassioned manners as I used to laugh at them, 50 years ago."*

Although he painted them supremely well, Huggins never really enjoyed painting portraits – certainly, they kept the wolf from the door but they were also a distraction from the things he liked to paint. Huggins was never a wealthy man and was hardly in a position to refuse a lucrative commission and many of his portrait paintings could be found around the Liverpool area in the houses of wealthy merchants and businessmen who also purchased his miniatures on ceramic or glass ware of which he was an avid collector. Knowing what it was to be poor, once when a fellow artist, down on his luck, came to Huggins' studio to borrow some money the artist replied *"I have none myself but there is a picture you can take to sell."*

Huggins was 11 years of age when the first passenger rail service began from Edge Hill to Manchester in the 1830s and when the railway rapidly expanded in all directions, he was not slow to take advantage of the revolutionary method of travel. But although speeding along at a breakneck 30 mph held no fears for him, Huggins lived in dread of railway tunnels and on arrival at Edge Hill he always alighted and walked the rest of the way home. He did exactly the same thing when travelling from Chester to Birkenhead, alighting at Rock Ferry to avoid *"the passage underground."*

Huggins had a quirky sense of humour which was not always appreciated, particularly by his patrons who sometimes resented any additions to a painting they had commissioned. There was an instance of this when one patron commissioned a picture of a bull which was painted to Huggins' usual high standard, with a farmyard background and a notice board in the corner. At first glance there seemed little to complain about until closer inspection of the notice-board revealed a comic alternative to the conventional *"No Trespassing"* with Huggins' sign stating that on this particular farm *"Trespassers Would Be Persecuted."* Huggins' patron was not amused and painted over the sign in watercolour paints. Sometime later, Huggins was a guest in the house and noticed the change which had been made and said to his patron in a tone of assumed indignation *"Water Colour, I thought so. Somebody has tampered with my background – they are always doing it!"* Whether or not his patron appreciated Huggins' comedic dressing down is not recorded.

On another occasion, Huggins and a small number of fellow artists were browsing around the art exhibition in Post Office Place when the landscape artist and friend of Huggins, Robert Tonge, approached one of Huggins' farmyard paintings and remarked *"That's the first time I ever saw a purple donkey."* When they came to one of the paintings by Tonge, Huggins wasn't long in gaining his revenge and pointing to the picture he said *"What's that Tonge?"* in reference to a heap in one corner of the canvas. Tonge replied *"That's just rubbish"* and Huggins laughingly said *"Quite right, that's what I would have said it was."*

The artist's wife by Huggins

A Strange Critique

Cheetahs by Huggins

Huggins exhibited his work in Manchester, Dublin, Edinburgh, Glasgow and of course Liverpool but rarely in London. However, he did on one occasion exhibit his paintings in several rooms of a gallery in London where it was seen by the art critic Martin Hardie who went on to write a review of Huggins' paintings in a magazine named *The Queen*. The London media and their art critics were at that time notoriously insular and had little time for artists from outside the capital who they condemned as *"provincials"* so it was a pleasant surprise when Hardie went on to write a knowledgeable and scholarly resumé of Huggins' career. Hardie was totally familiar with the artist's diversity of talents and began by saying Huggins was: *"the embodiment of at least three personalities; in one phase he is as an animal painter who in solemn and solid paintings of horses outdoes Landseer and Herring. I have never seen a horse better painted than in Old Friends; it has a sensitiveness to open-air light which Landseer never possessed. Then he broke off to paint subjects in the grand style such as Adam and Eve. In his third and greatest phase, the provincial who knew nothing of Monet, Manet, Renoir and Pissarro plays with light like any impressionist; giving all the glitter and iridescence of sunshine on trees and cattle or fowls, catching the fugitive magic of light rays playing on receptive surfaces."*

While the prose was a little pretentious, there was no doubting the sincerity of Hardie's commendable comments and it was astonishing how well he seemed to know Huggins' work and life. He went on to praise Huggins' other paintings in the exhibition, paying special attention to his paintings *The Monarch of the Meadows, Portrait of a Lady, Landscape With Cattle Near Helsby* and several others. If Huggins ever read Hardie's article he may well have blushed when the critic even wrote of the *"purple donkey"* episode and coloured even more when he after reviewing the paintings Hardie stated that *"the greatest revelation of all is Huggins."*

After writing in such glowing terms of Huggins and his paintings it came as something of a shock when Hardie's critique ended in something so ridiculous and facile that it could have been written by somebody completely different and his summary only served to underline the pretentious attitudes to *"provincials."* In one single sentence Hardie described Huggins as a genius and then in a preposterous phrase he wrote *"the pity of it is that he should have so prosaic a name."* Hardie continued his theme by quoting Matthew Arnold's withering condemnation of *"such hideous names as Higginbottom, Stiggins and Bugg"* and went to state without a hint of absurdity that *"Huggins is an unfortunate name by which to remember an artist whose own perceptions were so spirited and delicate."*

Despite or perhaps because of such nonsensical articles in the media, Huggins never really made much of an impact in London and remained a *"provincial"* throughout his life. It's probably true to say that the old adage *"it's not what you know but who you know"* was more relevant then that it is now and it is probable that if Huggins had somehow acquired just one prestigious patron in London then his reputation would have soared and fame and fortune would have followed. To this day, northern cities and in particular Liverpool are often accused by the southern media of insularity and an *"us and them"* attitude towards London and the south. The above article by Hardie, although bad enough, was far less condescending than most, and was only one of many at that time which belittled northern endeavour, and there is a multitude of evidence to prove that the suspicion between north and south which exists today was fostered during the Victorian era.

Bebington Church by Huggins

The Leaving of Liverpool

In 1861 Huggins went to live with his brother Samuel in Chester and it was undoubtedly Samuel's influence which brought about Huggins' interest in architecture which in turn led to Huggins' masterly paintings of Chester and its Cathedral in the Victorian era. Huggins remained in Chester until 1876 when he took a house in Betws-y-coed. Huggins was beginning to suffer badly from rheumatism at this time and it hardly helped his condition that the house he chose was situated above a stream. Despite his worsening condition Huggins continued painting with his delightful *Fairy Glen* exhibited at the Liverpool Academy in 1877. The following year, Huggins was forced to move to what he believed to be more congenial surroundings in the Vale-of-Clywd but once again he made a poor choice and he complained that in the mornings when he opened the shutters there were *"sometimes mushrooms as large as a soup-plate growing out of the carpet."* The stone floors were cold and the house was freezing, so much so that Huggins *"never ceased to shiver all winter although 14 fires were kept constantly going."* Things went from bad to worse when Huggins' wife died in the house in 1878 and he retired to Chester once again, living in a village two miles south of the town called Christleton, on the River Dee, where he lived in a large house called Rock House which is still standing today, one of many tributes to Victorian building skills. It was said that Huggins kept a menagerie of wild animals in the cellar which he would paint from life, but in his twilight years, Huggins was declining physically of *"atrophy of the muscles"* which could have been any number of things, and was finding holding a brush difficult until finally he was forced to stop work altogether. On the 25th February, 1884, William Huggins breathed his last and was buried in St James' Church, Christleton, with his brother Samuel and sister Hannah. The headstones are unusual in that they are Grade II listed and on that of William Huggins is carved the inscription:

William Huggins, Historic Animal Painter of acknowledged eminence.
A just and compassionate man who would neither tread on a worm or cringe to an Emperor.

Some of Huggins' unfinished works were later completed by artists who were his inferior while others were fraudulently copied but Huggins reigned supreme as a Liverpool artist who is all but forgotten and of the large collection of his paintings in the Walker Art gallery there is not one on display - all of them are in storage including the portrait of William Spence.

Near Helsby by Huggins

The Man Who Bought The Tinted Venus

"The thing is but a statue after all!"

– Pygmalion and Galatea

Venus Verticordia.
Fitzwilliam Museum, Cambridge

William Schwenck Gilbert (1836–1911)

The *Tinted Venus* is probably John Gibson's best-known and best-loved sculpture. It was certainly loved by Gibson who laboured over it lovingly for five years working to some esoteric formula laid down by Winkelmann and meditating over every undulation and curve in his painstaking quest for perfection. Lady Eastlake likened Gibson to Pygmalion, in his obsession with the *Venus* and there's little doubt that Gibson's attachment to his statue went far beyond the realms of normality.

The Tinted Venus had its origins in a statue which Gibson had made years earlier for a wealthy client named Joseph Neeld (1789 - 1856). In 1828, Neeld had inherited an estate and a fortune in money which he used to build a mansion called Grittleton Manor near Chippenham, and in 1833 he entered Gibson's studio in Rome searching for additions to his new home. Neelds asked Gibson to make him a *Venus* and after his usual ponderings on the subject, Gibson created a statue called *Venus Verticordia*. Gibson's statue was a figure of the legendary Goddess, holding an apple bestowed on her by Paris, dressed in a mantle with a tortoise at her feet – although Gibson never realized it at the time, it was in effect the prototype for *The Tinted Venus*. The literal meaning of *Venus Verticordia* was *"Venus, the turner of men's hearts"* and could be further interpreted as *"turning men from sex and vice to virtue."* The Goddess Venus, had over the years, been variously venerated as the Goddess of sex and fertility, the epitome of virtue, the emblem of prostitutes, and the symbol of sexuality – she was in fact, all things to all men. Dante Gabriel Rossetti represented his *Venus Verticordia* as a temptress in his 1863 painting but there's no doubt that to Gibson, Venus was never anything but a modest and maidenly exemplar of womanhood, symbolised

175

by the tortoise at her feet, which was an ancient emblem for the *"steadfastness of woman,"* presumably in opposition to the raging sexuality of men – Gibson's version of the Goddess bore no resemblance to Canova's seductive *Venus Victrix*. Joseph Neeld insisted that his statue should be exhibited at the Royal Academy before he took possession of it, and the *Venus Verticordia* was shown at the 1838 Exhibition before entering Neeld's mansion. The *Venus Verticordia* is now on display in the Fitzwilliam Museum, Cambridge.

In the winter of 1850, Robert Berthon Preston and his wife, entered Gibson's studio, also looking for artworks for their home in Liverpool. Gibson described Mrs Preston as *"pretty and amiable"* and acknowledged that she was a skilled artist, which was praise indeed from the acclaimed sculptor. Robert Berthon Preston's wife's name was Eleanor Leonora, née Rogers (1833 – 1891) and the couple, after marrying in the parish church of Windermere in November 1850, were undoubtedly on honeymoon in Rome when they entered Gibson's studio where the *Venus Verticordia* was still on display. The Prestons commissioned a copy of the statue, little knowing that it would be seven long years before they received it and slightly different to the sculpture they had ordered.

If Stones Could Speak

Memorial to Robert Berthon Preston, Holy Trinity Church, Wavertree

There's a large family crypt in the churchyard of Holy Trinity Church, Wavertree, Liverpool, and in the manner of many Victorian memorials in England it is weather-beaten and uncared for with the ivy surrounding the crypt rising up the sides of the slab for all the world like waves lapping at a rock in the sea. Picked out in lead lettering, the names are still visible but some of the numbers are missing, making the dates unclear, and soon the names themselves will vanish. It's hardly a fitting monument to an old and venerable family which dates back to the Conqueror, has ancestors who have fought in the English Civil War and others in The American Civil War on the Confederate side, contained knights of the realm and has been conspicuous in all walks of life throughout the ages. The Preston family crest is a castle with an eagle rising into the skies and the motif *"leaving the towers of earth we soar God willing to Heaven"* and the wall-plaque within the church dedicated to this particular branch of the family has the ancient crest above the memorial. The memorial is dedicated to Robert Berthon Preston, the son of Robert Preston (April 26th, 1792 - 22nd July, 1825), and his wife Ellen Sarah Preston (née Berthon) (1801 - 1846). Robert Preston and his father also called Robert Preston both lived in a mansion called Fir Grove, West Derby, which is now demolished but in its heyday stood on the corner of a much-changed Alder Road and Blackhorse Lane.

Ellen Sarah Berthon and Robert Preston married on the 14th September in 1819, little knowing that their married life would only last for a scant 6 years; however, their brief marriage produced three children – Ellen Jane Berthon Preston (March 5th 1822 - 1838), Jeannette Berthon Preston (Sept 14th 1823 - June 7th 1837) and Robert Berthon Preston (June 25th 1820 - 8th April 1860) who are all commemorated on the stone slab, with the very last name on the stone being that of Eleanor Leonora Preston. Because this story has as its subject matter the Preston's first child, Robert Berthon Preston, it would be a simple matter to leave the people named on the stone slab of the family crypt to rest in peace, but the reality is that the brief information on the slab is only the first chapter in a long and complex story and the more observant reader of this tale will have noticed that Ellen Sarah Berthon is none other than surgeon Henry Park's grand-daughter. Given that there are multitudes of the Preston clan surviving on both sides of the Atlantic it's rather surprising that none of them tend to their ancestor's crypt, and the repetitive use of the same names make research a frustrating task; there's also little doubt that it requires a certain amount of concentration on the part of the reader but hopefully it will all be worthwhile. The saga of the Prestons also puts into context Robert Berthon Preston's background and his place in the world and illustrates clearly that the Victorian aristocracy were no less vulnerable to the plagues that beset life in that era than the meanest of slum dwellers.

When Ellen Sarah Berthon Preston's first child, Robert, entered into the world, she insisted that her maiden name should be retained and thenceforward all her descendants can be easily identified by the name *"Berthon"* inserted before the name *"Preston."* Ellen Sarah was only 18 years of age when she first married Robert in Bangor Cathedral and if the dates on the slab in Holy Trinity Church were legible they would reveal that she was only 24 years of age when she was widowed in 1825 with three children, aged 5, 3 and 2 respectively – aged just 33, Robert died suddenly while in France at Passage, lot-et-Garonne, Aquitaine. Following a respectable six year period of widowhood, Ellen Sarah married again on the 21st June, 1831, at the Church of St Philip (now demolished, St Philip stood on the north side of Hardman Street from 1816 to 1882) to a cousin, William Robert Preston of Aigburth (1805 - November 24th, 1869). Still only 30 years of age, Ellen Sarah went on to have a further seven children with her second husband, who remains an enigmatic figure in the Preston hierarchy – born in Walton, little is known of William Robert Preston who died at Minstead Lodge, Lyndhurst, Hampshire, an opulent Victorian mansion and grounds which are still in use today. One or two of the dates of the children are confusing, with her first child by William, Emily Berthon Preston, having several different birthdates – the explanation could be that Emily was born in 1830, before the couple had married. The following are the six children with the dates of their lives as best as I can decipher – the anomalies in dates are because Horatio, George, Henry and William were all baptised on the same day in 1837 in St Peter's Church, Church Street, Liverpool.

Emily Berthon Preston (1830 (or 1834) - 2nd Dec, 1841)
William Berthon Preston (1834 - still living in 1870)
George Berthon Preston (1835 - 1855)
Henry Berthon Preston (1836 - 1896)
Horatio Berthon Preston (1837 - 14th April, 1855)
Frederick Berthon Preston (27th July, 1838 - 1838)
Florence Berthon Preston (1844 - 1889)

There seemed to be a curse on the Preston family whenever they travelled away from home - Ellen Sarah's eldest daughter by her first husband, Ellen Jane Berthon Preston, died in Sorrento on March 5th, the same day and month that she was born, in 1838, aged just 17, and Frederick Berthon Preston was born on July, 1838 and died on 25th October, 1838, just 4 four months old – also in Sorrento. The scanty information concerning this period brings up more questions than it answers – for instance, why did both Frederick and Ellen Jane die in Sorrento and what were they doing in Sorrento in the first place when Ellen Sarah was heavily pregnant? But it was also strange that when Emily Preston died on the 2nd December,1841, at just 12 years of age, she also died in Sorrento, which begs the question why Ellen Sarah and William chose to return to such a sad place, three years after the deaths of two of their children. It is well within the bounds of possibility that the children were suffering from tuberculosis and Ellen Sarah and William were following the accepted method of moving to a more clement climate – given that Jeannette Berthon Preston had died, aged just 14 in 1837, the Prestons may have wanted to do their best to avoid any further tragedies. By 1841, Ellen Sarah Berthon Preston was still only 40 years of age, and of her 10 children 4 of them were already dead. There would be others who would die young but Ellen Sarah would not live to see it – she died on the 17th May, 1847, aged 46 and is buried alongside her first husband in Holy Trinity Church, Wavertree, Liverpool.

The Crimean War lasted from 1853 to 1856 with the siege of Sebastopol draining men and resources from the British and French for a whole year from September, 1854, to September, 1855. Sometime in the midst of the conflict two more members of the Preston clan ventured abroad. On the 14th April, 1855, Lieutenant Horatio Berthon Preston of the 88th Connaught Rangers was killed *"in the trenches by a rifle shot"* and in August, 1855, one month before the siege was lifted, Lieutenant George Berthon Preston of the 97 Foot, Earl of Ulster Regiment, was also killed on the final attack on the Great Redan on the 8th of September, 1855. Their brother officers thought well of both men and raised memorials where they had fallen but the fact remained that two more of Ellen Sarah's children had died young, Horatio aged 17 and George aged 20.

Of her 4 remaining children, Henry Berthon Preston (1836 - 1896) married Sarah Caroline Grey Berthon and they had six children together; little is known of William Berthon Preston but he married Frances Anne Maria Shute in 1870 and was evidently in the army as Major Preston of the Bombay Staff Corps. He was promoted to Lieutenant Colonel in November, 1873. Evidently, he had a son named William Deane Berthon Preston who married in New Zealand in 1899, by which time William père had died. Florence was the last of Ellen Sarah Berthon's children and she also died comparatively young, aged 45. The 4th surviving member of Sarah Ellen's children was her first-born child by her first husband Robert Berthon Preston.

Robert Berthon Preston (1820 - 1860)

It was said that the sudden death of his father at the age of 33 when Robert Berthon Preston was just 4 years of age had a profound effect on him throughout his lifetime. Coupled with the early deaths of his sisters and the chequered nature of the Preston family's longevity, his father's early demise made Robert only too aware of the fact that he too was a player in the

Preston lifespan lottery. It was also said that Robert's incipient dread of sharing his father's fate was the thing which spurred him on to living his life to the full.

Robert's education commenced in England but the greater part of his school years were spent in Geneva where he picked up several foreign languages and moved from place to place as he grew older. Robert was known to have a fine intellect, a grasp of many varied subjects and was unusual in that he combined a flair for mathematics and engineering with a love of the arts, and he returned to Liverpool a well-rounded, energetic and intellectual individual. Robert's engineering skills were put to good use when he inherited a large share in the firm of Fawcett, Preston and Company, from his grandfather and spent a great many years supervising in the foundry. Robert's grandfather, also Robert Preston, had died in 1833, and Robert took up the reins at Fawcett Preston circa 1848 on completion of his education.

The Phoenix Foundry, located at the rear of Duke Street, between Lydia Ann Street and York Street, had already been well established when the Preston family bought shares in the company in 1820, making machinery for the sugar trade in the West Indies, steam-hammers, steam locomotives and later on even a steam motor car. During Robert Preston's time as principal partner at the Foundry, he supervised the construction of ship's engines for the *Nubia, Alma, Orissa, Behar* and *Ottawa*, all ships belonging to the Peninsular and Oriental Company (later the P and O Line), as well as engines for the French steamships *Simois, Jourdain, Borysthene* and *Meandre* belonging to the Messageries Imperiales, a French steamship company – most of the ships were built at John Laird's yard in Birkenhead. The Phoenix Factory founded in 1758 was originally a subsidiary of the famous Coalbrookdale foundries in Shropshire until its Quaker founders relinquished ties with the Liverpool factory in 1793 when they began to manufacture armaments. Over the years, the factory had continued to supply armaments, principally for the Napoleonic Wars and the many conflicts of the Victorian era, and Robert Berthon Preston would have overseen the casting of mortars and arms for the Crimean War; Robert went on to take an interest in rifled guns which would later be supplied for ships built in Liverpool for the Confederacy during the American Civil War, as well as engines for many of the blockade-runners.

Following his marriage in 1850, Robert and Eleanor Leonora Preston went to live in a house in Bedford Street South and combined with his work at Fawcett Preston and Company Robert's life began to expand in all directions – in 1855 he became a Member of the Institution, the British Association and the Institution of Mechanical Engineers in Birmingham and he became a member of the Royal Southern and Mersey Yacht Clubs, as well as becoming a patron of the arts. He had still not received the *Venus* he had ordered from John Gibson but the sculpture was only a part of a rapidly expanding collection of sculptures and paintings which were filling his house. Also filling the house were the Preston's rapidly growing family beginning with their first child Leonora Frances Margaret Preston, baptised on 2nd July, 1852, at St Philip, the same Church of Robert's baptism, and somewhere around this time the family moved into No.10 Abercromby Square. The Preston's second daughter, Eleanor Jeannette Preston was also baptised at St Philip, on the 12th October, 1853. Robert appeared to have maintained close connections in Geneva and both of his two sons were born there – Robert Arthur Berthon Preston in 1856 and George Berthon Preston in 1859. One of the inescapable features of the mid-Victorian landscape is how the very wealthy often filled their homes with tangible reminders of loved ones in paintings or statues, and mansion houses across the land were replete with generations of family members in oils and busts. Although it is little documented, Robert Berthon Preston was acquainted with many of the artists and sculptors of the day and he commissioned works from several of his favourites.

After waiting five years for their *Venus* sculpture, the Prestons rightly felt that once it was completed, they should be able to welcome it into their home at last, but they were again doomed to be disappointed as Gibson refused to part with what had become his *Galatea*. Gibson had become obsessed with the Preston's *Venus* and what had started out as a straightforward commission had turned into a labour of love on which the sculptor lavished all his attention, chiselling a bit more here and titivating a little more there in his search for perfection, and of course, adding the famous *"tinting."* It was not the first time that Gibson had tinted a statue but he had never added colour to such an extent as this, knowing full well that it would cause a sensation when it was placed on exhibition. The statue which was now renamed *The Tinted Venus* remained in Gibson's studio, where he often mooned over her as *"an ethereal being with her blue eyes looking upon me. I forgot at times that I was gazing at my own production. There sat I before her long and often. How can I ever part with her!"* Eleanor Preston wrote letter after letter, each one more irate than the last, asking for their statue, but Gibson remained steadfast in his devotion to his *Venus*, and at one stage, sent Eleanor Preston a lyric poem by the reverend Edward Stokes, and wrote an accompanying letter with the astounding sentiment *"hoping that this poetry will keep you a little quieter for some time to come."* Eleanor Preston's expression when she received this letter can only be imagined and she again wrote angrily back, only to receive an even more outrageous reply – *"I am using you abominably bad, and I confess my sin, but the fact is, I cannot screw up my courage and send away my Goddess"* and finished with the jaw-dropping statement that *"it is as difficult for me to part with her as it would be for Mr Preston to part with you."* Gibson finally relinquished his beloved *Venus* and the Preston's received their statue in 1857, fully seven years after commissioning it in Rome. He made a further four full size replicas and four miniature versions of *The Tinted Venus*. Despite his reluctance to part with the Preston's long-awaited *Venus*, John Gibson received several other commissions from the Prestons for busts of Eleanor and Robert and their children which were dotted around the house.

John Gibson talking to Eleanor Leonora Preston with the Tinted Venus in the background.
The International Exhibition, 1862

Robert was still applying himself to his work at Fawcett Preston and Company, and beside a growing interest in chemistry and microscopes, he had also begun to make a study of ship-building, constructing models with a view to eventually building his own ship but the nemesis that had followed him all his life was gradually getting nearer and had only three years left at his work and at home to enjoy the statue he had commissioned on his honeymoon. The fate that Robert Berthon Preston had eluded for so many years finally came in the night of Sunday, the 8th of April, 1860, on a trip to Gloucester accompanied by Eleanor, and in a repetition of his father's death, Robert also died suddenly when he unexpectedly took ill and died in his wife's arms. Once again a member of the Preston clan had come to a premature end while travelling and the Preston family's fortunes had turned to dust − Robert was buried in Holy Trinity Church, Wavertree, on the 13th April, 1860.

Following her husband's untimely death, Eleanor looked after their collected art treasures and their four children at No.10 Abercromby Square until she later remarried Robert's cousin, Alderson Berthon Preston and in 1863 moved to No.2 Prince of Wales Terrace, Kensington, London, along with her children, and their 6 servants. It was a measure of the Preston's wealth when they moved into the newly-built Prince of Wales Terrace, which were then palatial homes of the aristocracy and command prices in the millions to this day.

Eleanor retained her own interests in the arts and maintained Robert's collection of sculptures throughout her lifetime and for a few weeks in 1862, John Gibson was reunited with his *Tinted Venus* when Eleanor placed it on exhibition in the London International Exhibition, which was virtually across the road from her home on the site of what is now the Natural History Museum, the Science Museum and the Victoria and Albert Museum.

Possibly to divert her mind from her sorrow and partly as a memorial to her deceased husband, Eleanor wrote to Benjamin Spence to commission a statue of their son, George, which he completed in 1861. Prior to shipping the statue which was entitled *Master George,* Spence wrote to Eleanor on the 27th February, 1861, telling her; *"I first modelled him in a leopard skin but I did not like it, neither did Gibson who advised me to put him in a little frock."* The thought of a little boy in a frock would seem unthinkable today but Spence omitted to add that the frock was also part of a classical costume and that *Master George* was to be portrayed as a neo-classical sculpture. The statue has since been lost but fortunately a preliminary sketch still exists of the little boy in a skirt.

The Preston's statue that they waited so long for later became an international sensation as *The Tinted Venus* and can be seen as the centrepiece in the Walker Art Sculpture Gallery just a stone's throw from its original home.

Robert Berthon Preston had fortunately not passed on the genetic tendency to die young as a list of his children will testify.

Sketch of Master George statue
by Benjamin Spence

182

Leonora Frances Margaret Berthon Preston (1852 - still living in 1871) – baptised at St Philip, Hardman Street.

Eleanor Jeannette Berthon Preston (12th October 1853 – died Isle of Wight, 3 September, 1938, aged 85).

Robert Arthur Berthon Preston (1855 - 1908) born in Geneva.

George Berthon Preston (1859 - 1940) born in Geneva. Retired from the 2nd Dragoon Guards, George was living at 27 Redcliffe Gardens, Kensington, in 1895.

Eleanor Leonora Preston returned to Liverpool on her own death, to be buried alongside Robert in Holy Trinity, Wavertree. John Gibson later sculpted a memorial to Mrs Preston and a bust of Robert – both now *"lost"* possibly within the vaults of the Walker Art Gallery.

The Tinted Venus

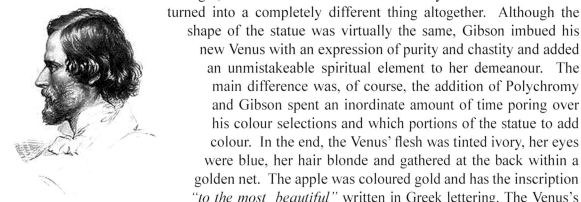

Gibson, by John Herbert Maguire

When Gibson began work on his replica of the *Venus Verticordia,* he began to see it in a completely different light, and what should have been a fairly mundane commission turned into a completely different thing altogether. Although the shape of the statue was virtually the same, Gibson imbued his new Venus with an expression of purity and chastity and added an unmistakeable spiritual element to her demeanour. The main difference was, of course, the addition of Polychromy and Gibson spent an inordinate amount of time poring over his colour selections and which portions of the statue to add colour. In the end, the Venus' flesh was tinted ivory, her eyes were blue, her hair blonde and gathered at the back within a golden net. The apple was coloured gold and has the inscription *"to the most beautiful"* written in Greek lettering. The Venus's tunic remained white with delicate lines painted along the hems. The tortoise has the inscription *"Gibson made me in Rome"* written in Latin on its shell. The finished work made the original *Venus Verticordia* look drab in comparison, and *The Tinted Venus* glowing with life and iridescent with subtle hues and tints, was not only a superb sculpture but a vindication of Gibson's passionate belief that all statues were once painted by the sculptors of the classical world. Although Gibson had revived the ancient art of tinting, he was sagacious enough to use restraint and subtlety in his work, knowing quite well that the ancient Greeks had been far more lavish with their palettes and used glass, precious stones, gold and ivory to embellish their statues – the Victorian world wasn't ready for such extravagance just yet and Gibson knew it. When the statue was finally finished, Gibson opened his studio to anyone who wanted to see the completed Venus and curiosity was at such a level that hundreds passed through, from the crowned heads of Europe, art connoisseurs down to Gibson's neighbours. Gibson's fellow sculptors, whose opinion he valued most, were most complimentary but all of them told the same story; they dared not follow his example in case they were unable to sell their works – it seemed that even in Rome, Gibson's tinting was controversial.

256   ILLUSTRATED TIMES.   AUGUST 16, 1862.

THE TINTED VENUS, BY GIBSON, IN THE INTERNATIONAL EXHIBITION.

The Tinted Venus at the
International Exhibition
– Illustrated London News,
August, 1862

The International Exhibition, Kensington, 1862

Room to Breathe

"...and the superb carriages of the rich with their refined and elegant ladies threaded their way among sections of the population so miserable and squalid that my heart ached at the sight of them. I had seen wealth. I had seen poverty. But never before had I seen the two so jammed together."

– Reverend Armstrong,
Unitarian Church, Hope Street, 1885

The Mother of Invention

There is a widely held belief that the magnificent parks which encircle the outer edges of Liverpool were the brainchild of a visionary and philanthropic city council dedicated to improving the lives of the poor people of the city. While there may be some truth in that view the prime reason for the creation of what became known as the greenbelt was that from the late 1700s onwards British cities, including Liverpool, were choking in a lethal fug of their own making, forcing a national initiative to deal with the problem. Coal fires in every household and establishment sent constant clouds of smoke high in the air through a myriad of chimneys which ranged from the plain square brick of the plebeian to the highly ornamental beacons of the privileged, and the common understanding was that the smoke was somehow dispersed and lost in some mysterious way into the ether. But the axiom that *"what goes up must come down"* never seemed to occur to a population which coughed its way through life and the reality was that the smoke descended under its own weight, and day and night the city was silently blanketed in a fine dusting of toxic chemicals. Visitors and residents alike complained of the hazy atmosphere which pervaded the city streets and not one person was immune from the effects of the lethal miasma, from the housewife cursing the effects on her washing to the pallid ghosts walking the streets with all manner of pulmonary diseases; it has been said that the unique Liverpool twang was brought about by the polluted atmosphere of the city streets – if that's true then it was a high price to pay for being different. But the real problem was the ever-growing number of court dwellings and overcrowded houses in which the smoke from their coal fires was only a minor inconvenience in comparison to the diseases which were rife – cholera, typhoid, tuberculosis, smallpox, mumps and

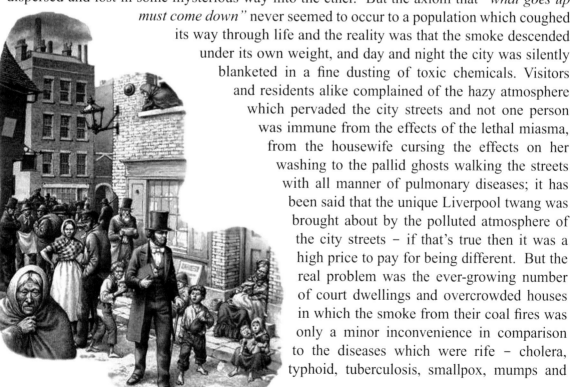

scarlet fever were just a few of the deadly accompaniments to everyday living. The insanitary living conditions of court dwellings where an earthen pit served for a toilet, often for over one hundred people, and the only water available was a cold water tap in the yard, combined with the chronic overcrowding to form a breeding ground for a myriad of contagious diseases.

If things were not bad enough with coal fires belching out their toxic fogs, the coming of the Industrial Age made matters worse and combined with a lack of legislation, from 1830 onwards, unsupervised factories and coal-fired trains spewed out an even more lethal chemical brew. It was a process which covered every building in Liverpool with sulfurous fumes, coating them in a black, tarry veneer which ruined the aesthetic value of everything it touched and it was a process which continued well into the following century until following the Clean Air Act of 1956 the beginnings of a return to a healthy environment began.

Other cities had similar agendas but as far as Liverpool was concerned, it was not by mere chance that the National Public Health Act of 1846 and the appointment of Dr William Henry Duncan (1805 - 1863) as the first Medical Officer of Health in Liverpool in 1847, coincided with the embryonic ideas for healthy outdoor spaces; and the Corporation of Liverpool's scheme for public parks was just one part of a grand plan to alleviate the sufferings of the denizens of the teeming rookeries of the city centre.

Court dwelling

An early solution to the problem of air pollution was the creation of landscaped *"squares"* which appeared to be fresh thinking by British town planners but had been a part of the Parisian landscape for centuries. Abercromby Square and Falkner Square were the Liverpool version of Parisian squares comprising a central landscaped area of shrubs, trees and floral displays surrounded by iron railings. The squares were surrounded by mansions which were far beyond the reach of even the hardest working artisans and were the homes of captains of industry, shipowners, factory owners and the well-heeled gentry of the town, each household with its own key to the gardens in their midst. Although the general public were banned from using the gardens and they were in fact the private domains of the aristocracy, it was a fact that when the city council had purchased the land for building, the price of the gardens was included in the cost and defrayed the expenses of landscaping and maintaining the garden squares. Falkner Square and Abercromby Square were extremely successful schemes, they attracted wealthy householders eager to escape the city smog and increasingly crowded city centre and willing to pay for the privilege. Whether the town planners and city councillors were influenced by the success of these squares is debatable, but knowingly or unknowingly Falkner and Abercromby Squares were the template for all the grand Liverpool Parks which followed. Princes Park, Sefton Park, Stanley Park and Newsham Park were in effect Falkner and Abercromby Squares on a grand scale and were funded in much the same way – the surrounding mansions were larger and the parks themselves were far more grandiose but the principle was the same with the surrounding property funding the landscaping and maintenance in much the same manner.

Abercromby Square prior to the modern Senate House

The Golden Age of Parks

Opened in 1847, Birkenhead Park on the Wirral is generally acknowledged as the first public park in the country and often quoted as the inspiration for New York's Central Park. Princes Park in Toxteth designed by Joseph Paxton, was built five years earlier than Birkenhead in 1842 but forfeited the honour of being the first public park by being in the nature of a private development although confusingly was open to the public. Significantly, the park itself was funded by the prospective buyers of the surrounding mansions who found the idea of a beautifully landscaped park an enticing inducement to buy. Although it was in effect a grander version of Abercromby Square and was built for the same reason − for the well-heeled to escape to more salubrious surroundings − Princes Park with its lake, boating house, tennis courts, landscaped areas and bedding schemes had all the elements of a Victorian park and became the template for every Liverpool park that came after.

Princes Park − circa 1900

The three great parks of Newsham, Stanley and Sefton were built roughly around the same time with Newsham Park being the first of the trio to be completed. The planning for Newsham began in 1846, the same year that the National Public Health Act came into force, when Liverpool Corporation purchased a 240 acre estate from the Molyneaux family at a cost of £85,000. At the heart of the estate was the Molyneaux mansion called Newsham House which narrowly escaped demolition by the park planners and later became the Judges' residence. In 1850, the

188

The windmill in Newsham Park.

Corporation acquired a neighbouring tract of land and together the two estates were intended to form the landscape upon which Newsham Park would arise. However, the wheels of local government grind slowly and the land designated for the park lay fallow for the next ten years – in which time there were several unforeseen incursions which would affect the original plans; in 1862, one portion of the land was neatly bisected by the newly-built Sheil Road while on the opposite side of the estate the Bootle railway line reduced the size even more. It was not until 1864 that work began on creating the park, nearly 20 years after its original conception, with Edward Kemp, a protégé of the great Paxton, chosen as the landscape architect with the expectation that Kemp would follow the example of his mentor and create a park similar to Princes Park. Again following the example set by Princes Park, the officers of Liverpool Corporation set aside tracts of land surrounding the park for sale to property developers, fully expecting a ring of prestigious mansions to arise around the park, both funding and enhancing the area at the same time. However, the council officers were in for a major setback when the land auctions were disappointingly low; it seems that the prospective purchasers believed the area to be less prestigious than Toxteth and the Bootle railway line made the land it backed onto virtually unsaleable – an unhappy situation for the Corporation but one that was quite serendipitous for a consortium of philanthropic gentlemen seeking a site for their projected orphanage. Once again Edward Kemp was forced to revise his plans for the park, on the one hand incorporating the unsold tracts of land into the park and on the other hand economising on features such as fountains, lakes and ornamental gates. It is intriguing to imagine the park as it would have been if so many eventualities had not forced Kemp into adapting his plans but it is to his credit that he managed to incorporate all the features of a Victorian park when Newsham officially opened in 1868, boasting an aviary, bowling greens, a bandstand, lakes, fountains, bedding displays and even a windmill which appeared to be a *"folly"* but was actually an ingenious piece of engineering which pumped water from one lake to another when the water in one lake overflowed; eventually a set of greenhouses was built near to Sheil Road which would make the park completely self-sufficient.

Stanley Park opened two years after Newsham Park in 1870 and once again Edward Kemp was the chosen landscape architect. It was unsurprising that the park was built upon similar lines to Newsham Park but there were many features which Newsham did not possess – a number of ornamental bridges overlooked the boating lake, a floral clock, the sunken garden with its hundreds of tiny sculptures, ornamental walls and overlooking it all the superb Gladstone Conservatory. In common with Newsham Park, Stanley also had a number of greenhouses which were hidden away from the public but were the means by which the substantial and complex bedding schemes were provided.

Stanley Park Terrace 1900.

J.A. Picton referred to it as a *"mania for building parks"* but in the latter part of the 1800s one magnificent park followed another and on the 20th May, 1872, Prince Arthur opened the finest park of all with the words *"For the health and enjoyment of the townspeople."* The park was of course Sefton Park and within the space of four years, three of the finest parks in the country had been built around the perimeter of Liverpool. Sefton Park was designed by the French landscape architect Ēdouard André and his Liverpool counterpart, Lewis Hornblower, and was and still is the jewel in the crown of a magnificent trio of archetypal Victorian parks. Built on a much larger scale than Newsham and Stanley Parks, Sefton was further embellished with ornate statuary, a diorama of J.M. Barrie's *Peter Pan* with a full-scale model of the pirate ship, 2 small cannon from the Royal Yacht *Victoria and Albert*, a Wendy House and a replica of Sir George Frampton's statue of *Peter Pan* in Kensington Gardens. The winding paths revealed one surprise after another to park visitors; limestone grottoes were a background to small ponds, swans floated gracefully among islands set in the series of lakes, the bandstand

*Mansion house surrounding
Sefton Park
– City Planning Dept*

which could only be reached by a small bridge, wooded copses of rhododendrons and other Victorian favourites, bowling greens, an aviary, a boating lake and even an area set aside for archery as well as the obligatory set of greenhouses. Overlooking it all was the crystalline and geometrically perfect Palm House which housed a host of tropical plants and orchids with statues by Benjamin Spence tastefully placed beneath the foliage. The outside corners of the Palm House each have a statue by the French sculptor Léon-Joseph Chavalliaud which include explorers Captain Cook and Christopher Columbus, navigators Gerardus Mercator and Henry the Navigator, botanists and explorers Charles Darwin, Carl Linnaeus and John Parkinson and landscape architect André le Notre. Whereas the idea of framing the parks with mansion houses was only successful to a degree at Newsham and Stanley parks, the plan worked to perfection at Sefton and besides funding the work in park proper the superb houses circling the park are architectural gems in their own right and the park and its necklace of stately mansions form a priceless heritage of Victorian industry and ingenuity.

*Mansion house
surrounding Sefton Park
– City Planning Dept*

It was difficult to imagine anything which could enhance the park any further and Sefton was the epitome of all that a Victorian park aspired to be; however, there was one more feature which was unique to Sefton which was a ring of sand between the houses and the railings set-aside for horse-riding after the fashion of Rotten Row, so that the horses from the stables in the mansion houses could be exercised or ridden by their owners on a course outside their front doors. Although over the years the riding track has served more as a giant sand-pit to generations of local children this is one element of Sefton Park which adds to a lingering suspicion that the wealthy and influential aristocracy living around the park were deferred to more than any of the ragamuffins from the city centre slums. There were several other factors which hinted at the same tacit class distinction – one of which was an unwritten dress code in which collar and tie were required before entry to the park. The other factor was one which was common to all the newly built parks; there is no doubt that the Corporation were to be commended for their creation of open spaces for the teeming masses in the city centre slums bursting at the seams, but when the idea was first mooted in the 1840s there was no form of public transport and there was no indication of how the people most in need of clean air and bucolic surroundings would get to them. The first tramways company only began in 1870 with horse-drawn vehicles and it is difficult to envisage any of them brimming with coachloads of what was termed *"the labouring classes"* to the parks especially since many of them hardly had two halfpennies to rub together and others whose priorities lay in other directions. In reality, the first years of the trio of public parks in Liverpool were the in the main the province of those who lived in the surrounding mansion houses. It was only when the city expanded outwards and affordable housing lapped at the gates of a Utopian suburbia that the parks were eventually peopled by those that they were originally built for.

Sefton Park entrance

Liverpool and its Corporation were not to know it but the trio of great public parks, Newsham, Stanley and Sefton, would soon be supplemented by an astonishing number of new parks across the city in an unprecedented era when private ownership proved too expensive and estates fell like skittles. In the Woolton area alone, Camp Hill, Clarke Gardens, Allerton Tower, Allerton Golf Course, Reynolds's Park and Calderstones estates all came into public ownership while further afield Sudley, Walton Hall, Croxteth and many others came under the aegis of Liverpool Corporation. The demise of the great estates was a phenomenon which was not unique to Liverpool and happened countrywide but in this city it left a legacy of parks which are unparalleled in their numbers and quality. Given the manner in which the great estates fell in such a short period of time and in such a dramatic fashion after the First World War it is quite surprising how little has been written on the subject, but the fact is that it was the end of a way of life for an aristocracy which had owned great swathes of land and lived in luxury for hundreds of years. There were traditionalists who mourned the passing of the great landowners but there were others who celebrated the downfall of the upstairs/downstairs regime and applauded the return of the land into public ownership. But while traditionalists mourned and subversaries rejoiced, a whole host of coachmen, ostlers, cooks, servants, and others found themselves without work and some whose housing was tied to their work found themselves homeless, and all were forced to look for work elsewhere. In a strange way the numerous gardening staff were better off than most, in that a Corporation with such huge tracts of parks needed staff to look after them and inadvertently acquired a highly- skilled workforce of specialist gardeners able to maintain stove-houses, orchids, herbaceous borders and bedding schemes while others were adept at growing fruit and vegetables and still more knowledgeable in the care of the tropical plants which were in such vogue at that time. For a few short years Liverpool Corporation employed a highly skilled workforce of gardeners raised on a Victorian work ethic which transferred easily to the Liverpool parks and from the latter years of the 1800s right up to the beginning of the 2nd World War – it was truly a Golden Era.

Peter Pan, Sefton Park, by Sir George Frampton

The opening of Stanley Park in 1870 was the subject of an article in the *London Illustrated News* with the accompanying drawing below. The ladies and gentlemen strolling around the park are all genteel families with not a working class family in sight.

Wealth and Poverty

The Great Chasm

"I'll fares the land, to hastening ills a prey,
Where wealth accumulates, and men decay."

– Oliver Goldsmith

The sinking of the Chimborazo in 1878 off the coast of Australia.
London Illustrated News

Life and Death at Sea

Successive maps of Liverpool from the Georgian era to the late Victorian era and beyond illustrate clearly an astonishing growth of streets and houses spreading outwards from what was once a pleasant littoral waterfront of fishing boats and cottages. There's no mystery as to why Liverpool expanded in such a dramatic manner – it was simply in accordance with the unprecedented growth of the maritime trade which turned the River Mersey into a highway for ships and boats of every shape and size, while hundreds of others were crammed into the docks loading and unloading their cargoes. Year after year, the farmland surrounding the city centre was further engulfed by a tide of humanity and the bucolic landscape covered over by an avalanche of bricks and mortar. A glance at a map drawn in 1850 shows the city centre transformed into a bewildering network of streets and houses creeping ever outwards, with no room for a grassy square or even the odd tree to soften the harshness of the environment. There seemed to be no end to the manic craze for building streets and houses and no idea where

*The bustle of the docks in Victorian times
by Gustave Dore*

it would all end but the population explosion created a demand which had to be met. In 1850 Princes Park still stood in splendid isolation but already the tide of houses was lapping at the foot of Park Road windmill while another was flanking the park from the river side as far as Northumberland Street and soon the park and its necklace of imposing houses would be surrounded on all sides by a labyrinth of new streets and a sea of back-to-back terraced houses. In the city centre itself while the prestigious homes of wealthy merchants in Duke Street and Hanover Street still maintained their respectable reputations, they had been engulfed by a maze of cheap court houses, both overcrowded and unsanitary. On the eastern side of the city the river of houses had flowed up to the heights of Mount Vernon and lapped at the base of the rustic heights of Everton Brow where wealthy merchants lived in isolated splendour – for the time being. And to the northern extremities of the city, Scotland Road was slowly being flooded with scores of streets, terraced houses and courts which would soon be densely overpopulated bringing all the ills that accompanied such conditions. A brief examination of the addresses of Liverpudlians at that time shows that people of means were also moving outwards to escape the noise and bustle of the waterfront; they moved to the still rural surroundings of Seaforth, Edge Hill, Ullet Road and Everton while in the main the city became populated by those who made their living from the sea – and there were many of them. The Liverpool of mid-Victorian times was in effect a city devoted in its entirety to maritime matters and most of its citizens worked in shipping in some capacity – whether it was going to sea attracted by the lure of exotic sounding names, or loading a cornucopia of strange cargoes, driving massive shire-horses or simply selling ship's stores, there was work for anyone who wanted it on quaysides swarming with dock labourers and cluttered with the paraphernalia associated with ships. But there was a downside to life on the docks, and in the days before Health and Safety and risk assessments injuries to dock workers were commonplace – but if the dockside could be a dangerous place then life at sea was immeasurably more hazardous and casualties were commonplace; the statistics for 1866 at a time when steamships were fast making sailing ships redundant were that British merchant seamen in that year numbered 196,371, of which there were 4,866 deaths with 2,390 of these from drownings – it was estimated that 75% of seamen at that time could not swim. Further statistics revealed that a deceased married sailor left a widow and an average of three children with the great majority of those families utterly destitute.

It was plain for all to see that some kind of relief was long overdue for the widows and orphans of seamen whose hazardous occupation led to their deaths and it was only fitting that those who had most knowledge of those deaths, in their ledgers and files and logbooks, namely the shipowners, who should be the prime movers in the creation of an orphanage. In an age when employees were killed or injured at work in any given occupation and received little if any recompense, and there was little if any obligation placed upon the employer to provide a safe working environment, the Liverpool shipowners had no legal requirements to do anything whatsoever, but it was to their credit that they did feel a great responsibility towards their seamen and they acted out of moral and not legal obligations.

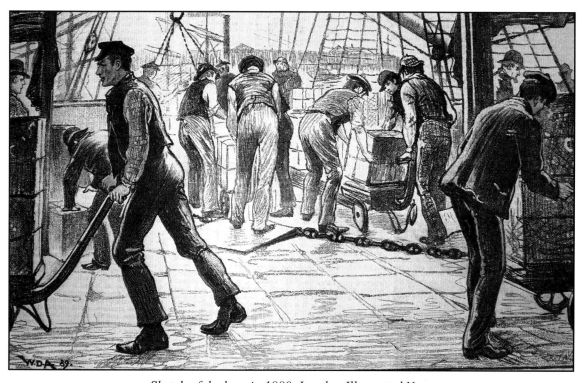

Sketch of dockers in 1889. London Illustrated News

Temporary Accommodation

Charitable institutions had been provided in the past but they were few and far between and in common with the projected orphanage were totally dependent on the goodwill of philanthropists and the financial donations of the wealthy. Egerton Smith, the founder of *The Liverpool Mercury,* saw the poverty in the city every day of his life and in 1830 founded a temporary dwelling place for the needy in Freemasons Row, a narrow street off Vauxhall Road, calling his refuge The Liverpool Night Asylum For The Homeless Poor. Nobody was excluded from the asylum which visitors were pleasantly surprised to find clean and well run, and at any one time there would be survivors fleeing the Irish Potato Famine, seamen, labourers, the homeless and a great many children, some of them orphans, with the numbers of boys greatly outnumbering the girls. As time went by and Vauxhall Road and its environs were overtaken by manufacturing industries and clusters of court dwellings, the area declined alarmingly since Egerton Smith first founded the asylum and in 1849 an onlooker described Freemasons Row in the following manner. *"The courts in this street defy description. The senses powerfully repelled approach; interior gained I found human inhabitants closely mixed up in a strange and sad confusion, with ruinous privies and cesspools of the worst and most offensive kind."*

It was hardly surprising that Freemasons Row and the surrounding streets were in the winter of 1849 afflicted with some of the worst cases of cholera yet seen in the city and in the same year the asylum closed its doors to be incorporated into an existing workhouse. Nevertheless, in its day, the asylum had housed many thousands of the most poverty stricken and had undoubtedly saved many of them from an early grave, and as basic as it was in its provisions for the poor, it was a marker for the forthcoming orphanage. In December, 1838, Egerton Smith had printed his ledger for the preceding 8 years – the figures make astonishing reading with no less than 122,736 souls finding refuge there.

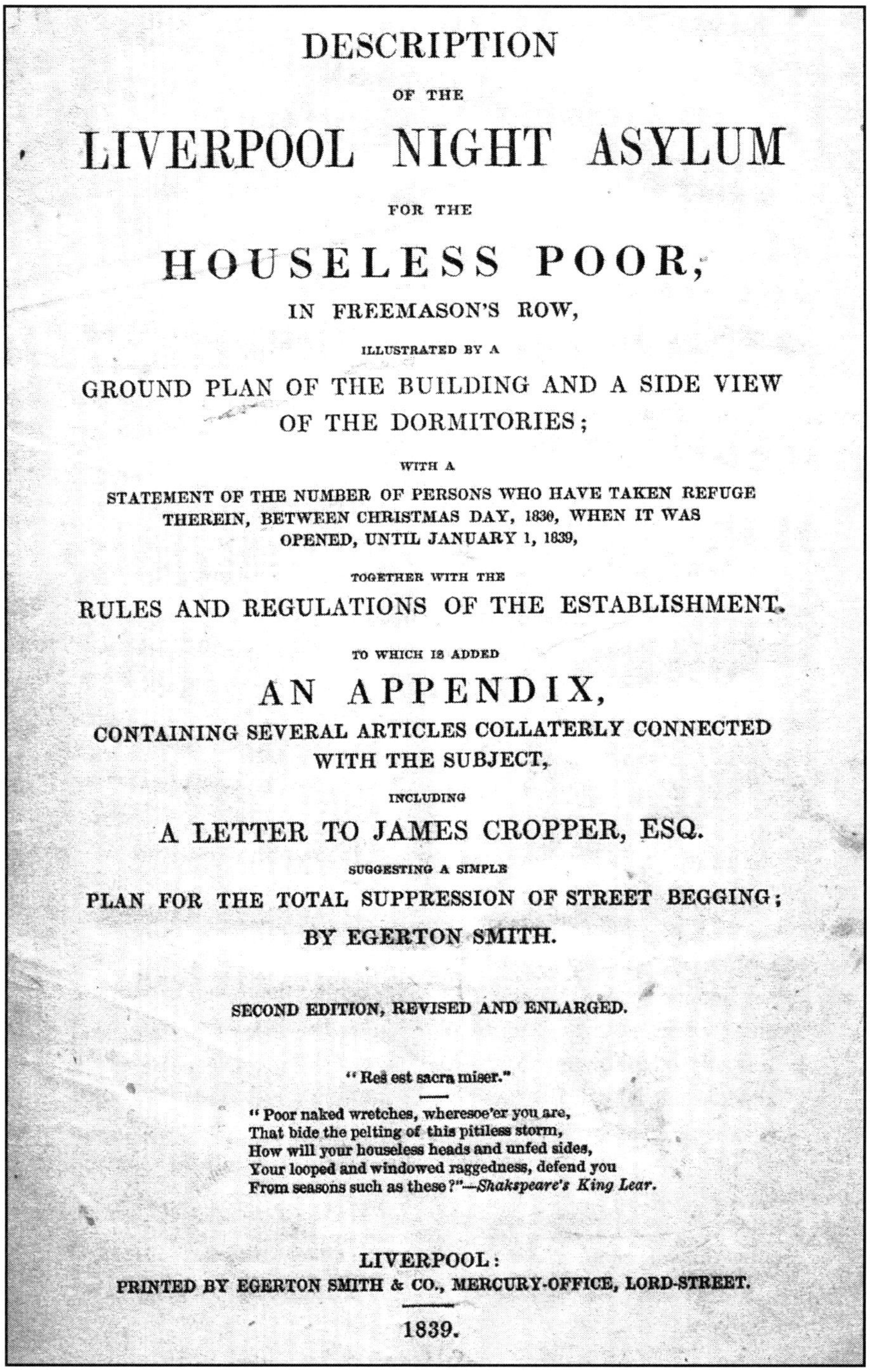

DESCRIPTION

OF THE

LIVERPOOL NIGHT ASYLUM

FOR THE

HOUSELESS POOR,

IN FREEMASON'S ROW,

ILLUSTRATED BY A

GROUND PLAN OF THE BUILDING AND A SIDE VIEW OF THE DORMITORIES;

WITH A

STATEMENT OF THE NUMBER OF PERSONS WHO HAVE TAKEN REFUGE THEREIN, BETWEEN CHRISTMAS DAY, 1830, WHEN IT WAS OPENED, UNTIL JANUARY 1, 1839,

TOGETHER WITH THE

RULES AND REGULATIONS OF THE ESTABLISHMENT.

TO WHICH IS ADDED

AN APPENDIX,

CONTAINING SEVERAL ARTICLES COLLATERLY CONNECTED WITH THE SUBJECT,

INCLUDING

A LETTER TO JAMES CROPPER, ESQ.

SUGGESTING A SIMPLE

PLAN FOR THE TOTAL SUPPRESSION OF STREET BEGGING;

BY EGERTON SMITH.

SECOND EDITION, REVISED AND ENLARGED.

"Res est sacra miser."

"Poor naked wretches, wheresoe'er you are,
That bide the pelting of this pitiless storm,
How will your houseless heads and unfed sides,
Your looped and windowed raggedness, defend you
From seasons such as these?"—*Shakspeare's King Lear.*

LIVERPOOL:

PRINTED BY EGERTON SMITH & CO., MERCURY-OFFICE, LORD-STREET.

1839.

Smith Egerton leaflet for the Liverpool Night Asylum

E. SMITH AND CO., PRINTERS, LIVERPOOL.

EIGHT YEARS' RETURN

OF THE

NUMBER OF INMATES EACH YEAR FROM THE OPENING OF THE PERMANENT NIGHT ASYLUM

FOR THE HOUSELESS POOR, IN FREEMASON'S ROW,

From December 25, 1830, to December 31, 1838.

	NUMBER OF BERTHS OR BEDS FOR						YEARLY SUMMARY.			
	Seamen.	Mechanics and Labourers.	Women.	Boys.	Girls.	Children.	Number of Berths.	Average number of Berths.	No. of both sexes admitted.	Actual number quitted.
From 25th December, 1830, to 1831...	11330	15587	3918	1348	792	576	33551	90	6237	6222
1832...	5998	7711	1507	658	330	262	16466	45	5204	5222
1833...	4104	5444	1260	529	225	207	11769	32	4028	4043
1834...	3216	4685	1207	527	234	261	10130	27	4074	4059
1835...	3653	4522	1016	434	201	262	10088	27	3684	3659
1836..	1638	5311	2095	595	361	559	10559	28	4667	4675
1837...	2466	8073	2915	962	559	806	15781	39	7480	7453
1838...	1575	7479	3118	876	582	762	14392	39	6892	6896
	33980	58812	17066	5929	3284	3695	122736	..	42266	42229

☞ From this statement it appears that the number of berths or sleeping accommodations provided during the eight years has been ONE HUNDRED AND TWENTY-TWO THOUSAND SEVEN HUNDRED AND THIRTY-SIX; and as the actual number of individuals was 42,266, it follows that the average stay of each individual has been between two and three nights.

Smith Egerton 8 year return

The first stirrings of activity towards the creation of an orphanage came at a meeting held in Water Street on December 16th, 1868, which was attended by Liverpool shipowners and members of the public and set out the aims of the embryonic committee. A joint resolution drafted by Ralph Brocklebank and Bryce Allan, both shipowners and well-known philanthopists was read out confirming *"the moral obligation resting upon the shipowners of this great port to provide for the protection and education of the Mercantile Marine orphan children resolves that an establishment for feeding, clothing and educating the fatherless children of seamen be brought before the merchants, shipowners and general public of Liverpool for support."* The resolution went on to say that there were already many existing institutions but they were so badly supported *"that they have to struggle for their very life."* There was nothing revelatory about the speaker's further remarks that *"these struggling and most admirable institutions are full to overflowing of rescued innocents and so are our streets and courts and alleys full to overflowing of perishing innocents"* – it was in fact common knowledge, but at a time when the gap between rich and poor had turned into a chasm, it was inevitable that institutions which relied on public donations would struggle in an environment where charity, of necessity, began at home. However, it was heartening for those present to hear that *"Liverpool will not be long without a Seaman's Orphan Institution"* and as a statement of intent it could hardly be clearer; but even more encouraging was the speaker's proposal for a temporary house while the building fund for the new accommodation swelled, which made it clear that this project was no nebulous idea to be forgotten somewhere down the line. The list of subscribers to the scheme read like a Who's-Who of Liverpool shipping – R. Brocklebank, James Beazley, John Farnworth, Clark Aspinall, Alexander Balfour, Bryce Allan, William Inman, David MacIver, J. Aspinall Tobin, George Henry Horsfall, H. J.Ward and C.H.E Judkins – all of them with one exception leading shipowners, fabulously wealthy and extremely influential in the town, and it was no exaggeration to say that they formed the bedrock of Liverpool's commercial empire at sea. The single exception was Captain Judkins who was a renowned Commodore of the Cunard fleet.

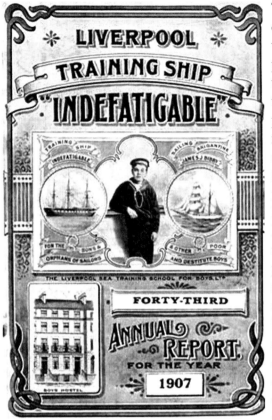

The man who was chosen as chairman of the committee that was drawn up was James Beazley who had already carved out a reputation for philanthropic works aimed at young people with the establishment of the training ship for officers the *Conway,* the training ship for boys from poor backgrounds, T.S. *Indefatigable,* and the reformatory ships *Akbar*, for Protestant boys and *Clarence*, for Catholic boys, all anchored in the Sloyne off Birkenhead. Beazley was not slow in following up the meeting in Water Street with a letter sent from his home at Fern Hill, Oxton, on February, 17th, 1869, addressed to all the committee members. The letter was short and straight to the point in which Beazley promised to donate the sum of £500 on the condition that every one of the other committee members donated the same sum by the 30th June, 1869, which *"would give £5,000 at once, which I propose should be specially held towards a building fund and I think if that sum was actually in hand and a suitable advertisement put out to landowners we should stand a good chance of having a site presented to us, or we might ask the Dock Board or the Corporation to give us some land."* Beazley's proposal was answered almost immediately and the £5,000 raised, supplemented by some donations from the better-off members of the public, allowed the search for temporary accommodation for the orphan children to begin at once. A suitable house was soon found at 128 Duke Street, on the corner of Kent Street – a large 3-storied building which was converted into rooms containing dormitories, kitchens, classrooms and staff accommodation. Following the addition of furniture and fittings the Liverpool Seamen's Orphan Institution came into existence on August 9th, 1869, and the first group of needy children admitted into the sanctuary of a caring foster home. By the end of 1869, there were 46 boys and 14 girls living in the Institution entrusted to the care of the matron, Miss McGregor, who was also in charge of the staff. From the initial meeting in Water Street in December 1868, it had taken just 8 months for the home to come into being – the Corporation of Liverpool were never able to act so speedily or efficiently and it was easy to see why such dynamism had brought the shipowners such success in their business dealings.

When Life Was Real and Life Was Earnest

The first President of the Institution was Mr Ralph Brocklebank and his first address to subscribers was on 25th January, 1872, where he emphasised that the education of the children was a paramount requisite of their care; it was a stricture which would remain in place throughout the whole existence of the Orphanage. Brocklebank was quite precise concerning the educational procedures for the children, beginning with the requirement that entry to the Orphanage would only begin from the age of 6 up to the age of 14 which made it clear that higher education was precluded from the curriculum. From the list on the curriculum it was quite obvious that the programme was designed to provide a solid grounding in basic educational subjects which would be attractive to any prospective employer and at the very least would provide the orphan children with some survival skills inherent in Victorian life – it was as quoted by Brocklebank, a curriculum for an age *"when life was real and life was earnest."* The hours of learning were to be from 9 o'clock until 12 and from 2 o'clock to 4 with another hour of tuition in the evening with the lessons comprising scripture, writing, composition, arithmetic, reading, history, grammar, geography, mapping, dictation and bookkeeping. Free hand drawing and mechanical drawing were also taught in the expectation that the boys would enter into engineering work, possibly aboard ship. The children were also taught *"to clean knives, to clean plate, to scrub floors, to wash their own linen, to knit, to mend their own clothes and also to make bread"* – all subjects useful to a life in service. There was little time left for recreation and the regime seems harsh by present day standards but it was not the present-day – it was a work ethic far more demanding than that of today and the *"tough-love"* regime would one day see the children leave the orphanage far better prepared to survive in a Victorian environment. But even in Victorian times the value of recreation was recognized as integral to any child's upbringing and as time went by the number of the children's *"treats"* increased, especially with the clergy taking an increasing interest in their welfare; there was no shortage of toys and gifts at Christmas, trips to the pantomimes were always popular, there were *"magic lantern"* shows and in summertime there were boat trips organized and paid for by the officers and crews from ships sailing the Mersey.

The Official Opening

While the children were being cared for at Duke Street, in the background the momentum for a permanent building had taken on a life of its own and became virtually unstoppable when on 7th April, 1870, the City Council gifted 7,000 square yards of land in Newsham Park specifically for the Orphanage. The land was of course the tract near to the railway line, which may not have been suitable for the landed gentry but was perfect for the Orphanage Committee who never imagined a few trains going by as anything of a problem, and plans were soon set up for the building itself. The design and planning for the Orphanage was given over to Alfred Waterhouse (1830 - 1905) whose reputation as an architect was impeccable. Born in Mossley Hill in July, 1830, Waterhouse was a champion of Gothic architecture who was commissioned to build Manchester Town Hall at the same time as the Orphanage – a workload which never bothered him as he was a prolific designer and had built up an impressive portfolio throughout the 1850s and 1860s which astonishingly ran into hundreds of different works across Lancashire and Wales and beyond as his reputation increased. The contract for building the Orphanage was won by a firm named Haigh and Company and with the foundation stone laid on September 11th, 1871, by Ralph Brocklebank.

In the same year of 1871, there was an epidemic of scarlet fever and smallpox throughout Liverpool city centre. The grossly overcrowded living conditions meant that any disease was difficult to contain and almost impossible to isolate so that when the diseases began to affect the children in the Duke Street orphanage it was a cause of great concern which prompted thoughts of an infirmary for the new building in Newsham Park. Ralph Brocklebank had already donated huge sums of money to the orphanage and there seemed no end to his generosity when he also paid for a sanatorium which opened in 1879, and if any good came of the periodic epidemics in Liverpool then it could be seen in Newsham infirmary. On 31st January, 1874, the building was nearly completed and 63 of the children from Duke Street joined with 46 new recruits to be the first children to enter into Newsham Park Seamen's Orphanage. By March 27th, 1874, the number of children in the home had risen to 200 but the admittance of the projected number of 400 orphans was hampered by the building still awaiting completion and once again more funds were requested by the Committee. The waiting list for the orphanage far exceeded its capacity and 62 children were being supported on an Outdoor Relief List which also required an extra budget.

Despite these setbacks the Institution was formally opened on September 30th, 1874, in a ceremony performed by The Duke of Edinburgh, Alfred, the 4th child of Victoria and Albert (1844 - 1900) – commonly known as *"The Sailor Prince"* which made him a fitting Royal to open the Liverpool Seamen's Orphanage. The opening ceremony was a grand affair which took place on a gloriously sunny September day; the roads leading to the building were lined with 1500 officers and men from the ships of the various shipping companies; there were contingents from H.M.S. *Caledonia* the naval guard-ship anchored in the Mersey and others from the Royal Naval Volunteer Reserve founded in 1859; still more in attendance were from the Royal Naval Artillery Volunteers and 100 men of the 19th Regiment of Foot arrived from Chester with their band. At 3.30 p.m. preceded by lancers *"at a sharp trot,"* the Royal party were received by Ralph Brocklebank at the chapel entrance and presented to James Beazley and members of the Committee. Following a rousing chorus of the hymn familiar to mariners across the globe, *Eternal Father Strong to Save,* which echoed throughout the chapel, the Duke inspected the orphanage before entering the huge dining hall filled with guests and the children wearing a small commemorative medal to mark the occasion. Following the obligatory speeches which must have caused some impatient shuffling among the children, Liverpool Seamen's Orphanage was officially declared open.

Chapel plaque - now in Our Lady and St Nicholas Church

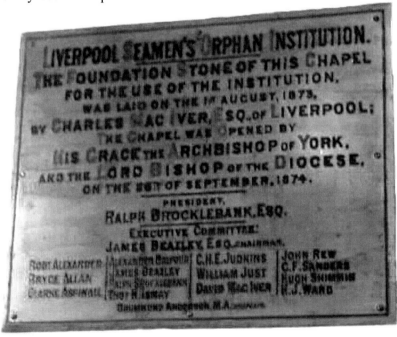

The opening of the orphanage by Prince Alfred, Duke of Edinburgh, 1874

A Strange Speech

There was a great deal of enthusiasm and goodwill for the new orphanage and when it was put forward that an adjoining infirmary and chapel were not only advantageous but virtually essential, the City Council readily agreed to cede the extra land required. The foundation stone for the chapel was laid on 1st August, 1873, by Charles MacIver (1812 - 1885) who had donated £1,000 to its construction. He used a commemorative silver trowel with an ivory handle made especially for the occasion by the renowned silversmith, Joseph Mayer of Lord Street – the trowel was inscribed *Presented to Charles MacIver Esq. on the occasion of his laying the foundation stone of the chapel of the Liverpool Seamen's Orphan Institution, 1st August, 1873.*

Charles MacIver
by Hubert von Herkomer 1882

Charles MacIver lived in the Mansion House, Calderstones, which later became Calderstones Park. Charles MacIver had in partnership with his brother David MacIver (1807 - 1845) and in association with Samuel Cunard, founded the celebrated Cunard Line. David MacIver (1840 - 1907) was the eldest son of Charles MacIver and his wife Mary and followed in the family tradition which went back centuries by founding his own shipping line in 1874. There is a common thread which runs through successful Victorian industrialists and that is the extraordinary amount of dynamism they applied to their work and the energy they applied to other aspects of their lives – apart from running his shipping line, David was chairman of the Liverpool Steamship Owners Association and President of the American Chamber of Commerce, a director of the Great Western Railway, a major in the 11th Lancashire Artillery Volunteers, an alderman and J.P. for Liverpool, commodore of the Royal Mersey Yacht Club, M.P. for Birkenhead and later M.P. for Kirkdale, and of course patron to many charities, most importantly the Seamen's Orphanage. David MacIver was just 23 when he married Ann Rankin (1842 - 1869) of Bromborough in 1863, and she was just 20 years of age. They had one child together and the future looked bright for the young couple, but David had more reason than most to support the Seamen's Orphanage when in 1869, aged just 27, Ann died in a tragic and futile accident when she drowned while bathing in the sea off Beaumaris, Anglesey. MacIver married again in 1873, to Edith Eleanor Squarey (1853 - 1940) and in the best traditions of Victorian family life, went on to produce 11 children.

Following the laying of the foundation stone ceremony, the whole group including the orphan children went inside the Chapel where hymns were interspersed with the usual speeches from several dignitaries. The event was marked by a touching gesture from an orphan girl who stepped up to place a silver coin in the collection box, followed by the whole of the assembled children who all followed her example; it seems that on the previous day, the ever-generous Mr Brocklebank had presented every child in the orphanage with a freshly-minted silver coin as a souvenir of the occasion and the children had mutually decided that their coins would be better served collectively for the Chapel fund. The final speech was made by Charles MacIver himself and following some conventional remarks he went on to say that *"The Chapel would be indisputably a Protestant Chapel, subject to the laws – the known and declared laws of the Church of England"* – a vow which was met with enthusiastic applause from his audience. Seemingly encouraged by the warm reception for his views MacIver expanded on his theme and his speech concluded in a startling manner by mocking the rituals of the Catholic Church *"the confessional would never be allowed"* was just one of his lesser statements while *"a ritual in full blast* (which referred to Mass) *would be destructive of all moral and social life and order if practised in a Protestant Church"* was another.

By today's standards, MacIver's speech was insulting and inflammatory but the most remarkable thing of all was the reaction of his audience which included hundreds of impressionable children who universally greeted his anti-Catholic diatribe as something quite normal. And in many ways it was normal because it has largely been forgotten that religious prejudice throughout Liverpool at that time was widespread in every walk of life. It was a remarkable fact that from the Reformation of the 16th century onwards, Catholics could barely practise their religion and it was only following the Catholic Emancipation Act of 1829 that Catholics were allowed to sit in Parliament or indeed play a part in many facets of English life. Although the Catholic Emancipation Act was a beginning, it took more than an Act of Parliament to eradicate the widespread religious bigotry which was most apparent in Northern cities such as Manchester, Glasgow and Liverpool, and the situation was to become even worse from the 1840s onwards with the massive influx of Irish Catholics escaping the potato famine. Thrown together in mutual poverty with many of them out of work, Catholics and Protestants became ever more hostile in the warrens of court housing in Liverpool, resulting in a simmering separatism which often spilled over into fist fights and sometimes all out brawls. It didn't help that Charles Darwin's revolutionary book on evolution, *On the Origin of Species*, published in 1859, was used in some quarters to demonise the Irish as a backward species, and it is a sad fact that the Victorian era was one of sectarianism and prejudice where pillars of the community such as Charles MacIver were able to mock the Catholic Church and be cheered for their efforts. From the turn of the century onwards Catholics and Protestants became more tolerant of each other but religious prejudice in Liverpool continued well into the 1930s in a world where marriage between Catholic and Protestant was as acrimonious as that between the Montagues and Capulets and football teams were quantified as leaning to one religion or the other. Although it was fast dying away, even as late as the 1960s and 1970s there were lingering vestiges of prejudice, until Bishop David Sheppard and Archbishop Derek Warlock worked together in harmony to eradicate the remaining religious divisions in Liverpool and the goodwill they fought to bring about can never be overestimated – there is a statue, fittingly in Hope Street, commemorating both men.

Religious graffiti.
St Andrews Street 1967. Liverpool Echo

A Gothic Orphanage

Although almost all of Alfred Waterhouse's buildings are typically grand and imposing, invariably incorporate aspects of Gothic architecture and include a tower wherever possible, the architect was quite capable of introducing *"softening"* elements into his designs; The Natural History Museum which has all of the above features and manages to have two towers has become a well-loved icon in South Kensington, London, while the Liverpool University Victoria Building with its ornate, gilded clock tower and terracotta and Ruabon stone brickwork is strikingly decorative. The interior of the university's Victoria Building is reminiscent of the interior of the Victoria and Albert Museum, also in South Kensington, with colourful tiles, curved columns, glazed brickwork and ornamental arches where the words *"cheerful"* and *"welcoming"* come to mind.

Unfortunately, there was little that could be construed as cheery or welcoming about Waterhouse's orphanage; the building was undoubtedly imposing and grand with the architect's hallmark tower next to the entrance but somewhere along the way Waterhouse had forsaken those architectural touches which are so endearing to well-loved buildings and had managed to conjure up the popular conception of what a Victorian orphanage looked like – austere and functional and to small children probably frightening. Apart from a few small sandstone sculptures there were few reminders that the building was the Seamen's Orphanage. Inside the building everything seemed to be designed on the grand scale making small children appear even smaller, with a massive dining-hall, reminiscent of Oliver Twist and Mr Bumble, at its heart and it's almost certain that no minstrels ever played in the minstrel's gallery overlooking the great hall. Economics undoubtedly influenced Waterhouse's design for the orphanage, not least in his choice of common brick and the lack of ornamentation, but if it were not for the softening influence of the lake and the pleasant parkland surroundings, Liverpool Seamen's Orphanage could well have been described as more forbidding than welcoming.

Sketch of the orphanage. Liverpool Record Office

And The Rains Came Down

*"Wherever you go, no matter what the weather,
always bring your own sunshine."*

– *Anthony J. D'Angelo*

Distinguished Visitors

ᴀᴛᴇᴅ ᴏᴍᴏᴏᴀᴜᴇ ᴀᴇʟ ғᴀʏᴅ, sᴜʟᴛᴀɴ ᴏғ ᴢᴀɴᴢɪʙᴀʀ.

The Sultan of Zanzibar.

In the following years the standards which had been defined within the confines of the Duke Street establishment transferred seamlessly to the spacious new building in the park where they were refined and improved with the help of an increasing number of benefactors; doctors, dentists and *"friends"* gave up their free time on a voluntary basis and every Sunday morning James Beazley took the ferry from his home on the Wirral to attend the service in the chapel. As applications for admission to the orphanage increased the Committee were forced to become more selective, and children were turned away when it was believed that they could be looked after at home with assistance and grants of money and donations of clothing, while others were precluded because their religions would have caused difficulties in supplying their needs. Before long there were actually more children being assisted outside the orphanage than were inside and as with all charitable institutions past and present many staff hours were spent dreaming up new methods of sourcing money. Prize-giving day was held each year in the Town Hall where the Lord Mayor presented prizes to boys and girls who had been outstanding in academic or sporting prowess, while an appreciative crowd of orphanage boys dressed in sailor suits and girls in long, blue dresses and white pinafores, clapped and cheered. At the end of the day the children received oranges and buns, but for the orphanage staff the occasion was always a chance to highlight the work carried out at the orphanage and its financial demands. Other visitors to the orphanage were the Judges, but what the staff and children made of one exotic visitor from a land which seemed so unimaginably remote as to be a land of fable, would be difficult to imagine; at the invitation of Queen Victoria, the Sultan of Zanzibar spent several months in England in the summer of 1875, where it was the intention to inveigle him into signing a treaty which would lead to the end of the slave-trade in Zanzibar. The Sultan was entertained in cities across the country and treated as an honoured guest at Westminster and on the 8th July, 1875, was an object of wonder to the children in Newsham Park Orphanage when he was invited to see how children were looked after in a civilized society.

A decade later, the orphanage would be visited by the far less flamboyant figure of Queen Victoria who made up in dignity and bearing for what she may have lacked in resplendent robes and knives in her sashes.

The Visit of Queen Victoria

In May, 1886, the grandly-named International Exhibition of Navigation, Commerce and Industry was ready to open to a public which was happier to refer to it as The Shipperies Exhibition. The site of the Exhibition was adjacent to Botanic Park on Edge Lane and for all its magnificence, which lasted throughout the summer of 1886, today there is nothing to show that the Shipperies ever existed – apart from the architecturally superb Shipperies public house on Durning Road which today stands forlorn among a sea of modern mediocre buildings, and even in its derelict days is far more handsome than any of its surroundings. The Exhibition was a celebration of Liverpool achievements in manufacturing and industry with a particular focus on maritime matters in which the city was acknowledged as the busiest port in the country if not the world, and the Queen herself would open the Exhibition. Queen Victoria and her retinue of Prince Arthur, (the Duke of Connaught), Princess Beatrice, the last of Victoria's children, and her husband, Prince Henry of Battenburg, and General Sir Henry Ponsonby, left Windsor aboard the 10 past midnight express train arriving at the specially built siding at Exhibition Road at 6 minutes to eight on the morning of Monday, 10th May, 1886. Exhibition Road stood between Wavertree Road and Picton Road, roughly where the Littlewoods Building now stands, and it was from there that the Royal party left for their temporary lodgings in Newsham House.

The Queen's carriage leaving the Exhibition

On the following day, Tuesday, 11th May, the rain came down in torrents as the Queen arrived to open the Exhibition where she was visibly moved as she was welcomed by 50,000 cheering schoolchildren. The Queen opened the gates of the Exhibition with a golden key and knighted the Lord Mayor, Sir David Radcliffe, who had welcomed her to Liverpool on her previous visit to the city as long ago as 1851. She was then driven around the wonders of the Exhibition which included among other things *"a captive balloon,"* a Gypsy camp, an Indian village, an Ashanti village, an African village, exotic animals and a 170 foot tall replica of the Eddystone Lighthouse. In the evening, a grand banquet was held in the Town Hall where the latest technology was employed, with every speaker having a telephone so that the speeches could be relayed to the Queen who had stayed at Newsham House. The Duke of Connaught was presented with a ceremonial sword and Prince Henry of Battenburg was reported to be delighted with a new hunting whip.

On Wednesday, the 12th of May, the torrential rain was accompanied by a vicious gale which had blown up in the night when the Queen once again set out from Newsham House. Passing through a floral arch, her first destination was the nearby Seamen's Orphanage where the children were assembled and a band played the national anthem. The Queen, the Duke and Prince Henry were shown around the various facilities by the matron, and as a mother herself, Victoria was interested in speaking to some of the children. When the time came to depart the Queen dutifully signed the visitor's book with her name and all her titles which ran into quite a list – Order of the Indian Empire, Order of the Garter, Order of the Bath, Order of the Thistle, were just a few – but this was one occasion when Victoria *was* amused; when the time came for the matron to sign the book, several lines down from the Queen's titles she carefully wrote her own name which was simply *"Fanny."* Leaving the orphanage Victoria's carriage went onto the Shipperies Exhibition once again for a short time until she left for a tour of the streets on her way to the city centre; despite the rain the Queen and her party drove in an open carriage along Exhibition Road and on to Wavertree Road and Tunnel Road passing through *"a district occupied by industrious artisans"* as the journalist of *The Penny Illustrated Paper* wrote so succinctly. On they travelled past Princes Park, along Princes Boulevard to Catharine Street, Myrtle Street, the Philharmonic Hall, Hardman Street and down Leece Street, passing Rodney Street which was pointed out as her Prime Minister, William Ewart Gladstone's birthplace – a fact which would not have impressed her greatly as the Queen and Gladstone's relationship was always frosty at best. As the carriage passed the Adelphi Hotel and entered Lime Street the Royal party passed beneath one of several handsome floral arches before reaching a decorative canopy between the lions of St George's Hall where the Queen was greeted by thousands of well-wishers who had braved the dreadful conditions for a sight of their sovereign and filled the plateau and street to overflowing. It went without saying that it was a shame that the weather was so bad because a great deal of thought and effort had gone into making a theatrical display on the grand scale where St George's Hall was transformed into a vast stage with floral arches at every entry and exit point – London Road, Lime Street, Byrom Street and Dale Street. There was also a grand arch on Castle Street on the approach to the Town Hall. The city was *en fête* but the rain was unrelenting.

Lime Street decorations

Queen Victoria and preparations for her river cruise

Following the obligatory welcoming speeches the Royal party set off once again, this time down William Brown Street, *"skirting the Irish Quarter close to Scotland Road where many Irish men and women. many with shawls on their heads, cheered the entourage."* From Byrom Street and the be-shawled Irish ladies, the carriage travelled down Dale Street and onto Woodside landing stage where, despite the wind and rain, the Queen embarked on the steamship *Claughton* which was flanked by the steamers *Alert* and *Vigilant* for a river cruise. The river was filled with ships of all shapes and sizes but the Queen's main interest was in Brunel's famous folly, *The Great Eastern* which was anchored in the river. When Victoria viewed the once proud *Leviathan,* the great ship was owned by Louis Cohen of Lewis's department store in partnership with James Baines whose career was also drawing to a sad end. Baines had once walked the quays of Liverpool waterfront as the proud owner of the Black Ball Line whose clipper ships *Marco Polo, Lightning, Champion of the Seas* and many others had enthralled the Liverpool public who lined the docksides each time a Baines' ship sailed into the river. Both Baines and *The Great Eastern* were desperately trying to recapture some of the old magic that had once surrounded both of them and the giant ship was now a showboat open to the public. Baines had persuaded Louis Cohen to purchase the ship for a sum of £15,000 which seemed a poor investment until Baines reminded Cohen of the numbers of visitors to the city in the year of the Shipperies Exhibition which ran from May to November. In the event, a staggering 2.6 million visitors attended the Shipperies Exhibition and many of them went on to see *The Great Eastern,* making the venture a financial success for both men. In a strange twist of fate *The Great Eastern* began to be dismantled on January, 1889, on the beach at New Ferry, and 2 months later on the 8th March, 1889, James Baines died in Nile Street, which was also demolished later as part of the building programme for the Anglican Cathedral. James Baines' headstone is in Toxteth Cemetery where his name can still be seen with difficulty after years of English weather have played havoc with the sandstone headstone.

Later in the day, with her duties fulfilled despite the horrendous weather, the Queen returned to Newsham House from where she would return to Windsor on the following day. The same evening, Lady Radcliffe presented the Queen with a gold bracelet encrusted with diamonds and in return Lady Radcliffe received two engravings of the Queen in state taken from the original oil-paintings. On Thursday, 13th May, the Queen departed leaving £100 for charitable purposes.

Underneath The Arches

The constant rain and wind had made life difficult for the workmen building the canopy and arches in the city centre but they were completed in time for her visit, with the arch leading out of Lime Street and up London Road the most decorative and meant as an impressive and bold finale to her visit. Passing on their way to work people had become used to walking beneath the arch which was 70 foot in height and could hardly be avoided as it straddled the width of London Road. By Saturday 8th May, two days before the Queen's arrival in the city, the carpenters and workmen had departed, confident that their work was finished, and people passed under the huge arch headed for their workplaces. Unusual for the time of year, the gales had been blowing fiercely for days and accompanied by heavy rain had become just a passing nuisance, until at 8.30 a.m. an exceptionally strong gust of wind caught the wooden structure and blew it down. The arch fell down so suddenly that although several people were agile enough to leap out of the way a number of others were crushed and badly injured beneath the heavy beams; a young dressmaker's apprentice, Clara Andrews, was lucky to suffer only an injured foot and shock; a young boy was knocked unconscious and taken to the Northern Hospital; several horses pulling a tramcar were injured although the passengers miraculously escaped injury; while *"an omnibus driver named John Melly was also conveyed to the Northern Hospital where it was found that some ribs were fractured, his ankle sprained and he was also suffering from contusion of the legs"* but the real drama was reserved for the driver of the parcel's post van. *The Penny Illustrated* made it the subject of an engraving on the front-page of the paper and described the scene vividly within its pages; *"He was coming with his vehicle down London Road when within a yard of the structure he saw it shaken violently by the wind and fearing its demolition he urged his horse to pass through the archway as it was then too late to turn back. At this instant, down came the arch with a terrific crash, smashing the parcel's post van and injuring the driver."* The postman inside the van emerged uninjured but the heroic van driver and the other three injured people were all taken to the Northern Hospital and it is to be hoped all recovered from their ordeal.

The arch must have been repaired with some haste as an engraving in *The Graphic* some days later showed the Queen passing beneath the same arch surrounded by crowds of cheering people.

The ornamental arches had evidently been used on previous occasions such as the visit here of the Prince and Princess of Wales in 1881 approaching Castle Street, having opened Langton Dock

It was only on her return to London that the Queen was informed of the accident and she sent her good wishes to those involved for a speedy recovery but there must have been a few city council members who breathed a sigh of relief that the arch had not fallen down when she had passed beneath it. And a day or so after the Queen had left for London, the winds abated, the sun came out and the world moved on.

Liverpool International Exhibition, 1886

Lime Street celebrations for the Queen

The Penny Illustrated's sensational reporting of the disaster

The Orphan's Tale

"Not everyone can be an orphan."

–Andre Gide

After the Lord Mayor's Show

The visit of Queen Victoria was an undoubted highlight in the then short history of the orphanage and there's little doubt that the interest shown by Royalty and other luminaries raised the profile of the Institution, which went from strength to strength in the following years. Always seeking new sources of income, in 1892, the committee came up with a new plan when they put forward the idea to include the boys in the Government schools education programme which qualified them for the inclusive Parliamentary grant. Several years later, in 1898, the girls were put forward for the same scheme. Nevertheless, the committee still clung to their own agenda which ran concurrently with the children's formal education, and while the boys were taught carpentry and shoemaking the girls were still trained in domestic science. In 1896, the boys were allowed to travel to the public baths but Victorian sensibilities died hard when it came to the opposite sex and the girls were not given the same opportunity. The boys proved to be excellent swimmers and it may well have been their success in several swimming galas against local schools which brought about the building of a swimming pool in the grounds of the orphanage which opened in 1900.

Remembrance of Things Past

In 1903, 30 years after the opening of the orphanage, a boy named Frank Watmough entered the institution at the stipulated age of 7 years – it was probably of little consequence to a small boy who had his own problems but Queen Victoria had died in January, 1901, and Edward VII (1841 - 1910) had succeeded to the throne. Frank was no different to any of the other boys in the orphanage and he would no doubt have passed his formative years there leaving nothing but his name in the yearly ledgers but for one thing – unlike most of the other children, Frank left a record of his days in the Seamen's Orphanage, a document which was all the more remarkable for having been written when Frank was 100 years of age. Given the Victorian connotations associated with the word *"orphanage"* it would be easy to fall into the trap of believing that Frank Watmough's account would be replete with tales of caning and cruelty but there is very little of Dotheboy's Hall or Salem House here. That's not to say that the orphanage was undisciplined, it was, in fact, just the opposite, but its justice was always fair and in conjunction with a structured routine gave the children a sense of order in the world. Given that his testament of his eight years within Newsham Seamen's Orphanage was written so many years afterwards and at such an advanced age it would be excusable if there had been omissions or mistakes but Frank's tale is astonishing for its wealth of detail and his personal and often moving reflections upon life in the orphanage. It is a remarkable proof of the education system within the orphanage that Frank's text is beautifully hand written with not one spelling mistake and perfectly spaced on unlined paper – a writing style learned 100 years ago which has remained with him and is all the more poignant for its simplicity. Born in 1895, Frank wrote his memoir in 1995, and his experiences left such an indelible impression that his testament could well have been written yesterday. When Frank entered the orphanage in 1902, the principles laid down in 1868 were still very much an integral part of its existence and when he left eight years later he stepped out into the world armed with a good education, a sense of responsibility and the confidence to take his place in society. No doubt there were orphanages somewhere in England which had some resemblance to those described in innumerable Victorian novels where kindness and caring were notably absent but Newsham was not one of them.

The orphanage frontage at the turn of the century

First Day at School

A century later, Frank was quite phlegmatic about the circumstances which led him to enter the orphanage, but although he never said so, that forbidding Gothic building must have been a daunting prospect as he walked with his mother along Newsham Drive and into an unforgettable phase of his life. Frank's story begins with the reason why he entered the orphanage in the first place and from this point onwards it is only fitting that he tells his story in his own words which I have transcribed just as he wrote it – interspersed with the story is the odd comment from myself here and there.

"I remember very little of my first 8 years of childhood and have very little memory of my father because as a seafaring man he was always at sea for long voyages. I know my mother told me once that during the Boer War, I think it was, his ship was converted into a troopship and he was away months at a time. But coming home from one of these voyages the ship had sprung a leak and all hands were up to their waists in water trying to keep her afloat. My father safely returned home but took a chill which developed

into bronchitis and died. I would be about seven years of age then and I had a younger brother and sister. It was a sad position for my mother to be in, no money from the shipping office, and so she was advised to let me go into the Liverpool Seamen's Orphanage in Newsham Park."

The forbidding entrance

Frank's memories of his first day at the orphanage are of a bewildered young boy travelling by train and walking along Newsham Drive with his mother for an interview with the matron, and like all young boys he never gave a thought to his mother's feelings as she was forced to relinquish her child into the care of an institution. But her sad situation was the precise reason why the orphanage came into being. Following what must have been a tearful farewell to his mother Frank and six or seven other boys were taken to be bathed in a communal bath then fitted out in new clothes and taken to the dining room which would become a very familiar place in the next few years. One of the most stunning features of the orphanage building is the sheer size of the dining hall with its huge windows and dizzyingly high ceilings and it is not surprising that Frank noticed this feature right away. From the very beginning he was also aware of the rigid ceremonials of mealtimes and would later realize that each part of life in the orphanage from rising to going to bed was of necessity a regimented ritual.

"The master on duty blew the whistle and every boy and girl said grace. The whistle blew again and that was the one they had been waiting for to eat their tea. We new boys and girls were waited on by several women. It was a huge dining hall with tables and forms from one end to the other. I had never before seen so many boys and girls together for at that time there were about 200 boys and a similar number of girls, all orphans, victims of the cruel sea. Whether I ate my tea or not I don't remember because something happened that I have never forgotten. Having of course been used to leaning back on a chair at home I forgot it was a form I was sitting on, I leaned back and over I went onto the floor giving my head a nasty crack. I was soon picked up and was none the worse except for a lump that was rapidly getting bigger and the exclamations of sympathy from the girls nearby becoming very embarrassing for we were at the girls end of the room. And that was how I made my first bow to the ladies – backwards.

Here I might as well give you a picture of the layout of the tables and forms. They were situated lengthways with four tables the length of the room and four tables the width of the room. Each table was arranged to seat 50; 25 each side. It was a lovely big room and if I remember rightly, it had stained glass windows. There was an organ at one end, which would make anyone think that the Services may have been held there on Sundays before the Chapel was built. At the other end was a balcony with a clock in the centre. The food was wheeled in straight from the cookhouse, to the centre of the room and placed at the end of each table, and was served on plates at the end of the table by women attendants and then passed down the line, but no one was allowed to start till grace had been said. During meals the Master would stand on the side of the room in line with the doors, one leading to the boy's school the other to the girls. Each boy knew his own place and the arrangement was that the senior boys would be on the far table from the Master, in seniority of entrance to the school, which was No.1 company, and so on down to No.4 company, with the new boys in front, and when a boy left the school all the others would move up one. When the meal was over, and the boys marched out to the adjoining room they formed up in exactly the same lines as they were in the dining room, so that every boy knew his place there as well."

Bullying was as prevalent then as it is now and the Masters in the orphanage had adopted a method of prevention which would be worth considering today in some schools.

The Great Hall

LIVERPOOL SEAMEN'S ORPHANAGE

PATRONS : HIS MAJESTY THE KING.   HON. SIR ALFRED WILLS

NUMBER OF CHILDREN, 320. RECEIPTS FROM PUBLIC ANNUALLY ABOUT £14,000.

MATRON   -   MRS POSTANCE

	BREAKFAST 7.15 TO 8 A.M. — DINNER 12 TO 12.30 —— TEA 5.45 TO 6.15		
SUNDAY	1 THICK SLICE OF DRY BREAD. 1 MUG OF COCOA	STEWED BEEF AND CABBAGE, RICE PUDDING	1 THICK SLICE OF BREAD AND JAM
MONDAY	PORRIDGE WITH ONE MUG OF MILK BETWEEN 2 CHILDREN	CORNED BEEF AND POTATOES OR 1 PLATE OF RICE AND PRUNES	1 THICK SLICE OF BREAD AND TREACLE, MUG OF COCOA
TUESDAY	BREAD AND MILK	LENTIL SOUP	1 THICK SLICE BREAD & DRIPPING, 1 MUG MILK AND WATER
WEDNESDAY	AS SUNDAY	SUET PUDDING AND TREACLE (1 HELPING)	AS TUESDAY
THURSDAY	AS MONDAY	FISH AND POTATOES OR BEANS AND STEW	AS TUESDAY
FRIDAY	AS SUNDAY	COLD MEAT & POTATOES OR BEANS AND STEW	AS TUESDAY
SATURDAY	AS SUNDAY	PEA SOUP, BREAD AND CHEESE	BREAD AND TREACLE, MILK AND WATER

A SMALL PIECE OF BREAD ALLOWED FOR BOYS' SUPPER.

"Normally the Master now dismisses the boys but this being New Boy's night he would call them out in front of him. He would say a few words of welcome to them, and ask the first boy in the line his name. I don't remember now whether I was first or not but supposing I was. I told him my name and he made me stand on the raised platform around his desk, facing the boys. He said 'This is Frank Watmough, now take a good look at him.' Then he asked me if I knew any other boy in the school, when I said 'No Sir' he asked for a volunteer to be my Guardian. If a boy put his hand up in response he would say 'Good, then I hold you responsible for him.' If no one volunteered, he would name one of the senior boys to act as Guardian. Each new boy went through the same procedure. Sometimes a new boy would already have a brother in the school. I was Guardian for my brother when he came in three years after me. This was a splendid arrangement for it was an awful feeling for a new boy not to have anyone there that he knew, someone to put him wide to the Do's and Don'ts. A good Guardian didn't have to be with him all the time, he couldn't, but his advice and protection often saved a lot of heartache.

There was another reason for this system also. As we have all experienced during our school-days there is always the bully and the trouble-maker who often made life uncomfortable for the young boys, especially the new ones and life could be miserable unless you had someone to stand up for you until you were big enough to stand up for yourself. When the last of the new boys had been introduced the Master would dismiss the assembly and the Guardians were free to show their charges around the school, and return them to join the rest of the boys in their games or other interests till the whistle blew for supper at 9.00 clock. Supper over, a prayer was said and we all joined in singing a hymn, the most favourite being Abide With Me, Fast Falls The Eventide and then off to bed.

But that was easier said than done when I tell you that there was one dormitory on the first floor landing, one on the second, and two on the third or top floor, with 50 beds in each, you will realise the number of steps some of us had to climb to go to bed. But don't think it was a scramble to get to bed, everything had to be done in order, one step at a time. After marching out of the assembly room, across the corridor to the steps, the seniors first, the long climb began. Left Right, Left Right, Left Right the time being given by the master.

Now that all the excitement was over you can imagine the new boy's reaction on entering the big dormitory and being shown to his bed. If he has been used to sleeping alone or perhaps with a brother in a small room it is quite a shock to come into a room of that size with 50 beds in it, 25 each side. In the centre of the room were three low double-sided racks for the boys' clothes and shoes.

As they filed into their respective dormitories, the boys had to stand at the foot of their beds, till the Master was sure they were all in their places, then he would blow the whistle which was the signal to undress. Every article of clothing had the boy's name on it and these had to be made up into a neat and proper pack, all alike, and placed on the rack, every boy having his own particular place – with his shoes and socks on the floor in front of his clothes. Then with only a nightshirt on would hop into bed. They were good beds but no such thing as a hot water bottle, all the rooms being centrally heated with hot water pipes all round.

All lights were out now, most of the boys already asleep and now that the excitement was all over we had more time to think of what had now happened to us. Some boys would perhaps react different to others, some of a harder nature than others depending on their home life. Speaking for myself I don't remember much of my first eight years as I told you earlier. I know I lived in Walton. I remember going to Arnott Street School, I remember a grocer's shop in Spellow Lane, the man would give me a bag of broken biscuits for a penny, but that is about all I can remember. I had every reason to believe that my mother loved me but lying there wide awake I was only just beginning to realise that I wouldn't be going home again and I couldn't understand why I didn't cry when my mother had left me with the matron but now being of a sensitive nature I buried my head under the clothes and gave vent to my pent-up feelings."

Frank's memoir of his first day at the orphanage is so thorough and detailed that the experience was left indelibly imprinted on his young mind. The impression is of wonderment at the whole thing and throughout his day Frank seemed to be holding up well, but impressions even in writing can be deceiving and it is only in his final sentence that Frank finally reveals how traumatic it was to leave his family. But there was little time for sentiment among the diverse personalities of the boys and Frank had to adapt quickly to the rough and tumble of a completely different environment to the one he had been used to.

New Friends and old Masters

The girls in their sailor suits

"I had no time to think about myself the second day, so much happened and I felt more resigned to my new life. I was now making friends with boys of my own age, more than ever I knew before, and life was becoming much more interesting. But it takes all sorts to make a world and in every school you find boys of different temperaments and characters. I remember one boy who never seemed to keep a friend very

long, he was of a surly nature, with a positive grudge against discipline which often got him into trouble with the Masters.

I suppose we all had our unhappy moments, one time or another, it wasn't all sunshine, but it is an old and true saying that 'life is what you make it,' but more often than not, it is more true to say 'life is sometimes what others make it for you.' During the years I was in the school I remember two boys who ran away for some reason best known to themselves but they eventually came back as their mothers would have to notify the authorities even if they wanted to keep the boy.

But I never forgot one sad incident because it happened to a boy who slept in the same lock dormitory as I was in. When the whistle blew at six o'clock one morning his bed was empty. It was thought at first he may have gone to the toilet but as he did not return it was reported to the Master. A search was made and his body was found on the ground outside. It appeared he had got out of a window and attempted to climb down the rain-water pipe but had evidently slipped or lost his footing. No boy admitted having known of his intentions or seen him go. If they had I don't suppose they would have said so.

But on the whole, as time went on and we got used to the discipline and routine of the school, life became much easier. In a school of that kind there had to be discipline of course and as long as you keep to the rules you keep out of trouble. But like every other school, quarrels would occur which sometimes ended in a fight. When that happened the contestants would be ushered down to the bottom playroom where there was less chance of the duty Master seeing them. The news spread like wildfire and more and more boys were lining up all round the room. More often than not some boy would inform the Master and he would come down and stop the fight and maybe mete out some punishment for it was against the rules. But I remember one fight and they weren't three minute rounds either, they were a fight to the finish till one of them gave in. I happened this time to be opposite the door when the Master came in. He beckoned to the boys around not to say anything and slowly made his way up the room. When he got near the contestants he gave a blast out of his whistle that gave then such a fright they broke away immediately. He said 'Well, you do look a pretty sight. Do you feel any better now you've knocked spots off one another? Next time you feel like scrap let me know first and I will bring two pair of gloves and we will do it properly, now shake hands and go and get a wash and brush up.' One boy clapped and we all joined in. It was a liberty but the Master just smiled and walked out. That action on the part of the Master won for himself more respect and confidence from the boys than any punishment would have done.

The Beazley plaque

I remember one Master who came from a training ship. He brought a lot of canes with him and was too fond of using them on the least pretence. One night a couple of the boys went into his room when he

221

was off duty and broke all the canes. There was a court of enquiry of course but no one knew who had done it. After I had left the school, my brother told me that the same thing happened again when this Master brought more canes, and he never found out who did it. When he realised he was now dealing with a different kind of boy and a different kind of school, his attitude changed and my brother told me he became one of the best Masters.

But I must say this about the Headmaster, Bob Mylie, he was very strict but also very fair-minded with us. I had occasion to be called into his office once for breaking a window. I managed to convince him it was an accident or I thought I did but he gave me a lecture on setting a bad example to younger boys and said 'I am now going to give you a punishment for your carelessness that you won't forget.' I started to dither wondering what was coming. Then he said 'Go and stand on the form in front of the clock for one hour and watch the flight of ages pass.' I thought I had got away with it nicely but you try standing on a form nine inches wide that has unsteady legs which made it wobble every time you changed the weight from one leg to the other and watch those sixty seconds change to sixty minutes and every minute like one hour – my back ached for a week after. He was right when he said I would never forget it. I wish he was alive today to read this, Oh, how he would laugh."

Although it must have been daunting for Frank to enter into a world where initially at least every boy was older and therefore tougher, it was clear that he was very resilient and adapted easily to life at the orphanage. From the above descriptions of some of the boys it was obvious that being without parents the one thing they lacked most was discipline, which had brought about a philosophy of tough-love into the orphanage. Frank goes on to describe typical days in the orphanage which alternate between physical work, education and sport.

School days and Sports Days

The boys in their sailor suits

"I have not told you yet how the hours between six o'clock in the morning and supper time were employed. Well! first all the cleaning on the boys' half of the school had to be done by the boys. The flights of steps and corridors had to be washed and the classrooms swept and dusted. A rota was made out for each week and boys were allocated to each of these jobs, sufficient boys on each job so that the whole of the work would be complete by 7.30 a.m. and every broom, mop, bucket and duster, back in the cupboards. They were like ants. This was the first eye-opener the new boys had of their new life, their turn would come soon enough.

Then at 7.30 a.m. every boy had to be down in the wash-house, washed and shoes polished and up in the Assembly room by 7.50. Any boy that was late his name went on the defaulters' list. Prayers were said then all marched into breakfast. School was at 9 o'clock by which time we all had to be in our respective classrooms. Dinner at 12.30 p.m. School again 1.30 p.m to 4.30 p.m and tea at 5 o'clock. After tea we were free till supper-time. I may say we were free but not all because there was a lovely swimming bath on the premises and whenever a Gala night was being held in Lister Drive Baths our teams would get into training in our own baths during the evenings beforehand. The boys one evening, the girls the next. Swimming was also part of our lessons and classes would take it in turn. Every boy learned to swim. The Headmaster taught them all. I could do almost anything in the water and although I never won a race I earned for myself the nickname Water Rat. One year I took part in a competition for Life Saving and was presented with The Royal Humane Society Medal which my daughter still has after all these years. Friday evening was bath night. There was a huge bathroom downstairs with, if I remember rightly, six baths, each of which would take about 18 boys. We would strip off first in the dressing room and form two lines at the door and the Master would let the first 18 in for No.1 bath, second 18 No.2 and so on. You can imagine there was always a scramble to be among the first because you had the longest time in the bath. The Master took care to keep clear of the baths or there would be some accidental splashing with 'Sorry Sir.' There was no school on Wednesday afternoons which was supposed to be sports day. In the winter we had a football team and we would play on Train Park at the back of the orphanage. Volunteers were asked to play against the team and there would be no shortage of them because there was a chance of being found a job to do if you didn't. I was in the team one season and the master tried to get us interested in Rugby but that did not appeal to me, you can call it a man's game if you like but give me football every time. In the summer we had a cricket eleven but I wasn't too keen on that either. But what about the boys who didn't go to the park, well, as the classrooms, assembly rooms and dormitories were not in use this was the best time to give the floors of each room a good scrubbing. A rota had been made out and this is where the list of defaulters came in handy."

Although the boys were required to scrub their own floors, no doubt in preparation for scrubbing decks aboard ship, the job of washing and ironing their laundry fell to the girls, which *"was part of their training."* Frank was too young to know anything of the Women's Suffrage Movement which was becoming militant in the early years of the 20th century, and while the movement's main aim was to gain the vote, it was the perceived role of women as domestics which also fuelled their campaign. Frank was fortunate to enter the school when it had its own Chapel, swimming pool and sanatorium and would never have known the work and fund-raising it took to achieve all these things. It would be interesting to know the age of the *'elderly lady'* called Nurse Emma, whose surgery was at the end of the playground – she was probably about 40ish or even younger.

Through the Looking Glass

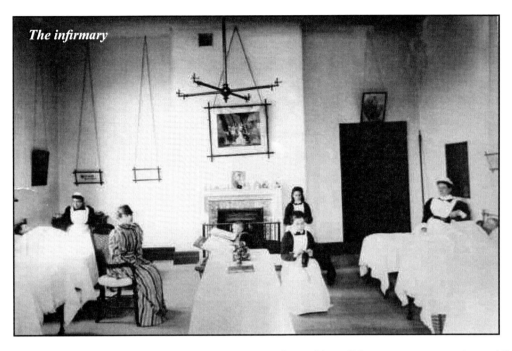

The infirmary

"There was a joiner's shop at one end of the playground for making all the necessary repairs and if a boy was interested he could apply to the master and arrangements would be made for him to have instruction during Wednesday afternoons.

We had our own laundry as well over on the girls' side which was part of their training. We had a change of underwear, night-shirt and bedding every week, all done by women and the girls. We had our own Sanatorium in the charge of a Red Cross nurse, for boys and girls who needed hospital treatment but for cuts and bruises and upset tummies there was a surgery at the end of the playground in the charge of an elderly lady, Nurse Emma. She was like a mother to us and not only cured our bodily ailments but many a boy went to her with his troubles and she sent him away in a much happier frame of mind, and there was always a bag of sweets in her desk. But no boy liked going into the Sanatorium, we were a bit scared of Nurse Jones who was of a much harder nature than Nurse Emma. I had to go in once with a nasty cut on my forehead over my right eye, fortunately for me she was due for leave and Nurse Emma came to take over.

But what I think scared a lot of the boys, especially the younger ones, was the legend handed down over the years. To get to the toilet you had to pass the foot of a short flight of stairs leading up to a room and the legend was that when you got to the top you would see a looking glass on a table and if you looked into the glass you would see the face of the devil. Well I was only a youngster myself at the time and as much scared as any boy and to get to the toilet I would run past the stairs both ways glad to get safely back to bed. After a couple of restless nights I said to myself 'I don't believe it' and plucking up courage I was determined to find out for myself. I crept slowly out of the ward when everything was quiet and looked up the stairs my nerves all on tension then gently climbing the steps till I reached the door and there was the looking-glass on the table and for a moment I was too scared to move. But with one quick step to the glass I looked, only to see the face of a very frightened looking little boy. But it shows how a story of that kind can play havoc with a young boy's mind and after that if ever I heard of a new boy having been told the story I would put his mind at rest."

Frank appeared to throw himself into every facet of life in the orphanage and in some ways it was a voyage of discovery for him but at the same time it is noticeable throughout Frank's story just how compassionate he is to the plight of some of the other boys.

A New Discovery and a Holiday

"Now we also had our own Fire-Escape ladder, and a team of the senior boys were trained how to use it. Once or twice a week we would go through the operation of wheeling the ladder to one of the dormitories, raising it up till it reached the top windows, then one of the boys would be told to climb. Some boys were scared of the idea, some would get so far then come down. This was to find out those who had the courage and were not afraid of heights. I am not saying I had the courage but that was the first time I found out I was not afraid of heights and so on many occasions I was called on to take that position. At first we practised bringing down a dummy but the day one boy volunteered to come down over my shoulder I felt the butterflies in my tummy. I don't know what he felt like but we arrived safely. It was a good precaution in the event of a small fire but by the time one boy had been rescued the Fire Brigade would have arrived and our ladder would have only been in the way.

Once a month it was visiting day when our Mothers or other relative would come and sit with us in the assembly room. They were allowed one hour and could bring us sweets, books, games and money which they invariably did but there was always a boy who had no visitor for some reason or other so those of us who were more fortunate would share our gifts with him. It was of course nice to see our Mothers again but the parting would often open the old wound which we thought had healed. There was nothing we could spend the money on, so it was put into the care of the Headmaster and called the Stamp Account then when we wrote a letter home which we were allowed to do he would put a stamp on the envelope and take the cost from our account.

Once a year during the summer months we had a month's holiday. If our Mothers could afford to keep us we went home, if not then those boys and girls were taken on a train journey to Willesden for a holiday in the country. We were dressed in our best uniform, with a sailor collar and hat like the Navy with a ribbon around the hat with gold letters "Seamen's Orphanage." We were given strict instructions to take great care of our uniforms and be a credit to the school. We were given a navy-blue kit-bag in which to put our everyday suit, a set of clean underclothes and socks and night-shirt and anything else from our box that we wanted to take home. Any money that might be left in the account would be given to use as pocket money. We were just getting used to being home when it was time to go back again but as we got older we didn't mind that for I think we missed the companionship of the other boys and the routine of the school."

Ralph Brocklebank

225

Acid Tests and Fussy Eaters

"As far as schooling was concerned, we didn't progress from standard to standard according to seniority but by ability. This gave the Headmaster a chance to rate what a boy was worth when his time came to leave the school. I must say we were given a very good education with a much wider range of subjects both literal and practical than any boy would have received in any Elementary school at that time.

We had a good Chemistry Master but he was too fond of experimenting on us. I recall one day he was explaining the properties of a certain acid. I can't remember the name now but he had a small stick of it in his hand and going around the class told some of us to hold out our tongue and he pressed the stick on it. It burned a little at first but when we went into dinner which was suet pudding with syrup we couldn't eat it as our tongues were raw with the acid. When the duty master asked why we couldn't eat it we had to tell him and show our tongue. He told us to go to the Surgery right away and either he or Nurse Emma must have reported it to the Head because he never did it again.

About my third year in the school a new Gymnasium was built alongside the covered playroom. It was a fine building with all the latest equipment and Physical Training eventually became part of our schooling. I remember as a senior boy taking part in an all-round competition. Points were given for every event and when all points were summed up another boy beat me by one.

Singing lessons were also part of our schooling and the Master who held this responsibility was Master of standard seven and Deputy Head and whom we only knew as Pip. He had that nickname when I went into the school and even when he was made Headmaster to the boys he was always just Pip. I remember one hot afternoon when he had given us a problem in algebra to work out and when he looked up his head was down on his desk, he seemed to have fallen asleep. The boys began to whisper and nudge one another when he suddenly woke up and aimed his book into the middle of the class. This caused a roar of laughter in which he couldn't help joining himself.

But the singing lessons were very necessary for us because we had to rehearse the Anthem and Hymns for morning and afternoon services in the Chapel on Sunday. Sometimes Pip would have the junior boys only and teach them how to read music. He would draw five lines on the board and against each line would put a letter starting from the bottom, E.G.B.D.F. and by each space F.A.C.E. and told us the best way to remember them was Every Good Boy Deserves Favour if he Keeps His Face Clean. Then he would explain the crotchets and quavers etc until we gradually began to understand their values. We liked these lessons, it was like a language of its own, which it certainly is. It was better than Sums, History and Geography. On Saturday evenings there would be a final rehearsal in the Chapel, all the boys and girls in their respective places. Before Prize-Day at which there was always a number of men and women present who I suppose were on the Orphanage Committee. We had our own brass-band and the instruments were kept in a small room at the end of the assembly room with a glass frontage. I would often stand looking at those instruments, hoping some day I would be able to play one. When I reached my third year, having by now learned to read music, I plucked up courage and asked a Master if I could join the band. He said 'Well, if you are so keen to join, I will mention it to the Band Master.' He was true to his word and I became one of the band for the next three years.

Every year the Pilots of the Port of Liverpool sponsored a concert in the Philharmonic Hall in aid of the Orphanage. Professional artists had been engaged but the children did a lot of the singing and the band had their share of the music. I remember one year an amateur operatic group playing scenes from H.M.S. Pinafore and Pirates of Penzance with the band and children joining in the chorus. We had been rehearsing for weeks beforehand. But part of the pleasure was the journey down to the Hall on horse-drawn wagonettes, and on leaving the Hall after the concert, being given a bag of refreshments which we ate in the wagonettes while we were jogging along merrily homeward, singing the chorus of some of the songs we had joined in during the concert. What a night to remember. But it was not only the Pilots who took such an interest in the school. When some years later my brother went to sea he told me there were collecting boxes on all the liners and merchant ships.

At Easter a big Chocolate Egg would be on show in a shop window at the bottom of Bold Street with a notice that it was for the children of the Liverpool Seamen's Orphanage and at tea-time on Easter Sunday there would be a piece for each of us on our plates.

When my brother came to join me I was his Guardian. For quite a while Monday was a bad day for him. It was always porridge for breakfast and a chunk of bread. When the other boys had finished and marched out he was still there, his porridge uneaten. The rule was that if a boy left his meal untouched it would still be there when he went in for dinner. It very seldom happened but now it had, so I would save my piece of bread and wait my opportunity then finish his porridge and give him my bread. That was alright but it was unfortunate that for dinner the same day we had broth and a chunk of bread and that was something else he couldn't fancy so I would save my bread again and eat his broth. After two or three weeks the women helpers saw what was going on and would quietly give him more bread and remove his porridge and broth."

Leaving the Orphanage

"I have up to now only alluded very briefly to the Chapel, so now is the moment to give you a fuller picture. It was built later at the end of the main building. It was a lovely Chapel built in the form of a cross, the girls were seated on one side of the cross and the boys on the other. One afternoon Service I remember a missionary coming to speak to us who had only recently come back from abroad. I was never fond of sermons, we got so used to listening to the Do's and Don'ts, but as soon as this Minister started speaking I was all attention. He gave as his text just one word OTHERS and made us spell it out letter for letter. He went on to give us a picture of the kind of country he had come from and the kind of people he had been living with, the children naked, the men and women with very little covering, living out in the open in a land covered in sand, no shelter from the sun, forgotten by the rest of the world. He told us of the difficult task they had in ministering to the physical needs of these people, they were in short supply of medicines and lack of food was the cause of so many of the complaints, and it was left to the Church and their voluntary helpers to try to make it known. I was so impressed by what he told us that throughout my life I have tried as far as lay within my means to keep that word OTHERS as a guide to my feelings, intentions and actions.

During the whole of the six years I was in the school, at the morning service in the Chapel, a retired Royal Navy Officer, Captain Stubbs, would be there in the same pew. After the Service he would sometimes come into the school with us and when we were assembled he liked to talk to us. I remember one cold winter's day, he sounded as if he had a cold too. He advised us never to neglect a cold but go and see the nurse because there was once an epitaph on a tombstone which read; 'It was a cough that carried him off, and a coffin they carried him off in" so boys don't neglect a cough. On another visit he was talking about ambition, the desire to get on in life. He said all boys had different ideas of what they would like to be when they grew up but it never somehow turned out that way. But there is an old proverb which states 'What thou doest do well.' He said he was going to give a prize to the boy who made the most progress during the next twelve months. Well, I don't think any of us gave it another thought, twelve months was a long time to look forward to but eventually the day came, when true to his word he turned to the Headmaster and asked him to name the boy who had been considered to have made the most progress during that time. To my great surprise I heard my name mentioned. There was a lot of clapping as I went forward to receive my prize and it was a proud moment for me when Captain Stubbs took my hand to congratulate me. The prize was what was then called a Gladstone bag, a good handy bag which I made good use of for many years when I started work.

Here I might mention that once a year the boys and girls who were near the age for Confirmation had to attend preparation class with the Chaplain beforehand. Then on the appointed Sunday afternoon when mothers and relatives were present the Bishop of Liverpool would officiate at the ceremony. No boy or girl left the school without being confirmed.

Another subject of our lessons was drawing to see if any boy had artistic talent. We were allowed to roam anywhere on our side of the building and make our own choice of subject. I had more of an eye to architectural drawing than flowers and ornaments and many an hour did I spend pleasantly in both the Chapel and the Dining-Hall. These lessons continued weekly till the time I was now getting near to my leaving the school. It was quite a coincidence that just at this time the architect who made the plans of the gymnasium applied to the Headmaster for a boy to work in his office. I learned later that all my drawings were inspected and to my surprise I got the job."

Out into the World

Frank left the orphanage with some regrets as he had thrived in the company of other boys, accepted the discipline with good grace and embraced every opportunity that was on offer, but in common with every other child who left he soon had to adapt to a working life. Frank was slightly unusual in that the job he was going to had nothing of a maritime connotation but many of the boys went to sea in some capacity or other; *"naturally we were encouraged to take to the sea as a career and if a boy chose the Navy which some did they were sent to the training ship Indefatigable which at that time was stationed by the Menais Bridge, Anglesey."*

The ever-resourceful Frank built upon his early drawing skills and went on to become a draughtsman in his first place of work which was situated in Westminster Chambers on the corner of Dale Street and Crosshall Street. He later fulfilled most of the aspirations which the orphanage had for their pupils by becoming an engineer, (although ideally the education system would have preferred a ship's engineer) and he proved his fearless attitude towards heights was not just youthful bravado by often scaling the electric pylons which were springing up across the country and reached the pinnacle of his profession in more ways than one.

Frank served in both the First World War and the Second World War and married and had a daughter, Doris. Doris is still living today as our much-valued neighbour and friend, inching slowly towards her own centennial year Living to the age of 103, Frank, often returned to the orphanage, taking his wife and daughter with him to the Services in the Chapel which he loved so much.

Differing Attitudes

There are dozens of sites on the Internet devoted to Victorian orphanages and each and every one of them is condemnatory of the Institutions that they describe. Almost all of them describe a litany of cruelty, hunger and deprivation as the normal way of life in such places and in some instances accuse the philanthropists who funded the Institutions in the first instance as self-serving egotists. There is no doubt that there were many Institutions which were lacking in many aspects of child-care and others which fell short in other ways but it does seem remarkable that every Institution in the country should be universally described as something borrowed from a Charles Dicken's novel. The common perception of a Victorian orphanage stems in great part from Dicken's novels in which a host of sadistic overseers take delight in making the children's lives as miserable as possible and one wonders if some of the later descriptions of Victorian Institutions borrow from this sensationalised version of the truth; it seems inconceivable that every dinner-lady doled out as little food as possible, that every tutor was a martinet and that every Committee member was a money-grubbing fraud. There are also one or two descriptions of Newsham orphanage itself in which former inmates of the Institution state that they hated the place but on closer examination their reasons are quite spurious and they probably *"hated"* it as some pupils *"hate"* school. I much prefer Frank Watmough's summary of Newsham orphanage which probably speaks for the silent majority who attended there.

"I don't know the date of that old building or anything of the former history but I am sure the founders of that orphanage and its supporters could not in those early years have realised the enormity of what they had set out to do nor at that time visualise the thousands of children who eventually received the benefits of their efforts. I was only one of 200 boys who moved from the bottom to the top in six years and when I think of the thousands of boys and girls who passed through the portals of that old building over the years when it was an orphanage who received as good if not better all-round education than most schools could provide, creating in us a self-confidence and a spirit of independence, along with a sense of respect to our elders and a belief in God, then we have a great deal to be thankful for to all those who over the years helped to make all this possible."

The End of an Era

"Look back over the past with its changing Empires that rose and fell, and you can see the future too."

– Marcus Aurelius

The Carpathia coming to the rescue of the Titanic courtesy of Ted Walker

Repercussions

Events at sea had always had a direct effect upon the orphanage's resources and when the *Titanic* struck an iceberg and sank on the 15th April, 1912, it was initially feared that the subsequent burden placed upon the orphanage would be stretched to the limit; many of the officers and crew of the *Titanic* were after all from Merseyside and it would be to the orphanage that their widows and orphans would look to for help. However, the Lord Mayors of Liverpool and London eventually formed a National Relief Fund which shouldered the financial burden, although there were children orphaned by the disaster who would find themselves placed in Newsham Seamen's Orphanage. Some of the better-known Merseysiders who were aboard the Titanic when she sank were Captain Edward J. Smith who lived on Marine Terrace, Waterloo – coincidentally his house was just a stone's throw from the opulent mansion of Thomas Henry Ismay (1837 - 1899) founder of the White Star Line and father of Bruce Ismay – Captain Smith died while Bruce Ismay survived only to face a lifetime of criticism.

John Frederick Preston Clarke (1883 - 1912) was the base viola player in the orchestra which continued to play until the ship disappeared beneath the waves, with their final rendition of *"Nearer My God to Thee,"* since entered into the legends of the sea. Clarke lived at No.22 Tunstall Street between Smithdown Road and Earle Road and just as he has passed into history so Tunstall Street has since been demolished in 2012, one hundred years after the sinking of the *Titanic.*

Frederick Fleet

Another Liverpool man who sailed aboard the *Titanic* was Frederick Fleet (1887 - 1965) who was the first man to spot the iceberg which tore the ship asunder. Fleet never knew his father and when his mother ran away with a boyfriend to Springfield, Missouri, he was passed from foster parents to orphanages, one of which was Newsham, and finally Barnado's, until he joined one of the training ships at the age of twelve. Fleet remained aboard the training ship until he was sixteen when he signed on the *Oceanic* as a look-out, transferring to the *Titanic* on the eve of its maiden voyage. The *Titanic* sailed on April 10th, 1912, and on the night of the 14th April, which he described as one of the most beautiful he had ever seen, Fleet was the first lookout to spot the black mass looming in the distance, telephoning to the bridge the fateful words *"Iceberg, right ahead."* Fleet would also reveal at the inquest that he had never been issued binoculars. Fleet survived the sinking of the *Titanic* and after a brief service aboard the *Olympia* he decided to leave the White Star Line behind him and signed on for other companies, finishing his life at sea in 1936 when he went to work for Harland and Wolff in Southampton, as a ship-builder. Given that associations with the *Titanic* were for many years seen as something shameful it seemed a strange choice of career move for Fleet to work for the builders of the *Titanic,* especially since the disaster had haunted him for the rest of his days. After such a difficult start in life it was to Frederick Fleet's credit that he continued to work all his life but fate was never good to him and in his final years he was reduced to selling newspapers on the streets of Southampton. On 28th December, 1964, Fleet's wife died and a few days later her brother gave him notice to leave the house they had all shared – two weeks later Fleet ended his own life by hanging and died at the age of 77, abandoned in old age as he had been in infancy. The police report stated that of the rope Fleet had used *"the splicing seemed to have been done in an experienced seaman-like fashion."*

The First World War and Royal Accolades

When one single incident could have such a potential impact upon the life of the orphanage the advent of the First World War was enormous and affected every facet of the management; the education curriculum was interrupted by the numbers of teachers who left for the trenches, while the devastating loss of merchant ships in the North Atlantic meant there was a subsequent loss of income from the onboard collection boxes, and not least was the vastly increased applications for help from widows whose husbands had been lost at sea. All these things placed a huge strain on resources but the orphanage struggled on through it all just as it had always done and by the end of the war in 1918 the orphanage was home to 265 children with a further 733 receiving help in their own homes. With the war over, life in the orphanage gradually returned to normal and while educational facilities changed in accordance with government policies and various other changes came about, they were always built upon the solid foundations laid down half a century previously in Duke Street.

In March, 1919, the staff and children were honoured with a visit by one of England's naval heroes, Admiral Sir David Beatty (1871 - 1936) who was staying at Newsham House with Lady Beatty. Whether the children understood the relevance of the Admiral's career is open to

question but he had a great deal in common with those boys who had left the orphanage to go to sea, becoming a cadet on the training ship *H.M.S. Britannia* at Dartmouth at the age of 13.

One month after Admiral Beatty's visit on 14th April, 1919, the orphanage celebrated its Jubilee with the 50th annual meeting in the Town Hall where Sir William Forwood recalled the men *"who stood out prominently in its history"* mentioning James Beazley, its founder, Ralph Brocklebank, its first President, Charles MacIver, Bryce Allan, Drummond Anderson, its first Chaplain, Captain Stubbs, Ist Secretary, Robert Allan, Mrs Postance and Mr Mylie, *"our much-respected Headmaster."* Frank Watmough had his own list of worthies who he said had influenced his life at Newsham more than any others – they were *"the Master Pip, Headmaster Bob Mylie and Nurse Emma."* Sir William Forwood resigned soon afterwards and his place was taken by the son of the founder also named James – James H. Beazley, one of the dynasty of Beazleys who were prominent at the orphanage from beginning to end.

With Transatlantic passenger liners and merchant ships able to travel safely once again donations began to flow freely as before and the orphanage began to return to its normal routine. The great and the good of Liverpool continued to support the orphanage and it was undoubtedly their influence in high circles which brought about invitations to celebrities such as Admiral Beatty which undoubtedly boosted the morale of both the staff and children. On 17th March, 1921, there was another Royal visit to the orphanage – on this occasion by

The statue of Queen Mary above the Mersey Tunnel

Queen Mary and Princess Mary. The visit led to King George V bestowing the title of *"Royal"* on the Institution and from that time onwards it was known as The Royal Newsham Seamen's Orphanage. Queen Mary would return to Liverpool on the 18th July, 1934, accompanied by the King, for the opening of the Queensway Tunnel – their commemorative statues are tucked away to the rear of the entrance where they are rarely seen. Also in 1921, a new facility in the form of a gymnasium was built at Newsham; the contractor was the firm of Jones and Sons whose workshops were situated on the exact place where Franceys Marble Works once thrived at the bottom of Brownlow Hill.

The Second World War

By 1938, war clouds were once again gathering over Europe and the orphanage Committee were not slow to react to any danger to the children; they were in fact remarkably prescient to potential perils which were not in place during the First World War; within the timescale of just 20 years aircraft had evolved from the flimsy First World War bi-planes and tri-planes which had acted as spotters and fought dog-fights over the French countryside into long-distance fighters and bombers which would cause so much damage to British cities, and for this reason alone the Committee decided that evacuation of the children in the orphanage was a priority. Throughout the history of the orphanage whenever difficulties have arisen there has always been someone to answer the call and on this occasion it was with great generosity that Mr and Mrs Royden offered the use of their large house and extensive grounds at Hill Bark estate, Frankby, on the Wirral, to house the children. The offer was accepted gratefully by the orphanage Committee and the summer of 1939 was spent preparing Hill Bark for the arrival of the children. The Royden's remained in their home throughout the whole process and looked on good-naturedly while the building of facilities and air raid shelters went on all around them and on the 11th September, 1939, the children arrived at their new home. The children adapted easily to life at Hill Bark and treated the whole experience as a great adventure, but despite their great relief at making the children safe, the Committee were nevertheless faced with a multitude of difficulties which were proportionately more extensive than the problems engendered by the First World War. There was the same loss of staff when teachers were called up and the financial difficulties were worse than ever but the scale of the conflict placed an even greater strain on resources and as early as 1941 the orphanage had admitted 18 children and over 100 more had applied for help in their own homes.

Searchlights over Liverpool

Somehow or other, just as they had done during the First World War the staff muddled through and through it all maintained the highest standards in all things especially the children's education which they had always prioritised. However, when the war finally ended and the staff and children may have believed that they would transfer back to Newsham and continue life as before, things would prove more difficult than anticipated. The first difficulty that the Committee encountered was the considerable damage to the buildings by errant bombs; the damage was proof of the wisdom of moving the children and while there may have been considerable consolation in knowing that lives had probably been saved the Committee was faced with a building which was unuseable in its present condition. The worst damage was to the Chapel which lay derelict until 1963 when it was decided that demolition was the only option.

The bombs which had rained down upon Newsham were collateral damage and the real targets were the nearby industrial areas and the railway line; it was strangely ironic that the Victorians refused to commission mansions near to the railway line because of the smoke and noise, but they would never in the wildest nightmares have envisaged that the flying machines they had read about in H.G.Wells' science-fiction tales would one day become reality. However, there was little time for musing on Victorian sensibilities and as pragmatism took the place of dismay the Committee began the work of restoration with a professional assessment of the damage and the provisional costs of repair. Contracts were subsequently issued to firms and a date of 1948 was set for completion and the return of the children to the school. But times were changing far more rapidly than they ever had after the First World War and there were elements entering into the equation which would affect the school far more than both World Wars had done.

Frank Watmough's feelings summed up neatly how Liverpudlians viewed the wreckage of their city after the 2nd World War.

"After I left the school I would often walk down to the Pierhead and get onto the Overhead Railway which ran along the full length of the docks to Seaforth. The shipyards were then a hive of industry. I left the school in 1910 so I am now speaking of the years before the 1918 war after which of course everything changed. But how sad it is now to see our once great city struggling under its present knockout blow. But not for long, for there are already efforts being made toward recovery and given the right kind of leadership at the top we should regain our former supremacy as one of the greatest cities in the country. But as to becoming a great seaport again, that is. I'm afraid, too far away in the distant future to make any rash predictions."

A Sea Change

The provisional date for the completion of the building works and the return of the children to Newsham coincided with the advent of arguably the greatest social reforms that Great Britain had ever seen. The Beveridge Report targeted the five giants of *Want*, *Disease*, *Squalor*, *Ignorance* and *Idleness* and addressed the problem of each one boldly and innovatively. It was the Labour Government's finest hour when the Welfare State came into being in a series of reforms which took in every aspect of life in Britain and would eventually affect every citizen in the land to a larger or greater degree at some point in their lives. The National Health Service was the flagship of the reforms and for the poverty-stricken who could barely afford the 2/6d for a visit to a G.P. it was like a light shone into the darkness; the numbers of people who had died over the years for want of a few shillings was unknowable but for the first time in history health care was available to all and not the sole province of the wealthy. Concurrent with the inception of the N.H.S. were a raft of benefits which included Family Allowance, National, Insurance, National Assistance, Council Housing, Town and Country Planning and not least Education. Perhaps the strangest thing about the birth of the Welfare State was that it came about at a time when Great Britain was financially, structurally and socially on its knees, and Liverpudlians were still picking their way through the rubble of bombed debris' and often rebuilding shattered lives during its gestation period. The Welfare State was nothing less than revolutionary and its affects were almost immediate – it was no coincidence that the dreaded workhouses became an anachronism soon afterwards and the working-classes acquired a new-found dignity.

As far as the orphanage was concerned, the new legislation was so far-reaching that it affected every facet of its governance; Family Allowance, free school meals and all the other benefits meant that a supervising parent, usually a mother, was reluctant to admit a child to the orphanage when she could now cope at home and the numbers of applications dropped dramatically. The education of the children had always reigned supreme in the running of the orphanage but following the legislation regarding education not only was there now a shortage of children to teach but the changes were so challenging as to be insurmountable; the school was completely unprepared for the introduction of the 11+ but the law which stated that it was illegal for any child to live in an institution under the age of eleven impacted greatly on the orphanage and to complicate matters even more it was now not permitted for children beneath the age of eleven years of age to attend the same school as children above that age. Taken in its entirety, the new legislation was too much to deal with for the Committee and they reluctantly concluded that the children would not be returning to the orphanage.

On 25th July, 1949, the Annual General Meeting took place as usual and Colonel J.G. Beazley informed the Committee that closure was inevitable and two days later on Wednesday 27th July, the Royal Newsham Seamen's Orphanage no longer existed.

It was an indication of the affection that the Committee members, the staff and even the children felt for the orphanage when there was a general air of sadness about its closure but looking at the situation from a greater perspective there is a great deal to be pleased about when an orphanage becomes redundant. However, the genuine desire to help young people had always been present among the Committee members and while they could easily have walked away from Newsham with their heads held high they continued with their philanthropic works, channelling their efforts into different directions; the children of sailors lost at sea no longer needed feeding, clothing or educating by the orphanage but there was a niche for helping those boys and girls who aspired to Higher Education and the Committee turned their attentions to helping them in every way possible. In 1969, a member of the Beazley family was still on the Committee in the orphanage's centenary year and the work continues to this day.

In 1951, the Royal Newsham Seamen's Orphanage building was sold to the Ministry of Health for the sum of £125,000 and developed a psychiatric unit as its primary function. For a short time, the building became an old people's home and Frank Watmough, who still took an interest, believed *"what better use could be made of such a fine building than to give a little comfort to our elderly citizens in the twilight of their lives."* There was a great deal of irony in noting that the Institution had originally been founded for the welfare of children and ended being responsible for the welfare of old people. The building remained in use as a hospital until 1992 and in 1997 the building was sold to a property developer. In 2015, despite being a Grade II listed building, Newsham is in a state of dereliction – whether it will ever be resurrected from its moribund condition is anyone's guess.

From There to Here

If Victorians thought that flying machines were literally just *"flights of fancy,"* then to Surgeon Henry Park, manned flight must have been an unimaginable concept. Henry Park was born at the beginning of an era of unprecedented growth for Liverpool, at a time when he could never have predicted how fast or far the city would rise from its centuries old slumbers to become the second city of the Empire. It is an inescapable fact that the growth of Liverpool was based upon the incredible wealth engendered by the slave-trade but it is also no coincidence that the rise of Liverpool's maritime empire ran in tandem with the rise of the British Empire, and within a time frame of around 250 years Liverpool grew faster than any time in its history, from little more than a sleepy fishing village to a dynamic maritime city. None of the people who appear in the chapters of this book would have been fully aware of the metamorphosis going on around them; fully occupied with their own projects, the artists, sculptors, politicians, slave-traders, bankers, sailors and all the rest could never see the big picture and it is only from the vantage point of history that an understanding of the growth of Liverpool can be grasped. Although there were no Huns at the gates and no cities were sacked, the British Empire was slowly and inexorably coming to an end during the lifetime of Frank Watmough, and just as Liverpool's maritime empire had risen with the British Empire, little by little it also declined accordingly.

Through the lives of the Liverpudlians of the past 250 years or so, we do have some idea of where we have been, but where Liverpool is heading in the next 250 years is anyone's guess and we are as unknowing as Henry Park was all those years ago.

Bibliography

A Medical History of Liverpool from   T. H. Bickerton
the Earliest Days to the Year 1920

Annals of a Traveller   Jay Levinson

A Short History of the First   George McLoughlin
Liverpool Infirmary

Biographical Notes of   J. Cooper Morley
Liverpool Artists

Birkenhead News 1914

British Library online

Bruce Castle Museum Archives

Edwardian Biography, Liverpool   W. T. Pike

Friends of Williamson Tunnels

Grace's Guide to Industrial History

Guide to the Studios of Rome   Columbia University Libraries

Henry Moore Foundation online

Historic Society of Lancashire and Cheshire

History of Edge Hill   Charles. R. Hand

In a Welsh Border House,   Robertson Davies
The Legacy of the Victorians

Joseph Williamson Society

Liverpool and Slavery   Scouse Press

Liverpool As It Was 1775 - 1800   Richard Brooke

Liverpool History Society Journal No.13,   F. T. Forrest
The Waterhouse Heritage

Liverpool History Society Journal No.14,   Ann Truesdale
Edwin Lyon, A Forgotten Liverpool Sculptor

Liverpool Journal Nov, 24th, 1849

Liverpool Post and Mercury articles 1908   Edward Rimbault Dibdin

Liverpool Record Office

Liverpool, The Hurricane Port   Andrew Lees

Lost Liverpool website

Magpies, Squirrels and Thieves,   Jacqueline Yallop
How the Victorians Collected the World

Memorials of Liverpool   James Allanson Picton

Memoir of Miss Elizabeth Park 1840

Memoir of the Late Henry Park Esq   Anon
– Surgeon of Liverpool

Merseyside Painters, People and Places   Liverpool Record Office

New South Wales Art Gallery   Terry McCormack

Old Mersey Times

Public Sculpture of Liverpool   Terry Cavanagh

Recollections of a Nonagenarian 1836   James Stonehouse

Redburn   Herman Melville

The Gentleman's Daughter   Amanda Vickery
– Women's Lives in Georgian England

The Liverpool School of Painters   H. C. Marillier

The Making of Liverpool   Michael Fletcher

The Pool of Life   Maggi Morris and John Ashton

The Streets of Liverpool   James Stonehouse

The Trial of William Sparling and
S. M. Colquitt online

Victorian Society Report 2000

Wirral Record Office

Westmount Advertiser

Index

Abbot, Bill 154
Abercromby Square 64, 77, 119, 126, 180, 182, 187, 188
Abolition of slave-trade 20
Adelphi Hotel 62-65, 209
Aigburth Road 59
Ainsworth Street 66
Alanson, Dr Edward 42
Albert Dock 120, 146
Albert Memorial, the 82
Alder Road 176
Aliwal, battle of 98
Allan, Bryce 199, 233
Allerton Hall 74
All Hallows Church, Allerton 97
Almond Street 168
American Civil War, the 91, 124, 125, 146, 176, 179
American War of Independence, the 14, 43, 49, 91, 119, 121
Ancient Chapel of Toxteth, the 56
André, Édouard 190
Andsell, Richard 146, 150, 139
Apperley, Henry 84, 85
Apsley House 153
Arcole, battle of 20
Arnot Street School 220
Athenaeum, the 29, 32, 55, 95
Atherton, John 38
Atkinson, Tyndall 147
Atkins Thomas 165
Augereau, Marshal 21

Baines, James 211
Baker, Captain Peter 20
Balfour, Alexander 199
Bankes, James 93
Bankes, Meyrick 93, 94
Barry, J. M. 190
Basnett Street 42
Bastille, the 19
Battle of Britain 26
Battle of the Nile 20
Beamont, Doctor George 96
Beatty, Admiral Sir David 232, 233
Beazley, Col. J. G. 236
Beazley, James 199, 200, 202, 207, 221, 233
Bedford Street South 180
Bellingham, John 52

Benson, Moses 56-58
Benson, Ralph 56
Benson Street 103, 144, 145
Berthon, Ellen Sarah 49
Berthon, Peter 49
Bibby, John 97
Bidston 53
Birkenhead Park 188
Black Ball Line 211
Blackhorse Lane 176
Blake Street 63
Blenheim, battle of 20
Bluecoat Hospital 12, 13
Blue School for Orphans 146
Blundell, Bryan 58
Bold Street 18, 30, 36, 44, 46, 47, 55, 144, 227
Bolton and Leigh Railway 90
Bolton, John 53, 54, 57-60, 123, 125
Bonaparte, Napoleon 18, 34, 20-22, 25, 26, 28, 32-34, 47, 53, 66, 119, 153
Booth, Henry 18, 151
Booth, John Wilkes 161
Booth, Junius Brutus 161
Botanic Park 151, 152
Brandreth, Doctor Joseph. P. 42, 44, 46, 95, 96
Brassey, Thomas 104
Bridge, Edward 120
Bridge, Ellen 120
Brocklebank, Ralph 199-202, 204, 225, 233
Bromfield, Doctor James 38-40
Bronte sisters 80
Bronte Street 65
Brooks, Major Edward 53-60
Brooks, Rev. Jonathan 107
Brownlow Hill 13, 61, 62, 64-66, 69, 98, 139, 140, 144, 148
Brownlow Hill Workhouse 12, 64, 65
Brownlow Street 38, 65, 101
Brunswick Street 32, 90
Buckingham Palace 76, 106, 110, 113
Bullin, Christopher 120, 121, 126, 127
Bullin, Richard 121, 123, 126, 127
Burke, James 154, 155
Burns, Robert 105
Butler Street 165
Byrne, Simon 154
Byrom Street 11, 209, 211
Calderstones Park 204
Campbell, Mary 105

Camperdown, battle of 20
Canning Dock 16, 120
Canning, George 52, 57, 58, 87
Canning Street 13, 119
Cannon, Tom 154
Canova, Antonio 74, 75, 103, 101, 176
Cape St Vincent, battle of 20
Cardiff National Museum 77
Carmichael, Captain 54
Carnatic Hall 20
Carter, Jack 154
Castlereagh, Viscount R. Stewart 52
Castle Street 11, 18, 31, 32, 36, 59, 74, 124, 132, 209, 212
Catharine Street 148, 209
Catholic Emancipation Act 52
Chambre, Sir Alan 57
Chantrey, Francis 70
Chapel Street 68
Charity 93
Chatsworth 75
Chavalliaud, Léon-Joseph 191
Chester Cathedral 157, 173
Church Street 12, 18, 29, 32, 36, 44, 45, 55, 73, 74, 95, 101
Circus Street School 69, 70
Clarence Dock 120
Clarence Street 62, 66, 71, 158
Clarke, John Frederick Preston 231
Clarkson, Thomas 124
Clayton Square 18, 36
Cleveland Square 11, 120
Coburg Dock 120
Cockburn, Devereux Plantaganet 106
College Lane 38
Colquitt, Capt. S. Martin R.N. 56, 57
Colquitt Street 43, 88, 98, 144
Commutation Row 30
Conan Doyle, Sir Arthur 100, 155
Concert Street 30, 151
Cooke, George Frederick 124, 161
Cooper's Court 57
Cooper's Row 120
Copperas Hill 54
Cornwallis Street 57
Cosette 80
Coventry Street 73
Cranley, Peter 154
Cresswell Street 161
Cribb, Tom 88
Crimean War, the 36, 178, 179
Crosse, Rev. John 11
Crosshall Street 229

Crown Street 91
Crystal Palace, the 107, 111
Culloden, battle of 48
Cunliffe, Foster 38
Curwen, Samuel 15, 16
Custom House, the 92

Dale Street 11, 24, 32, 36, 38, 124, 209, 211, 229
Daniels, Alexander 162
Daniels, Elizabeth 162
Daniels, Mary Ann 149, 150, 162
Daniels, Penelope 162
Daniels, Samuel 143
Daniels, William 141-155, 157-162
Daulby Street 60
Davies, Robertson 135, 136
Davies, Wm. Rupert 135-137
Davy, Sir Humphry 158
Dawbarn, William 159, 160
Dawson, Dr. James 47
Declaration of Independence, the 91
Defoe, Daniel 9-12, 15, 16, 18, 34
Dickens, Charles 80, 86, 99, 156, 161, 230
Dillon, Gerald 120, 121
Dispensary, the 32, 44, 45, 95, 96
Doc Holliday 81
Duckett, Elizabeth 82, 83, 85
Ducket, Lucia 83, 85
Duckett, Margaret 82
Duckett, Thomas 79, 80, 82
Duckett, Thomas Jr 80, 82-86
Duke of Buckingham, the 53
Duke of Devonshire, the 75
Duke of Reichstadt, the 22
Duke's Dock 97
Duke Street 29, 54, 56, 57, 69, 179, 196, 200, 201, 202, 207, 232
Duncan, Dr. William Henry 186
Dunkirk 21, 26
Durning Road 208

Earle of Cardigan, the 53
Earle Road 45, 231
Earle Thomas 45, 53, 54, 59
Earl of Derby, the 38
Edge Hill 28, 34, 48, 62, 140, 151, 170, 196
Edge Lane 208
Edwards, Georgiana 118, 128
Elmswood, Dowsefield Lane 133
Evans, Elizabeth 90
Everton 28, 34, 44, 53, 143, 161, 196
Falkner Square 186

Fall Well, the 37
Father Nugent 63
Fawcett Preston and Co. 179, 180, 182
Fiennes, Celia 9, 11, 18
Finch-Hatton, George, 52
Fleet, Frederick 232
Foley, John Henry 82
Folly Fair, the 38
Fontenoy Street 66
Forsyth, James 108
Forwood, Sir William 233
Foster, John 29, 90, 139
Frampton, Sir George 190, 193
Franceys, Bros. 71, 73, 77, 79, 83, 87
Franceys Marble Works 66-71, 73, 74, 79, 89, 90-93, 100, 101, 139, 144, 233
Franceys, Mary 66, 67
Franceys, Samuel 66, 89, 90
Franceys Street 66
Franceys, Thomas 66, 67, 89, 90
Freemasons Row 197, 198
Frog Lane 11

Gambier Terrace 13, 119
Garthmyl Hall 128
Gascoyne Street 142
Gaskell, Elizabeth 80, 86
George II 48
George III 27, 28, 40, 48, 52, 66, 91, 119, 140
George IV 49, 91
George V 233
Georges Dock 13, 15, 120
Gibson, Benjamin 104, 107
Gibson, John 48, 57, 67, 70-77, 79, 82, 87-90, 101-104, 107, 108, 110, 112, 113, 126, 131, 140, 162, 175, 176, 180-183
Gibson, Solomon 49
Gildart, Richard 38
Gladstone, Sir John 25, 26, 33, 34
Gladstone, Wm. Ewart 25, 43, 209
Glorious First of June, battle of 20
Gore's General Advertiser 28, 32, 66, 97, 98
Gore, John 97, 98
Gore, Johnson 98
Gower, George.W. 104, 112, 114
Gower, Letitia Rossina 104, 112
Grafton Street 26
Grayson, Edward 55-59
Great Exhibition, the 67, 135
Great George Square 18
Great George Street Chapel 68
Great Richmond Street 12

Green Lane 71
Grinfield Street 140
Grove Street 91, 168
Guérard, Eugène von 83, 84

Hafodunos 76, 110
Haggerston Hall 133, 134
Haggerston Road 125
Hale Street 32
Hanover Street 31, 38, 119, 196
Harbreck House 125
Hardman, John 38
Hardman Street 177
Hardy, Thomas 21, 22, 99
Hartley, Jesse 13
Haslem Creek Receiving Stn. 84-86
Hawke Street 63
Hawthorne, Nathaniel 64
Haymarket 43
Heenan, Cardinal John 155
Hemans, Felicia Dorothea 48, 157
Henderson, Cornelius 139-141
Herculaneum Potteries, the 26, 90
Herdman, W. G. 139, 155, 157
Hick, Benjamin 90
Holme, Samuel 103
Holy Trinity Church 49, 176-178, 182
Hooton Hall 117, 129
Hope Street 205
Hornblower, Lewis 190
Hosmer, Harriet 108
Howe, Admiral 20
Huggins, Anna 163
Huggins, Elisabeth 163
Huggins, Hannah 174
Huggins, Samuel 163, 173, 174
Huggins, Samuel (père) 163
Huggins, William 94, 163-165, 167-174
Hunt, Holman 68
Huskisson, Eliza Emily 76
Huskisson, Wm. 57, 67, 76, 90, 95, 162

Illustrated London News, the 100, 184, 194, 195, 197
International Exhibition of Navigation, Commerce and Industry, the 208, 209, 211
Ismay, Bruce 231
Ismay, Thomas Henry 231

James Street 95
Jefferson, Thomas 91, 92
Jenner, Edward 47
Jericho Lane 159
Jericho Strawberry Gardens 42
Jerome, James 11
Jervis, Admiral Sir John 20
Jonson, Ben 53
Josephine, Empress 20
Joseph Mayer 150
Josephson, Joshua Frey 107-109
Joseph Wright of Derby 28
Juggler Street 11

Keane, Edmund 161
Kemball H. T. 141
Kemp, Edward 190
Kemys-Tynte, Milborne 99
Kent Street 57, 200
King's Dock 13
King Street 126, 127
Kipling, Rudyard 100
Knott's Hole 56

La Boheme 80
Lady Lever Art Gallery, the 77
Lafone, Henry 125
Laird, John 179
Laurel Street 168
Lavater, Johann Kaspar 26
Lavater, John Caspar 26, 27
Lawrence, Sir Thomas 153
Lawson, Andrew 68
Lawson, George Anderson 68
Leece Street 209
Legé, Frederick, A. 69-71, 73
Leigh, Henry Faithwaite 98
Leighton Hall 117, 118, 128-138
Leipzig, battle of 20-22, 29
Leyland, Christopher (Bullin) 117, 121
Leyland, Dorothy 121
Leyland, Ellen 127
Leyland, Margaret 120, 121
Leyland, Thomas 118-121, 123-127, 132, 133
Lichfield Cathedral 70, 71
Lime Street 37, 65, 147, 149, 165, 209-211
Lime Street Station 9, 46
Liscard 62
Liscard Manor 128, 129
Littledale, Elizabeth 58
Liverpool Castle 11, 12, 49

Liverpool Chronicle, the 37
Liverpool Infirmary 36, 38-40, 44-48
Liverpool Lantern, the 141, 142, 152-154
Liverpool Mercury, the 22, 25, 27-29, 31-34, 74, 140, 142
Liverpool Night Asylum for the Homeless Poor 48, 197, 198
Liverpool Seamen's Orphanage 199-204, 206, 207, 209, 215-237
Liverpool Tower 11, 35, 49
Liverpool University 64, 65, 206
Liver Street 32
Lodi, battle of 20
London International Exhibition 1862, 77, 111, 137, 181, 182, 184
London Road 30, 61, 209, 211-213
Longfellow, Henry Wadsworth 146
Lord Byron 53, 88, 157
Lord Street 30, 74
Louis XVI 19, 66, 119
Low Hill 28
Lunatic Asylum, 1st 12, 45, 65,
Lyceum, the 18, 30, 69, 119
Lydia Ann Street 179
Lyon, Edwin 139

Mace Jem 154
MacIver, Charles 203-205, 233
MacIver, David 199, 204
Malmaison 20
Mansion House, Calderstones 204
Marble Street 88
Marie Louise, Empress 22
Marine Terrace, Waterloo 231
Marmont, Marshal 21
Martindale's Hill 64
Mason Street 68, 140
Mather, John 27
Maury, James 91, 92
Mayer, Joseph 150, 203
McBride, John Alexander Patterson 67, 68, 162
McCartney, Dr John 56, 57
Medical Institution, the 46, 64
Mellard, Mary Margaret 97
Melville, Herman 18, 61
Mersey View 149
Metropolitan Cathedral 64, 65
Midland Bank Ltd 127, 132
Miller's Castle 149, 158
Miller, Wm. Spurston 149
Molyneux, Wm 121, 123
Monticello, Virginia 91, 92

Moore Street 11
Mosses, Alexander 144, 145
Mosslake Fields 58, 64
Mossley Hill 201
Mount Pleasant 12, 26, 64, 103, 128, 139, 148, 151
Mount Vernon 196
Mrs Bartington's Backbone Club 32
Mulberry Street 91, 168
Murat, Marshal 21
Myrtle Street 91, 168, 209
Mystic Society, the 32

National Museum of Wales 110
Naylor, Christopher John 107, 129, 131-134, 136
Naylor, Dora 129, 131, 132, 136
Naylor, Dorothy 128
Naylor, Elisabeth Mary 121, 128
Naylor, Georgiana 107, 129-131, 134-137
Naylor, John 106, 107, 117, 118, 121, 128-137
Naylor, John Wrench 121
Naylor, Margaret 131, 132, 136
Naylor, Richard Christopher 117, 118, 121, 128, 129
Naylor, Rowland 107, 128, 131-133, 136
Naylor, Thomas 121, 127, 128
Newington Street 44, 55
Newsham Drive 216, 217
Newsham House 188, 208, 209, 211, 232
Newsham Park 187-192, 201, 202
Newton, John 9, 12
Ney, Marshal 21, 24, 98
Nile Street 211
North John Street 30, 32
Northumberland Street 196

Ogden, Samuel 38
Old Dock 12, 15, 92, 120
Old Hall Street 11
Olivebank Cottage 48
Olive Street 91, 168
Oratory, the 68, 97, 98
Ormskirk 95-97
Osborne House 76, 106
Owen, Mary 147-149, 162
Oxford Street 168
Oyl Mill Field 38, 39

Palace of Westminster, the 76, 129
Paradise Street 11, 91, 92, 120
Park, Ann 43, 49

Park, Ann Green 43, 49
Park, Charlotte Catherine 43, 48, 49
Park, Edward 39, 41
Park, Elizabeth (wife) 42, 43
Park, Elizabeth (daughter) 43, 49
Park, Elizabeth (daughter 2) 43, 48, 49
Park, Ellen Green 42, 43, 49
Park, Henry 35, 36, 38-49, 55-57, 60, 89, 95, 177, 237
Park, Henry (son) 43, 49
Park, John Ranicar 43, 49
Park Lane 12, 18
Park, Mary Lyon 43, 49
Park, Mary (sister) 39, 42-44
Park (née Lyon) 39, 43
Park Road 196
Parliament Street 12, 13
Paxton, Sir Joseph 107, 130, 188, 189
Pembroke Place 60, 65
Perceval, Spencer 52
Percy Street 119
Phoenix Foundry, the 126, 179
Picton, James Allanson 17, 18, 67, 89, 94, 100, 107, 113, 143, 190
Picton Road 208
Pitt, Wm. The Younger 53
Pleasant Street 66, 67, 140, 144
Pleasant Street School 66
Poniatowski, Marshal 21
Pool of Liverpool 11, 12
Poor Law Acts 38
Post Office Place 30, 171
Pott, Sir Percival 41, 43
Powys Castle 117, 130
Prescot Road 65
Preston, Alderson Berthon 182
Preston, Eleanor Jeannette 180, 183
Preston, Eleanor Leonora 77, 126, 176, 177, 180-183
Preston, Ellen Jane Berthon 177, 178
Preston, Ellen Sarah (née Berthon) 176-178
Preston, Emily Berthon 177, 178
Preston, Florence Berthon 177, 178
Preston, Frederick Berthon 177, 178
Preston, George Berthon (1) 180, 182, 183
Preston, George Berthon (2) 177, 178
Preston, Henry Berthon 177, 178
Preston, Horatio Berthon 177, 178
Preston, Jeannette Berthon 177, 178
Preston, Leonora Frances Margaret 180, 183
Preston, Robert Arthur Berthon 180, 183
Preston, Robert Berthon 49, 77, 126, 176-180, 182, 183

Preston, Robert (grandfather) 176
Preston, Robert (père) 176, 177
Preston, William Berthon 177, 178
Preston, William Robert 177, 178
Prince Albert 76, 106, 110, 112, 154, 167, 202
Prince Alfred 85, 202, 203
Prince Arthur, Duke of Connaught 208, 190, 209
Prince Henry of Battenburg 208, 209
Princes Boulevard 209
Princes Dock 142
Princes Park 187-189, 196, 209
Princess Beatrice 208
Princess Mary 233

Queen Caroline 111
Queen's Dock 13, 120
Queen Mary 233
Queen Victoria 76, 82, 85, 104, 106, 110, 112,
133, 167, 202, 207-213, 215

Radcliffe, Lady 211
Radcliffe, Sir David 209
Radley, James 63, 65
Ranelagh Gardens 63
Ranelagh Street 139
Ranicar, Elizabeth 42
Ranicar, Ellen 42
Ranicar, John 42
Rankin, Ann 204
Redburn 18, 61, 62, 64, 65
Renshaw, Ann 44, 54, 55
Renshaw, Rev. Samuel 55
Richmond Row 156, 157
Rivoli, battle of 20
Robinson, Ellen-Jane 70, 71
Robinson, Ellen-Jane (daughter) 70,
Robinson, Marianne 70
Robinson, Mat 154
Robinson, Rev. William 70, 71
Rodney Street 13, 43, 91, 119, 209
Roe Street 37
Rookwood Cemetery 84-86
Roscoe, Street 103
Roscoe, William 12, 64, 74, 76, 87, 88, 90-92,
101, 107, 110, 124, 125, 140, 150, 168
Rossetti, Dante Gabriel 80, 86, 164, 175
Roughsedge, Rev. Robert Hankinson 39, 89
Royal Academy Liverpool, the 68, 73, 74, 79,
87-90, 163, 170
Royal Academy London, the 70, 71, 73, 83
Royal Teaching Hospital 60

Rupert Street 139
Ruskin, John 145
Russell Street 62, 139

Salamanca, battle of 29
Salthouse Dock 13, 16, 120
Sandbach, Henry Robertson 76, 110
Sandbach, Margaret 76, 110
Sandfield Park 159
Sayers, Tom 154, 156
School Lane 29
Scotland Road 11, 196, 211
Scott, George Gilbert 110
Scott, Sir Walter 58, 111
Seel, Thomas 38
Sefton Park 187-192
Sefton Palm House 106, 109, 110, 113, 191
Sefton Parish Church 77
Shaw's Brow 11, 38
Sheil Road 189
Sheppard, Bishop David 205
Sheridan, Richard Brinsley 53
Siddall, Elizabeth 80
Siddons, Sarah 161
Sinclair, Upton 81
Slater Street 29
Smith, Captain Edward. J. 231
Smithdown Lane 44, 140
Smithdown Road 45, 231
Smith, Egerton 197-199
Somerville, William 157-159, 161
Southey, Robert 58
Sparling, John 54
Spekelands 45
Spence, Benjamin 79, 87, 90,
100-114, 117, 126, 131, 132, 136-138, 140,
163, 174, 182, 191
Spence, Benjamin Edgar 114
Spence, Clara 90
Spence, Eleanore 90
Spence, James 90
Spence, John 90
Spence, John. C. 114
Spence, Margaret 90
Spence, Maria Lena 114
Spence, Mary 90
Spence, Rosina Letitia 104, 113, 114
Spence, Thomas 90
Spence, William 67, 79, 87-90, 93-97, 100,
101, 114
Spence, William Gibson 114
St. Aidan's Church, Billinge 97

Stanley Park 187-192, 194
St. Anne's Church, Cazneau St 87, 90
St Ann's Church, Gt Richmond St 12
Star Concert Hall, the 155
St. Bride's Church 148
St. David's Welsh Church 63
St. Domingo House 54
Steers, Thomas 12
Stephenson, George 18, 107, 151, 158
St George's Church, Derby Sq 12, 36, 49
St. George's Church, Everton 53
St. George's Hall 12, 18, 38, 46, 82, 107, 149, 209
St. James Cemetery 49, 76, 162, 165
St. James Church 12
St. James Street 66
St. John's Church 12
St. John's Gardens 12
St. John's Lane 45
St. Mary's Church, Birkenhead 68
St. Mary's Church, Edge Hill 151
St. Mary the Virgin, Leigh 42
St. Michael's Church, Barbados 90
St. Nicholas Catholic School 63
St. Nicholas Church 11, 35, 39, 89, 202
St. Nicholas Pro-Cathedral 63, 98
Stonehouse, James 53
St. Paul's Church 12
St. Paul's Church, Hooton 117
St. Peter's Church, Church St 12, 101
St. Philip Church 177, 180
St. Thomas Church 12, 42, 120
Stubbs, George 164
Sullivan, Barry 152, 153
Swetenham, Willam Henry 98, 99

Tadema, Lawrence-Alma 108
Tarleton Street 155
The Courier 28, 32
The Daily Post 143, 165
The Dismal Swamp, poem 146
Theed, William 18
The Grange, Woolton 133
The Graphic 212
The Lancashire Witch locomotive 90
The Old Fort 16, 27
The Penny Illustrated 209, 212, 213
The Playhouse Theatre 155
The Revolt of Islam, poem 169
The Rocket 18, 76
The Seasons, poem 103
The Theatre Royal 31, 124, 161
The Three Loggerheads, pub 157

The Tower, prison 36, 39, 40
The Ugly Face Club 14
Thompson, Wm. Abednego 154, 155
Thornycroft, Mary 110
Thornycroft, Thomas 82-84
Thorvaldsen, Bertel 103
Tithebarn Street 36
Tobin Street 63
Toulon, battle of 20
Tower Buildings 35
Tower Weint 35, 40
Town Hall, Liverpool 9, 11-14, 18, 26, 27, 29, 34, 207, 209
Toxteth 26, 188, 189
Toxteth Cemetery 211
Trafalgar, battle of 20
Tunnel Road 45, 209
Tunstall Street 231
Turmeau John 73, 74
Turmeau, John Caspar 74
Turner, Dr. Matthew 36

Ullet Road 196
Ulverston 57, 58
Union News Room, the 29, 69, 88, 119

Vauxhall Road 142, 197
Victoria and Albert Museum 77, 162, 206
Vine Street 91
Vittoria, battle of 21, 29

Walker Art Gallery 67, 75, 77, 98, 106, 109, 110, 112, 113, 135-137, 146, 149, 150, 155, 157, 162, 174, 182, 183
Walmsley, Lady 156, 162
Walmsley, Sir Joshua 148, 151, 153, 158
Walton Hall Estate 125-127
Walton Jail 160, 161
Ward, Jem 154-156, 159
Ward, Robert 67
Warlock, Rev. Derek 205
Washington, George 92
Waterhouse, Alfred 201, 206
Waterloo, battle of 21, 66
Waterloo Place 69
Water Street 11, 35, 39, 120, 199, 200
Watmough, Frank 215-230, 233, 235, 237, 238
Wavertree 48, 49, 55, 91, 176, 182
Wavertree Hall 151, 153, 168
Wavertree Lodge 48, 49

Wavertree Park 151, 152
Wavertree Road 208, 209
Webster Street 66
Wellington Column 68
Wellington, Duke of 21, 25, 29, 31, 32, 52, 153, 154
Wellington Road 26
Wellington Rooms 27, 64, 77
Wesley, John 9, 11
West Derby Menagerie 164
West Derby Road 165
Westleigh Hall 42
Westmacott, Richard 34
Westminster Hall 90, 101
Whitechapel 11
Wilberforce, William 124
Wilde, Oscar 145
William Brown Street 11, 18, 68, 113, 211
Williamson, Joseph 76, 140, 141
Williamsons Advertiser 20
Williamson Square 31, 124, 155, 157, 159, 161
Williamson Tunnels 139
Williams, Penry 112
Windus Way 158
Winstanley Hall, Wigan 93
Wirral 43, 47, 207, 188
Wolffe, Emil 110
Wombwell, George 165-167, 170
Wood, John 13, 14
Wood Street 142, 151
Woolton 42, 53, 133
Wordsworth, William 58
Wyatt, Richard James 102-105, 110, 112, 113

Yewtree Road 133
York Hotel 155
York Street 54, 125-127, 179

Books

A Catalogue of Plants in the Botanic Gardens at Liverpool 91
Heart of Midlothian 111
Les Misérables 80
Memorials of Liverpool 89
The Jungle 81
The Life and Pontificate of X 91
The Life of Lorenzo de Medici 91

Paintings

A Boy Blowing Bubbles 159
Adam's Vision of the Death of Abel 164
A Fisherman 159
A Girl Peeling Potatoes 159
A Girl Selling Oranges 159
A Gleaner 159, 162
An Oyster Woman 159
A Portrait of Mr Friend 159
A Portrait of William Somerville 159
A Sister of Charity 159
A View of Birkenhead Priory 144
Beggars 149
Candle-Light 159
Castles in the Air 161
Certainty 159
Cologne 134
Dead Game 163
Doubt 159
Faces in the Fire 159
Fairy Glen 174
Family Portraits 159
Fantine 80, 81
Fight Between an Eagle and a Snake 169
Girl by a Pedestal 149
Ironing Day 159
Joseph Mayer 149
Landscape of Cattle Near Helsby 174
Lion and Lioness 164
Lions 165
Macbeth 159
Medora 159
Napoleon Crossing the Alps 135
Old Friends 172
Othello and Iago 157

Picture of William 159
Portrait of a Lady 172
Reading the News 161
Samuel Weller 159
Shylock 157
The Artist's Wife 171
The Brigand 147, 159
The Card Players 159
The Colporteur 152
The Dying Gladiator 144
The Expulsion from Paradise 144
The Fight for the Standard 146
The Fisherman's Home 159
The Friar of Orders Grey 159
The Goldfish 159, 160
The Harbour at Dieppe 134
The Hunted Slaves 146
The Image Maker 159
The Irish Man 159
The Man at the Wheel 161
The Monarch of the Meadows 172
The Nun 159
The Prisoner of Chillon 157-159
The Sailor's Daughter 159
The Sailor's Sweetheart 159
The Savoyards 144
The Street Musician 159
The Temptation of Christ 135, 136
The Wedding Ring 148
The Widow 159
Three Religious Works 159
Tried Friends 169
Venus Verticordia 175
Venus Victrix 176
Volunteer Manoeuvres 83
Washing the Baby 149

Ships

Akbar 200
Alert 211
Alma 179
Behar 179
Borysthene 179
Britannia 233
Caledonia 202
Carnatic 20
Champion of the Seas 211

Chimborazo 195
Clarence 200
Claughton 211
Conway 71, 73, 200
Dove 97
Enterprize 121, 123
Fortune 123
Gudgion 57
Indefatigable 200, 229
John 57, 123
Jourdain 179
Kingsmill 34
Kitty 123
La Convention 123
Lightning 211
Liverpool 133
Louisa 123
Marco Polo 211
Mary Rose 167
May 142
Meandre 179
Mentor 20
Morley 107
Neptune 107
Nubia 179
Oceanic 232
Olympia 232
Orissa 179
Ottowa 179
Princess 56
Royal George 167
Sabrina 134
Simois 179
The Earl of Liverpool 123
The Great Eastern 211
The King George 57
The Lottery 123
Titanic 231, 232
Victoria 133
Victoria and Albert 190
Vigilant 211
Winifred 83

Statues

A Faun 108
A Girl on a Pedestal 150
A Greek Slave 108

A Hunter and His Dog 76
Albert (Prince) 82
Alfred in the Camp of the Danes 82
Andromeda 108
Aristides Showing the Shell to the Vates 90
A Venus of Medici 108
Beatrice Cenci 108
Bebington Church 173
Boadicea and Her Daughters 82
Boy and Kid 113
Caractacus Before Caesar 90
Centaurs Pursuing Dante 87
Cheetahs 172
Christian and the Lions 168, 169
Christ's Agony in the Garden 144
Commerce 82
Cupid Restraining Mars 75
Dora and Margaret 137
Dr Raffles 68
Flora MacDonald 113
Georgiana and her Two Sons 136, 137
Head of a Greek Helen 108
Hector and Andromache 102, 113
Highland Mary 103, 105, 106, 108-113, 130
Hippolytus 108
Huskisson 131
Icarus 138
Jeanie Deans 111, 113
John Laird 68
Lady Godiva 68
Lavinia 103, 104, 113
Liverpool 107
Master George 182
Mercury 73
Mr Spence 87
Navigation, The Arts and Commerce 69
Neptune Fountain 93
Night and Twilight 82
Oberon and Titania 113
Ophelia 104, 113
Peter Pan 190, 192, 193
Pharoah's Daughter 131
Prince Albert 110
Princess Louise 110
Psyche at the Well 110, 112
Puck 108
Queen Mary 233
Queen Victoria 82
Queen Victoria bust 107

Rape of the Sabines 108
Rebecca 113
Roman Hunter 108
Satan 70
Sir Robert Peel 80, 81
Sister's Pride 83
Sleeping Children 70, 71
Sleeping Venus 67
The Angel of Death 84, 85
The Angel of Mercy 84, 85
The Angel's Whisper 109, 110, 112, 113
The Death of the Duke of York 101
The Duke of Wellington 88
The Finding of Moses 107, 113, 131, 132, 136, 137
The Good Samaritan 96
The Lady of the Lake 108, 110, 113
The Marine Venus 113
The Model of a Female Hand 69
The Sleeping Children 70
The Sleeping Shepherd Boy 75
The Tinted Venus 77, 78, 126, 175, 180-184
Tom Cribb in an Attitude of Boxing 88
Twilight and Night 83
Ulysses 101
Venus and Cupid 117
Venus Verticordia 175, 176, 183
Young Hymen 87